INTRODUCTION TO PHARMACEUTICAL ENGINEERING

FOR
DEGREE COURSE IN PHARMACY OF ALL INDIAN UNIVERSITIES

Dr. Anant R. Paradkar

Professor of Pharmaceutics,
Bharati Vidyapeeth University,
Poona College of Pharmacy,
Erandwane, Pune 38.

INTRODUCTION TO PHARMACEUTICAL ENGINEERING	ISBN 978-81-85790-38-1
Twelfth Edition : August, 2015	
© : Author	

The text of this publication, or any part thereof, should not be reproduced or transmitted in any form or stored in any computer storage system or device for distribution including photocopy, recording, taping or information retrieval system or reproduced on any disc, tape, perforated media or other information storage device etc., without the written permission of Author with whom the rights are reserved. Breach of this condition is liable for legal action.

Every effort has been made to avoid errors or omissions in this publication. In spite of this, errors may have crept in. Any mistake, error or discrepancy so noted and shall be brought to our notice shall be taken care of in the next edition. It is notified that neither the publisher nor the author or seller shall be responsible for any damage or loss of action to any one, of any kind, in any manner, therefrom.

Published By :
NIRALI PRAKASHAN
Abhyudaya Pragati, 1312, Shivaji Nagar
Off J.M. Road, PUNE – 411005
Tel - (020) 25512336/37/39, Fax - (020) 25511379
Email : niralipune@pragationline.com

Printed By :
Repro India Ltd.,
Mumbai.

✦ DISTRIBUTION CENTRES

PUNE
Nirali Prakashan : 119, Budhwar Peth, Jogeshwari Mandir Lane, Pune 411002, Maharashtra
Tel : (020) 2445 2044, 66022708, Fax : (020) 2445 1538
Email : bookorder@pragationline.com, nirallocal@pragationline.com

Nirali Prakashan : S. No. 28/27, Dhyari, Near Pari Company, Pune 411041
Tel : (020) 24690204 Fax : (020) 24690316
Email : dhyari@pragationline.com, bookorder@pragationline.com

MUMBAI
Nirali Prakashan : 385, S.V.P. Road, Rasdhara Co-op. Hsg. Society Ltd.,
Girgaum, Mumbai 400004, Maharashtra
Tel : (022) 2385 6339 / 2386 9976, Fax : (022) 2386 9976
Email : niralimumbai@pragationline.com

✦ DISTRIBUTION BRANCHES

JALGAON
Nirali Prakashan : 34, V. V. Golani Market, Navi Peth, Jalgaon 425001,
Maharashtra, Tel : (0257) 222 0395, Mob : 94234 91860

KOLHAPUR
Nirali Prakashan : New Mahadvar Road, Kedar Plaza, 1st Floor Opp. IDBI Bank
Kolhapur 416 012, Maharashtra. Mob : 9850046155

NAGPUR
Pratibha Book Distributors : Above Maratha Mandir, Shop No. 3, First Floor,
Rani Jhanshi Square, Sitabuldi, Nagpur 440012, Maharashtra
Tel : (0712) 254 7129

DELHI
Nirali Prakashan : 4593/21, Basement, Aggarwal Lane 15, Ansari Road, Daryaganj
Near Times of India Building, New Delhi 110002
Mob : 08505972553

BENGALURU
Pragati Book House : House No. 1, Sanjeevappa Lane, Avenue Road Cross,
Opp. Rice Church, Bengaluru – 560002.
Tel : (080) 64513344, 64513355,Mob : 9880582331, 9845021552
Email:bharatsavla@yahoo.com

CHENNAI
Pragati Books : 9/1, Montieth Road, Behind Taas Mahal, Egmore,
Chennai 600008 Tamil Nadu, Tel : (044) 6518 3535,
Mob : 94440 01782 / 98450 21552 / 98805 82331,
Email : bharatsavla@yahoo.com

niralipune@pragationline.com | www.pragationline.com

Also find us on www.facebook.com/niralibooks

❋ Dedicated to ❋

"My Family Members"

PREFACE TO THE TWELFTH EDITION

The previous edition of this book has been well accepted by the student community. I am thankful to the teachers for their suggestions and appreciation of the book.

The new chapter on Extraction introduced in a previous edition has been well received. Topics such as supercritical fluid extraction and enfleurage are covered in this chapter.

I wish to place on record my sincere thanks to my publisher **Shri. Dineshbhai Furia** and **Shri. Jignesh Furia,** for their kind co-operation. I wish to acknowledge my colleagues and all those who have assisted in the completion of the book.

Suggestions from all corners of the profession are welcome. I am responsible for any deficiencies or errors that might have remained and would be grateful if readers would call them to my attention.

A. R. PARADKAR

■■■

PREFACE TO THE FIRST EDITION

Fast development in the pharmaceutical processing field is possible due to collaborative efforts of pharmaceutical technologist and chemical engineers. The basic purpose of studying "Pharmaceutical Engineering" is to develop the approach of application of mainly chemical engineering to the field of bulk drug manufacturing and pharmaceutical processing. The text covers all important unit operations with specific applications to the pharmacy. More emphasis has been given on principles, mechanisms and theories of different operations. Mathematical treatment is included wherever necessary so as to clarify the concepts.

This book is a sincere attempt to simplify the concepts of pharmaceutical engineering with more practical orientation. The topics are selected so as to cover pharmaceutical engineering curriculum of most of the Universities. Your suggestions regarding coverage of topics, typographical mistakes are most welcome.

I am grateful to Dr. S.S. Kadam, Principal Poona College of Pharmacy for encouragement provided by him during completion of this book. I extend my special thanks to Mr. S.G. Bidkar and Miss Meera Honrao for their valuable suggestions. I wish to thank Mr. Sagar Padhye, for assistance in preparation of manuscript and Mr. A.R. Ketkar for cover design.

I appreciate, the co-operation and interest taken by Mr. Dineshbhai Furia and Mr. Jignesh Furia of Nirali Prakashan.

Last, but not the least, I thank all the faculty members of Poona College of Pharmacy, Pune and Nagpur College of Pharmacy, Nagpur for their co-operation, encouragement and timely suggestions.

A.R. PARADKAR

INTRODUCTION

1.1 PHARMACEUTICAL ENGINEERING

Industrial processing of drugs and pharmaceuticals has gained significant importance in recent years. This has increased the interest in the engineering aspects of pharmacy. The objective of studying pharmaceutical engineering is to understand the engineering principles involved in the processing of drugs and pharmaceuticals. The pharmaceutical technologist may not have to design the process equipment in detail but he should understand how the equipment operates. With an understanding of basic principles of process engineering, he will be able to develop the new pharmaceutical processes and modify existing ones. The pharmaceutical technologist must also be able to make himself clearly understood by design engineers and by the suppliers of the equipment he uses.

Only a thorough understanding of basic sciences applied to the pharmaceutical industry can prepare the pharmaceutical technologist with ability to tackle the complex problems of pharmaceutical industry today. In pharmaceutical engineering, we mainly study chemical engineering with special relevance to pharmacy.

1.2 UNIT OPERATIONS

Processing in the drugs and pharmaceuticals or any other industry involves complex physical processes. The various physical processes of importance can be analysed by breaking into a small number of basic operations, which are called 'unit operations'. The unit operation considers only the physical changes that take place during processing. Application of concept of unit operations simplifies the study of pharmaceutical engineering. Instead of studying each process separately, the basic principles of unit operations can be applied in all processes where it is involved. Some important unit operations are fluid flow, heat transfer, evaporation, crystallization, distillation, mixing, size reduction, filtration etc. In many cases, the same general principles apply to many unit operations. For example, drying, evaporation and distillation all involve simultaneous heat transfer and mass transfer.

1.3 STOICHIOMETRY

The word "stoichiometry" was invented by Jeremias Richter in 1792. It is a combination of Greek words that mean finding the proportions of magnitude between materials that cannot be further divided. Thus, stoichiometry is the study of material balances, energy balances and the chemical laws combining weights as applied to industrial processes.

1.3.1 Material Balance :

"Material balance" is a mathematical treatment given to the data of a process or unit operation on the basis of law of conservation of mass. The law of conservation of mass states that *mass cannot be created nor destroyed*. Thus in a processing plant the total mass entering the plant must be equal to the total mass of material leaving the plant, less any material accumulated. If there is no accumulation, then the simple rule holds that "what goes in must come out". Unit operations can be treated on the same basis.

For example, if an aqueous extract of crude drug is concentrated by evaporation, then by application of law of conservation of mass,

Mass of extract entering evaporator per hr. = Mass of water evaporated per hr. + Mass of concentrated extract obtained per hr.

This is overall material balance for the evaporation process.

Similarly, the law of conservation of mass applies to each component in the entering material. For example in the concentration of extract, we can apply law of conservation to one of the component of the stream, suppose water then we cay say,

Mass of water entering evaporator per hr = Mass of water evaporated per hr. + Mass of water in concentrated extract per hr.

Some component in the system is such that it comes into the process in just one stream and leaves unchanged only in one stream. Such component or material is called a 'tie substance'. Presence of tie substance in the process simplifies the stoichiometric calculations.

1.3.2 Energy Balance

"Energy Balance" is a mathematical treatment on the basis of law of conservation of energy. The law of conservation of energy states that *energy cannot be created nor destroyed*. The total energy in the materials entering the system, plus total energy added to system, must equal the total energy leaving the system. This is a more complex concept than the conservation of mass, because energy can take various forms such as kinetic energy, potential energy, heat energy, electrical energy etc. During operation, some of these forms of energy can be converted from one to another. For example, mechanical energy of fluid can be converted into heat energy through friction. Mechanical energy of the fan is converted into kinetic energy of fluid. But the total sum of all these forms of energy are conserved.

Broadly speaking, there are two primary classifications of energy, potential and kinetic. Potential energy refers to the energy a body or a substance has, because of its position relative to another material or because of its components. This can be further broken down into internal and external potential energy ; for example, a wooden piece has a certain external potential energy when placed at a fixed distance from the earth's surface because of its ability to fall and strike the earth with a momentum dependent on its mass and speed. The wooden piece has internal potential energy because of its ability to give off heat when burned. Kinetic energy refers to the energy due to motion.

The flow of heat from one body to another may be considered as energy in transition. When heat flows from hot to a cold body, the internal energy of the colder body is increased and that of the hot body has decreased. Work is also another form of transition energy. This may be defined as the energy transferred by the action of a mechanical force moving under restraint through a tangible distance. Work cannot be stored as such, but the capability to do work can be stored as potential energy or kinetic energy. For exmaple, work has to be done for compressing the fluid, this fluid has capability to do the same when released from compressed state (i.e. allowed to expand). This is known as pressure energy of fluid.

The most common and important form of energy is heat energy. In operations such as drying, evaporation, humidification, distillation conservation of heat energy has to be considered and enthalpy i.e. total heat balance has to be developed. Heat is absorbed or evolved by some reactions in pharmaceutical processing but usually the quantities are small as compared to other forms of energy entering the processes, such as sensible heat and latent heat. Latent heat is the heat required to change, at constant temperature, the physical state of materials from solid to liquid, liquid to gas or solid to gas. Sensible heat is that heat which when added or subtracted from the material changes its temperature and thus can be sensed. Sensible heat is obtained by multiplying the specific heat with mass of the material.

As energy balances are complex, it is advisable to determine first those factors which are significant in the overall energy balance. The simplified heat balance can be developed by neglecting insignificant factors.

Fig. 1.1 : Energy Balance with respect to Heat Energy only

Thus, in nutshell, from these laws of conservation of mass and energy, a balance sheet for materials and for energy can be drawn at all times for unit operation. These are called material balances and energy balances.

1.3.3 Laws of Combining Weights :

The chemical laws of combining weights are to be considered when chemical changes occur during the process e.g. synthesis of drug. The relationship between the mass of reactants and products involved in the chemical reaction can be obtained by considering the equation for chemical reaction and the molecular weights of the materials involved. By going through the reaction and the conversions of materials at molar levels, the relationship between mass of reactant and product may be easily drawn. While applying the principles of stoichiometry to gases, the relationships among mass of material, temperature, pressure and volume are very important. Various gas laws are, considered such as perfect gas law i.e. $PV = nRT$, Dalton's law etc. As the operations associated with gases and chemical changes are not very common in pharmaceutical processing these are not considered here in details.

1.4 DIMENSIONS AND UNITS

The fundamental dimensions of any mechanical or physical quantity are conventionally expressed in terms of a set of three primary quantities, mass, length and time. Mass is denoted by [M], length is denoted by [L] and time is denoted by [T]. The square brackets in each case imply the dimension. For example, since area possesses both length and breadth, the dimensions are $[L^2]$, and typical units are square inches and square cm. Similarly, dimensions of volume are $[L^3]$, and typical units are cubic inches and cubic cm. Dimension is a descriptive word, a unit is a definite standard or measure of dimension. A unit is defined as a particular amount of the quantity to be measured. For example, milimeter, centimeter, inches, foot are different units indicating different but definite lengths, while the dimension common to all these units is length. Some basic units used are as follows :

The second (sec.) is the fundamental unit of time. The primary standard of length in United States is United States prototype meter 27, a platinum - irridium (90% platinum – 10% irridium) line standard having X - shaped section. One yard is 0.9144 metre and one foot is 1/3 yard. As per metric system, the standard meter is defined as 1,650, 763.73 wavelengths of the orange - red line of krypton 86.

Mass is the property of matter which causes the matter to resist acceleration. Mass is independent of earth's gravity. Weight is dependent on both earth's gravity and mass. One kilogram is, by international agreement the prototype mass of platinum - irridium located in Sevres, France. One pound is 0.45359237 kilogram.

All physical equations must be dimensionally consistent. This means that both sides of the equation must reduce to the same dimensions. Dimensions can be handled algebraically and therefore they can be divided, multiplied or cancelled. As equations are dimensionally consistent, dimensions of unknown quantities can sometimes be calculated. Dimensions and units are given in Table 1.1. The conversion of units are given in Appendix – I.

Table 1.1 : Dimensional analysis of various quantities and variables

Quantity	Symbol	M – L – T	Typical units

Area	A	L^2	m^2
Volume	υ	L^3	m^3
Velocity	V	LT^{-1}	m/sec.
Acceleration	a or g	LT^{-2}	m/sec^2
Angular velocity, in radians	ω (omega)	T^{-1}	sec^{-1}
Mass	m	M	$kg\ sec^2/m$
Mass density	D or ρ (rho)	ML^{-3}	$kg\ sec^2/m^4$
Weight	W	MLT^{-2}	kg
Force	F	MLT^{-2}	kg
Weight density or specific weight	w	$ML^{-2}T^{-2}$	kg/m^3
Discharge	Q	L^3T^{-1}	m^3/sec
Weight rate of flow	G	MLT^{-3}	kg/sec
Intensity of pressure or stress	p or σ (sigma)	$ML^{-1}T^{-2}$	kg/m^2
Modulus of elasticity	E	$ML^{-1}T^{-2}$	kg/m^2
Absolute or dynamic viscosity	μ (mu)	$ML^{-1}T^{-2}$	$kg/sec/m^2$
Kinematic viscosity	ν (nu)	$ML^{-1}T^{-1}$	$m^2/sec.$
Power	P	L^2T^{-1}	m - kg/sec.
Torque	T	ML^2T^{-2}	m - kg
Shear stress	τ (tau)	ML^2T^{-2}	kg/m^2
Surface tension	σ (sigma)	$ML^{-1}T^{-2}$	kg/m.
		MT^{-2}	

1.5 DIMENSIONAL ANALYSIS

Dimensional analysis is a scientific technique based on the principle of dimensional homogenity. It is useful to determine the relationship among the physical variables in certain types of processes. Dimensional analysis is very useful in determining dimensionless ratios, and relationship of variables in terms of dimensionless ratios.

Some simple dimensionless numbers or ratios are specific gravity, trignometric functions such as sine, cosine, etc. Table 1.2 shows some dimensionless numbers commonly used in pharmaceutical engineering operations to compare or correlate some mechanisms.

Table 1.2 : Dimensionless Numbers

Sr. No.	Name	Formula	Mechanism Ratio
1.	Reynolds Number	$\dfrac{D u \rho}{\eta}$	$\dfrac{\text{Inertial Force}}{\text{Viscous Force}}$
2.	Froude Number	$\dfrac{N^2 D}{g}$	$\dfrac{\text{Inertial Force}}{\text{Gravitational Force}}$
3.	Nusselt Number	$\dfrac{h_c D}{k}$	$\dfrac{\text{Temperature gradient at a boundary}}{\text{Temperature gradient across the fluid to boundary}}$
4.	Prandtl Number	$\dfrac{C_p \eta}{k}$	$\dfrac{\text{Molecular diffusivity of momentum}}{\text{Molecular diffusivity to heat}}$

In the above table :

- D = diameter (length parameter),
- u = velocity of fluid,
- ρ = density of fluid,
- η = viscosity of fluid,
- C_p = heat capacity
- h_c = convection heat transfer coefficient
- N = rotational speed in r.p.m.
- g = gravitational acceleration and
- k = a constant.

Buckingham postulated that "the number of dimensionless group's involved in a mathematical representation of a physical process is equal to the number of physical variables involved, minus the number of fundamental dimensions used to express them." Thus dimensionless analysis carried out to get the relationships.

But there are some exceptions to Buckingham's rule. Therefore, dimensional analysis is carried out by algbraic method. The results obtained by dimensional analysis can be used as guidelines to establish relationship among variables, but it should be confirmed only by experimental tests. Dimensional analysis is also very useful in checking equations, investigating validity of formulas and checking units. The study of dimensions and dimensional analysis will often help in making a description of physical phenomena easier and more convenient.

The algebraic method of dimensional analysis to generate equations is illustrated below :

For example, the discharge (Q) of a liquid, in volume per unit time, through a horizontal capillary tube is thought to depend upon the pressure drop per unit length ($\Delta P/L$), the diameter (D), and the dynamic viscosity (η); then in this case we can say :

$$Q = f\left(\frac{\Delta P}{L}\ D\ \eta\right)$$

or

$$Q = k\left(\frac{\Delta P}{L}\right)^a (D)^b (\eta)^c$$

The dimensions are as follows :

$$Q = \frac{Volume}{time} = [L]^3\ [T]^{-1}$$

$$\Delta P = Pressure\ drop = [M]\ [L]^{-1}\ [T]^{-2}$$

$$\eta = Viscosity$$
$$= [M]\ [L]^{-1}\ [T]^{-1}$$

For L and D dimension is [L].

Dimensional equation becomes :

$$[L]^3\ [T]^{-1} = \left([M][L]^{-2}[T]^{-2}\right)^a [L]^b \left([M][L]^{-1}[T]^{-1}\right)^c$$

a, b and c are exponents for three variables.

Equating the respective power for time, mass and length

Time [T] $-1 = -2a - c$

Mass [M] $0 = a + c$

Length [L] $3 = -2a + b - c$

By solving simultaneously the above equations, we get a = 1, b = 4 and c = – 1. By substituting values of exponent, the equation becomes

$$Q = k \frac{\Delta P}{L} \frac{D^4}{\eta}$$

From experimentation it was found

$k = \frac{1}{128}$ then equation becomes,

$$Q = \frac{\Delta P\, D^4}{128\, \eta\, L}$$

***

MANUAL CORRECTIONS

CH. 1

will be able to develop the new pharmaceutical processes and modify existing ones. The pharmaceutical technologist must also be able to make himself clearly understood by design engineers and by the suppliers of the equipment he uses.

units are given in Table 1.1. The conversion of units are given in Appendix – I.

Table 1.1 : Dimensional analysis of various quantities and variables

considers only the physical changes that take place during processing. Application of concept of

Potential energy refers to the energy a body or a substance has, because of its position relative

Dimensional equation becomes :

CHAPTER 2

FLOW OF FLUIDS

2.1 INTRODUCTION

Fluids are the materials which deform continuously or flow as long as the shear stress is applied, but are unable to achieve an equilibrium under applied shear stress.

Many materials in the manufacture of bulk drugs and pharmaceuticals are in the form of fluids. Similarly, there is increasing tendency to handle powdered or granular materials in the form in which they behave as fluids i.e. fluidisation. Thus, concept of fluids covers liquids, gases and fluidised solids. If stress is applied uniformly over all boundaries and if fluid decreases in volume showing proportionate increase in density, it is considered as compressible. Liquids for general purpose are considered non-compressible, and gases as compressible.

The study of fluids is divided into the :

(i) Study of fluids at rest i.e. *Fluid statics*.

(ii) Study of fluids in motion i.e. *Fluid dynamics*.

2.2 FLUID STATICS

2.2.1 Pressure

Pressure is an important property of a fluid at rest. Pressure is defined as force exerted per unit area. For a material, force exerted is equal to the product of mass and gravitational acceleration.

$$F = mg$$

For fluids, mass can be calculated from volume and density.

$$F = V \rho g$$

where, F is the force exerted, m is the mass of fluid, g is gravitational acceleration, ρ is density and V is volume of fluid.

Thus, this force exerted by the fluid due to gravity must be resisted by some supporting medium so that fluid remain in equilibrium. Lower levels of fluid must provide support for the fluid that lies above them. Fluid at any point must support the above. Thus, the fluid pressure i.e. force per unit area in a fluid is equal in all directions.

The pressure of fluid varies with depth. If we consider the fluid at depth Z below the surface and A as the area ; the volume of fluid will be ZA. Therefore, force exerted will be ZA ρ g. But total force is sum of the force exerted on the surface of the liquid and force of the liquid.

$$\therefore \quad \text{Total force} = A P_a + Z A \rho g$$

where, P_a is the pressure at the surface (atmospheric pressure).

$$\therefore \quad \text{Total pressure} = \frac{\text{Total force}}{A}$$

$$= P_a + Z \rho g \qquad \ldots (1)$$

Fig. 2.1 : Fluid Statics

This is *absolute pressure*. But, usually pressure is given in terms of pressure above or below atmospheric pressure, i.e. considering atmospheric pressure as datum line. *This gauge pressure*, it will be represented as

$$P = Z \rho g$$

As pressure varies with depth, the hydrostatic expression can be represented as

$$dP = -\rho g \, dZ$$

As liquids are incompressible, integrating the above equation within the limits P_1 and P_2 and Z_1 and Z_2 gives :

$$\int_{P_2}^{P_1} dP = -\rho g \int_{Z_2}^{Z_1} dZ$$

$$P_1 - P_2 = -\rho g (Z_1 - Z_2) \qquad \ldots (2)$$

Example 2.1 : Calculate the greatest gauge and absolute pressure in a spherical tank of 5 m diameter filled with arachis oil of specific gravity 0.95. (density of water = 10^3 kg/m^3 ; atmospheric pressure 1.013×10^5 N/m^2).

Solution :

$$h = 5m$$
$$\text{Specific gravity} = 0.95$$
$$\therefore \text{density, } \rho = 0.95 \times 10^3 \text{ kg/m}^3$$
$$g = 9.8 \text{ m/s}^2$$
$$\text{Gauge pressure} = h \rho g$$
$$= 5 \times 0.95 \times 10^3 \times 9.8$$
$$= 46.55 \times 10^3 \text{ N/m}^2$$
$$\text{Absolute pressure} = \text{Gauge pressure} + \text{Atmospheric pressure}$$
$$= 0.4655 \times 10^5 + 1.013 \times 10^5$$
$$= 1.4785 \times 10^5 \text{ N/m}^2$$

The pressure of fluid is also expressed in terms of *'depth or head'* of the fluid.

Example 2.2 : Calculate head of water equivalent to standard atmospheric pressure.

$$\text{Formula : } Z = \frac{P}{\rho g}$$

Solution :
$$Z = \frac{P}{\rho g}$$
$$= \frac{1.013 \times 10^5}{9.81 \times 10^3}$$
$$= 0.1033 \times 10^2 = 10.33 \text{ m}$$

2.2.2 Pressure Measurement :

Pressure of a fluid may be expressed as : *Absolute pressure* which the fluid pressure above the reference value of a perfect vacuum or the absolute zero pressure.

Gauge pressure represents the value of pressure above the reference value of atmospheric pressure. Thus it is the difference between the absolute and local atmospheric pressure. The atmospheric pressure at sea level is **760 mm Hg** or **14.7 psi** or 1.013×10^5 Pa (Pascals). *Vacuum* is the amount by which atmospheric pressure exceeds the absolute pressure.

Some common pressure measuring devices include :

(A) Manometers and
(B) Bourdon Gauge.

(A) Manometers :

Manometer is a simple device for measurement of static pressure. There are two types of manometer discussed here :

(i) Simple manometer
(ii) Differential manometer.

(i) Simple Manometer :

A simple manometer consists of a U–tube containing a suitable fluid as shown in Fig. 2.2 The difference in levels (h) between the two arms is an indication of pressure difference ($P_1 - P_5$) between two arms. The fluid to be used in manometer should have following properties:

(a) It should be non-corrosive and should not react with the fluid whose pressure has to be measured.

(b) It should have low viscosity and hence quick adjustment with pressure change, and

(c) It should have negligible surface tension and capillary effects.

Hence water or mercury are fluids of choice in manometer.

(a) U-tube manometer   **(b) Inclined manometer**

Fig. 2.2

The relationship between h and $P_1 - P_2$ can be established as follows : Let shaded portion contains fluid A and unshaded portion in tube contains fluid B. Let ρ_A and ρ_B are densities of fluid A and fluid B respectively, Z_1 and Z_2 are heights of liquid columns in two arms and $h = Z_2 - Z_1$. Now pressure at any point can be given by hydrostatic equation as

$$P = h \rho g \qquad \ldots (3)$$

Therefore for various points shown in Fig. 2.2 (a).

At point 1, P_1 : Pressure is P_1

At point 2, P_2 : P_1 + Pressure of fluid B column (ht . h + m) = $P_1 + (h + m) \rho_B \, g$

At point 5, P_5 : Pressure is P_5

At point 4, $P_4 : P_5 +$ Pressure of fluid B (ht. m) $= P_5 + m\, \rho_B\, g$

At point 3, $P_3 :$ Pressure at point 4 + Pressure of column of A (ht. h) $= P_5 + m\, \rho_B\, g + h\, \rho_A\, g$

But P_2 is equal to P_3 ; therefore

$$P_1 + (h + m)\, \rho_B\, g = P_5 + m\, \rho_B\, g + h\, \rho_A\, g \qquad \ldots (4)$$

$\therefore \quad P_1 + h\, \rho_B\, g + m\, \rho_B\, g = P_5 + m\, \rho_B\, g + h\, \rho_A\, g$

$\therefore \quad \Delta P = P_1 - P_5 = h\, (\rho_A - \rho_B)\, g \qquad \ldots (5)$

If fluid B is a gas (which is a general case) then $\rho_B << \rho_A$, therefore it can be neglected. Then equation 5 will become

$$\Delta P = h\, \rho_A\, g \qquad \ldots (6)$$

Equation show the relationship between ΔP and h is independent of height m and diameter of the U–tube ; provided P_1 and P_5 are measured in the same horizontal plane. It is suitable for measurement of moderate pressure.

At very low pressures, the difference in levels in two arms will be very less and difficult to read. Therefore, for small readings a modification of U–tube manometer, *inclined tube manometer* is used as shown in Fig. (2.2 b). The tube is inclined at some angle to the horizontal so as to magnify the linear displacement of fluid. Here, the length l along the inclined tube is an inclination of pressure difference $(P_1 - P_2)$.

Relationship between l and ΔP is as follows :

The vertical length (L) of inclined leg can be obtained by inclined length (l) divided by the sine of angle of inclination θ (if area A_1 of one limb is significantly high as compared to A_2 for another limb).

$\therefore \qquad l = \dfrac{L}{\sin \theta}$

$\therefore \qquad \Delta P = P_1 - P_2$

$\qquad \qquad \quad = L\, \rho\, g$

$\therefore \qquad \Delta P = l \sin \theta\, \rho\, g \qquad \ldots (7)$

(ii) Differential Manometer :

It is a manometer to measure small pressure differences. As shown in Fig. 2.3, the manometer contains two immiscible fluid B and C. The liquid levels in the top reservoirs remains constant due to the large chambers. The pressure will be given as :

$$\Delta P = P_1 - P_2 = h\, (\rho_C - \rho_B)\, g$$

The reading (h) will be high if fluid B and fluid C have nearly the same density.

Fig. 2.3 : Differential manometer

(B) Bourdon tube Pressure Gauges :

It is a mechanical pressure - measuring element. Such mechanical elements are designed to operate under a pressure change by bending, deforming or deflecting depending upon the pressure variation. Such elements are termed as 'transducers', because the3
y can take one form of energy from the measuring source and supply energy of a different kind to an indicating, recording or controlling system. A pressure guage may take energy from the air compressed in the cylinder and supply enough mechanical power to move a pointer across a scale to indicate or record the pressure in the cylinder.

Eugene Bourdon invented pressure gauge in 1851. He stated that a round tubing which has flattened and a bent circular arc will tend to return to its original shape when pressure is applied inside it. A simple form of Bourdon gauge (Fig. 2.4), consists of a length of thin - walled metal tubing which has been flattened to approximately an elliptical cross-section and then rolled into a C shape. The arc of the gauge is in between $180 - 270°$. The tube has a
pressure - inlet at one end and the other free end is sealed, it is called as the tip. The tube is made up of bronze, phosphur bronze, stainless steel, nickel alloys etc.

Under pressure the elliptical or flattened section tends to change its shape to a circular form. The deflection of the tip depends upon the radius of the bend, total tube length, Young's modulus of elasticity of the tube material and total tube length. Different configurations of Bourdon gauges include helical and spiral tubes apart from C - shaped.

Bourdon gauge has good sensitivity and repeatability. It is useful in the range of 10^6 to 10^8 Pascals.

(a) C-shaped Bourdon gauge   (b) Spiral Bourdon tube

(c) A helical Bourdon tube

Fig. 2.4 : Bourdon tube gauge

2.3 FLUID DYNAMICS
2.3.1 Mechanism of fluid flow :

Fig. 2.5 : Reynold's experiment

Osborne Reynolds performed experiment to study the flow of fluids (Fig. 2.5). In a glass tube, he introduced a dye into the flowing stream at various points. The observations and conclusions are as follows :

(i) In the region of low flow rate, the dye formed a smooth, thin straight streak down the pipe and there was no mixing at the perpendicular axis of the pipe. In this region, pressure drop per unit length is proportional to flow rate. This type of flow where all the motion is in the axial direction is called as *laminar flow* ; because fluid appears to move in layers or lamina.

(ii) In the region of high flow rate, the dye was rapidly mixed throughout the entire pipe. The rapid, haphazard motion in all direction in the pipe along with axial motion caused rapid mixing of the dye. In this region,

For Smooth pipe : Pressure Drop per unit length α (Flow Rate)
For Rough pipe : Pressure Drop per unit length α (Flow Rate)

This type of flow is termed as *turbulent*.

(iii) Reynolds observed a region of unreproducible results between the laminar and turbulent flow region. This region is termed as *transition region*. As the laminar flow occurs in a condition of stable flow form which may switch to turbulent flow due to effect of certain outside disturbance, like roughness of pipe wall, vibration of equipment etc. In the transition region, the flow is either turbulent or laminar. Depending on the conditions, it alternates between laminar and turbulent. The pressure drop in this region is very difficult to measure and it oscillates between the lower and higher values.

From these experimental observations, Reynolds concluded that there are two forces acting on the fluid in flow. These are :

(i) Kinetic or velocity or inertial forces which tend to maintain the flow in its general direction. This force is proportional to velocity pressure ρu^2 and

(ii) Viscous forces which tend to retard the general motion of fluid and introduce eddies. These are proportional to $\dfrac{\mu u}{D}$, where μ is viscosity of fluid and D is diameter of the pipe.

Reynolds claimed that the fluid flow changes with the change in these forces. The type of flow developed depends on the ratio of the forces, hence a dimensionless number, Reynolds number was developed.

Reynolds Number, $\quad Re = \dfrac{\text{Inertial force}}{\text{Viscous force}} = \dfrac{\rho u^2 D}{u\mu}$

Error! ... (9)

where, $\quad D$ = pipe diameter,

u = velocity of fluid,
μ = viscosity of liquid and
ρ = density of fluid.

Reynolds number can be modified for flows other than a pipe flow, by substituting the pipe diameter by a suitable length parameter.

2.3.2 Significance of Reynolds Number :

(i) For fluid flow through a pipe, flow remains laminar or stream line for values of Re upto 2100 ; whereas flow becomes turbulent at Re values above 4000. Between the values of 2100 and 4000, the flow pattern is unstable or transition region exists.

(ii) At constant velocity fluid can change from laminar to turbulent if pipe diameter is increased. Decrease in viscosity (due to temperature change) may also show similar effects.

(iii) Higher is the Reynolds number, greater is the relative contribution of inertial forces, whereas as lower Re values viscous effects predominate the inertial effects.

(iv) Reynold's number is important in determination of heat transfer by forced convection, frictional losses in fluid flow etc.

In the most of the pharmaceutical operations, fluids are in motion. These systems are to be analysed by applying material and energy balances.

2.3.3 Material Balance :

Consider fluid flowing through a pipe across two points, point 1 and point 2. Let a_1, ρ_1 and u_1 be cross-sectional area of pipe, density and velocity of fluid at point 1. Similarly, a_2, ρ_2 and u_2 denote same parameters at point 2. The material balance across the pipe between point 1 and point 2 is given as :

$$\rho_1 \, a_1 \, u_1 = \rho_2 \, a_2 \, u_2$$

Liquids are incompressible, therefore $\rho_1 = \rho_2$. Thus

$$\boxed{u_1 \, a_1 = u_2 \, a_2} \qquad \ldots (10)$$

This is known as *continuity equation* for liquids; obtained for material balance of fluid flow.

2.3.4 Energy Balance :

Fluid has some intrinsic energy itself and some interchange of energy occurs with the surroundings. The intrinsic energy of fluid include :

(i) Potential energy
(ii) Kinetic energy and
(iii) Pressure energy or flow energy.

The *potential energy* is the capacity to do work by reason of it's position relative to some centre of attraction. Thus potential energy of a unit mass of fluid at height Z above the datum level is

$$P.E. = Zg \qquad \ldots (11)$$

Kinetic energy is the energy of the fluid due to it's motion. If u is the velocity of liquid and m is mass ; then

$$K.E. = \frac{1}{2} mu^2$$

For unit mass of fluids it becomes

$$K.E. = \frac{u^2}{2} \qquad \ldots (12)$$

Pressure energy or flow energy is energy form peculiar to the flow of fluids. Fluid exerts pressure on it's surrounding. If volume of fluid is decreased, the pressure exerts a force which must be overcome while compressing the fluid. Thus work has to be done in compressing the fluid. Similarly, work can be done by the fluid under pressure if its pressure is released. This is known as Pressure energy.

Suppose fluid is present in a cylinder having cross-sectional area A, and it moves through distance L against pressure P (Fig.2.6). Then work done by the fluid is PAL. This work is done by AL volume of liquid having density ρ ; hence by AρL quantity of liquid. Work done by unit mass of liquid is pressure energy.

$$\therefore \quad Pr.E. = \frac{PAL}{A\rho L} = \frac{P}{\rho} \quad \ldots (13)$$

Thus $\frac{P}{\rho}$ is the pressure energy or work that can be obtained by unit mass of fluid during flow.

Fig. 2.6 : Pressure energy

Total intrinsic energy of the fluid is sum of potential, kinetic and pressure energy.

$$\therefore \quad \text{Total energy} = P.E + K.E. + Pr.E.$$
$$= Zg + \frac{u^2}{2} + \frac{P}{\rho} \quad \ldots (14)$$

Apart from this intrinsic energy fluid comes across interchange with the surroundings as
(i) Frictional losses,
(ii) Mechanical energy added by pumps, and
(iii) Heat energy due to heating or cooling.

2.3.5 Bernoulli's Theorem :

Application of law of conservation of energy to flow of fluids is Bernoulli's theorem. In other words, the energy balance of flow of fluids is known as Bernoulli's equation.

Fig. 2.7 : Development of Bernoulli's theorem

If we consider a system at uniform temperature conveying liquid from point A to point B. Points A and B are at heights Z_a and Z_b from datum line. u_a and u_b are the velocities of liquid at points A and B respectively. P_A and P_B are the pressures at A and B respectively. As liquid is incompressible, there is no effect of pressure on density (ρ) of the liquid. The energy balance can be written as:

$$\text{Energy of fluid at A} = \text{Energy of fluid at B}$$

$$(P.E.)_A + (K.E.)_A + (Pr.E)_A = (P.E.)_B + (K.E.)_B + (Pr.E)_B$$

$$\therefore \quad Z_a g + \frac{u_a^2}{2} + \frac{P_A}{\rho} = Z_b g + \frac{u_b^2}{2} + \frac{P_B}{\rho} \quad \ldots (15)$$

This is the Bernoulli's equation without friction where frictional losses are neglected and no addition of energy is considered.

But when fluid flows through a pipe it has to overcome the frictional resistance of the pipe wall and thus, there is loss of energy from the fluid energy resources. If we consider that F is the energy loss due to friction and W is the energy added by the pumps then Bernoulli's equation becomes:

$$Z_a g + \frac{u_a^2}{2} + \frac{P_A}{\rho} + W - F = Z_b g + \frac{u_b^2}{2} + \frac{P_B}{\rho} \quad \ldots (16)$$

This is the Bernoulli's equation for flow of fluids.

The equation can be expressed in terms of heads instead of energy as follows by dividing all the terms by g. When we get dimensions of length:

$$\boxed{Z_a + \frac{u_a^2}{2g} + \frac{P_A}{\rho g} + \frac{W}{g} - \frac{F}{g} = Z_b + \frac{u_b^2}{2g} + \frac{P_B}{\rho g}} \quad \ldots (17)$$

2.3.6 Applications of Bernoulli's Theorem:

(a) Determination of power requirements:

Bernoulli's equation can be used to calculate the power required, if the liquid has to be driven at certain rate through a system.

As per Bernoulli's equation,

$$\frac{W}{g} = \frac{u_B^2 - u_A^2}{2g} + \frac{P_B - P_A}{g} + (Z_B - Z_A) + \frac{F}{g}$$

If the sum of changes in velocity, pressure, height and frictional losses is said to be ΔH, then

$$\frac{W}{g} = \Delta H$$

$$\therefore \quad W = g \Delta H \quad \ldots (18)$$

Thus $g \Delta H$ is the work done on unit mass of liquid. Hence if we want to transfer mass m of liquid in time t, then total work required to be done or power required will be

$$\boxed{\text{Power} = \frac{mg \Delta H}{t}}$$

To get terms of volume, i.e. if Q is the volumetric flow rate (volume flowing per unit time)

$$Q = \frac{V}{t} = \frac{m}{\rho t} \quad \text{i.e. } m = Q\rho t$$

$$\therefore \quad \text{Power} = Q g \Delta H \rho \qquad \ldots (19)$$

This equation will be used to calculate power requirements.

Ex. 2.3 : Calculate the power required to pump castor oil from a vessel at ground level to a vessel at 3 meter above the ground using a glass pipe having diameter 4 cm and length 3 m. The oil has to be delivered at the rate of 12 lit./min. and frictional head for given length of pipe is 4 m.

Sol. : Sp. Gravity of Castor oil is 0.95.

$$\text{Frictional head for given length of pipe i.e. } \frac{F}{g} = 4 \text{ m}$$

Density of water = 1000 kg/m^3

$\therefore$ Density of castor oil = 0.95 × 1000 = 950 kg/m^3

$$\text{Volumetric flow rate (Q)} = \frac{m}{\rho t}$$

$$= \frac{1.2 \times 0.95}{950 \times 60} \text{ m}^3/\text{sec.} = 0.0002 \text{ m}^3/\text{sec.}$$

$$\text{Average velocity in pipe (u)} = \frac{Q}{\text{area of pipe i.e. } \left(\frac{\pi}{4}D^2\right)}$$

$$= \frac{0.0002}{\frac{\pi}{4} \times (0.04)^2} = 0.167 \text{ m/sec.}$$

As point A is at ground potential and kinetic energy at this point is taken as zero

$$\text{Velocity head} = \frac{\left(u_b^2 - u_a^2\right)}{2g}$$

$$= \frac{0.167 - 0}{2 \times 9.81} = 0.0085 \text{ m}$$

As point A is at zero datum level and point B is at 3 m height ; potential head is 3 m.

$$\text{Power} = Q g \Delta H \rho$$

$$\text{Total head } \Delta H = \text{Potential head} + \text{Velocity head} + \text{Frictional head}$$

$$= 3 + 0.0085 + 4$$

$$= 7.0085 \text{ m}$$

$\therefore \quad \text{Power} = 0.0002 \times 9.81 \times 7.0085 \times 950$

$$= 13.063 \text{ Ns}^{-1}$$

(b) Measurement of Flow Rates :

Bernoulli's theorem is used for the measurement of flow rate of fluids. The flowmeters are classified as :

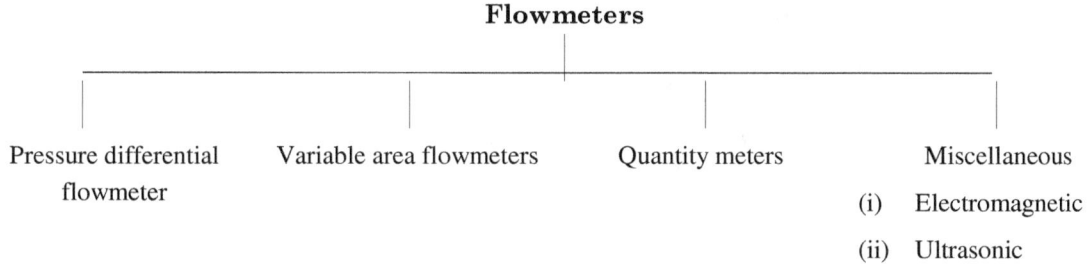

A. **Pressure Differential Flowmeter :**

Principle : When a fluid is passing through a pipe, it is exerting pressure in all directions. If a constriction is placed in the pipe, the fluid flows through this section more rapidly than when flowing through the rest of the pipe in order that the same quantity pass through. At the constriction, the kinetic energy of the fluid is greater and its potential energy is less so that its static pressure is less. Thus, if the pressure of the fluid at the suitable points on either side of the constriction, upstream and downstream, is measured, this differential pressure varies according to square of the rate of flow.

As shown in Fig. 2.8, the liquid is flowing through a pipe having constriction. If we consider in the pipe two points A and B,

where, a_1 and a_2 = cross-sectional area at points A and B respectively

u_1 and u_2 = velocity of liquid at points A and B respectively

P_1 and P_2 = pressures at points A and B respectively.

A and B are at same level from datum line. Therefore, potential energy of fluid at both points is equal.

Fig. 2.8 : Pressure differential

Hence, by applying Bernoulli's equation without friction we get,

$$\frac{u_1^2}{2} + \frac{P_1}{\rho} = \frac{u_2^2}{2} + \frac{P_2}{\rho}$$

∴ $$\frac{u_2^2}{2} - \frac{u_1^2}{2} = \frac{P_1 - P_2}{\rho}$$ ... (20)

From continuity equation, we know,

volumetric flow rate $Q = u_1 a_1 = u_2 a_2$

$$u_1 = u_2 \frac{a_2}{a_1}$$

Substituting this value of u_1 in equation (20) we get;

$$\frac{u_2^2}{2} - \frac{u_2^2 \left(\frac{a_2}{a_1}\right)^2}{2} = \frac{P_1 - P_2}{\rho}$$

$$\frac{u_2^2}{2}\left(1 - \frac{a_2^2}{a_1^2}\right) = \frac{P_1 - P_2}{\rho}$$

$$u_2^2 = \frac{2(P_1 - P_2)}{\rho\left(1 - \frac{a_2^2}{a_1^2}\right)}$$

$$u_2 = \sqrt{\frac{2(P_1 - P_2)}{\rho\left(1 - \frac{a_2^2}{a_1^2}\right)}} \qquad \ldots (21)$$

But $\qquad Q = u_2 \, a_2$

$$Q = a_2 \sqrt{\frac{2(P_1 - P_2)}{\rho\left(1 - \frac{a_2^2}{a_1^2}\right)}} \qquad \ldots (22)$$

But while deriving this equation we have not taken into consideration frictional losses and losses due to change in kinetic energy. Thus, a constant is introduced called as 'discharge coefficient' and now equation becomes :

$$\boxed{Q = C_D \, a_2 \sqrt{\frac{2(P_1 - P_2)}{\rho\left(1 - \frac{a_2^2}{a_1^2}\right)}}} \qquad \ldots (23)$$

Discharge coefficient varies with type of flow and nature of constriction. C_D value lies between 0.95 to 0.99 for turbulent flow and it is still lower for laminar flow.

Various flowmeters based on pressure differential principle mainly include :
(i) Orifice meter
(ii) Venturimeter and
(iii) Pitot tube.

(i) Orifice Meter :

This is the simplest and widely used pressure differential flowmeter. It consists of a simple plate with an orifice which is fitted between adjacent flanges of the pipe. The orifice constricts the fluid. Thus when fluid passes through an orifice, it's kinetic energy increases and pressure energy decreases. A manometer is connected with pressure taps, one above and one below the orifice plate.

Fig. 2.9 : Fluid flow thorugh an orifice in a closed pipe

As shown in the above Fig. 2.9, the fluid passes through an orifice giving a stream having minimum cross-sectional area called as 'vena contracta'. The pressure taps are placed across points A and B (B is at vena contracta). If we apply equation (20), we can not determine the exact area (a_2) at point B i.e. vena contracta. We know cross-sectional area at A and at orifice but not at vena contracta, therefore, area a_2 is related to area at orifice by following equation :

$$C_C = \frac{a_2}{a_o} \qquad \ldots (24)$$

where a_o is cross-sectional area at an orifice and C_C is called as 'coefficient of contraction'.

Coefficient of discharge (C_D) for an orifice meter takes into consideration C_C, frictional losses and losses due to kinetic energy changes. Thus equation (20) for an orifice meter becomes

$$\boxed{Q = a_o \, C_D \sqrt{\frac{2(P_1 - P_2)}{\rho\left(1 - \frac{a_o^2}{a_1^2}\right)}}} \qquad \ldots (25)$$

If $a_o << a_1$ i.e. orifice diameter is very less as compared to pipe diameter then $1 - \frac{a_o^2}{a_1^2}$ is almost equal to 1. Equation 25 will become,

$$Q = a_o \, C_D \sqrt{\frac{2(P_1 - P_2)}{\rho}} \qquad \ldots (26)$$

But $P = h \rho g$, for incompressible liquids. Therefore

$$P_1 - P_2 = h_1 \rho g - h_2 \rho g$$

$$\Delta P = \Delta h \rho g$$

Substituting value of ΔP in equation (26), we get

$$Q = a_o \, C_D \sqrt{2 \Delta h g} \qquad \ldots (27)$$

For an orifice meter value of C_D is around 0.6,

Generally, the plate is fitted in a pipe so that the orifice is concentric with the bore, this is changed in some conditions. When flow rate has to be measured for suspensions or dirty fluids, a plate of the eccentric type is used. The orifice is located with the lower edge coincident with the inside of the bottom of the pipe, so that solids are not obstructed in their passage.

An orifice meter plate sometimes has an additional small hole ;

(i) For gas flow rate measurement, the plate is placed with the small hole below the orifice so that condensate will pass through this hole.

(ii) For liquid flow rate measurement, plate is fitted with the hole above the orifice so that gases can pass without forming the pockets.

Advantages of Orifice meter :

(i) It is versatile and can be used for measurement of almost all gases and liquids. It is most suitable for clean gases and non-viscous liquids at moderate flow rates.

(ii) It can be used over a wide range of flow rates.

(iii) It is simple, inexpensive, and easy to install.

Most important disadvantage of an orifice meter is that, it produces permanent loss of head i.e. more resistance to flow. Therefore, it requires higher pumping cost if used for longer period. Therefore, orifice meter is not suitable for permanent installation.

(ii) Venturi Meter

Sudden constriction of flow of fluid is a major disadvantage of orifice meter, this is overcome in a venturi meter where gradual decrease in cross-sectional area is achieved.

A venturi meter consists of two cones, an entrance cone on upstream side and a discharge cone or a diffuser on downstream side. These two cones are joined by a short length of pipe called throat section. The difference in pressure is measured before entering the fluid in the entrance cone and the throat section as shown in Fig. 2.10. The entrance cone gradually constricts the fluid and the diffuser carries out gradual expansion thereby reducing loss of head, reducing turbulence. Volumetric flow rate of fluid can be calculated by using
equation (23).

Fig. 2.10 : Simple venturi meter

Main advantage of venturi meter is gradual constriction and expansion of fluid reduces the head loss considerably in a venturi meter, therefore, power loss is less with the flow meter. But it is relatively expensive and difficult to install.

(iii) Pitot Tube :

This pressure differential flow meter is also sometimes classified as insertion meter. Pitot tube is a narrow tube supported in a pipe with the head bent in such a way that the open end or impact opening directly faces the oncoming fluid. (Fig. 2.11)

In the pitot tube, B is a stagnation point where velocity of fluid becomes zero. The pressure is measured at point A (P_1) and point B (P_2). Then by using the equation (20), we get

$$-\frac{u_1^2}{2} = \frac{P_1 - P_2}{\rho} \quad (as\ u_2 = 0)$$

$$\therefore \quad u_1^2 = \frac{2(P_2 - P_1)}{\rho} \quad \ldots (28)$$

Fig. 2.11 : Pitot tube

Advantages of Pitot tube :

(i) As tube is very small as compared to the pipe diameter, it does not produce considerable loss of head.

(ii) It is inexpensive and easy to install.

Limitations of Pitot tube :

1. This insertion meter determines the velocity of fluid at point. The mean velocity in the pipe can be measured by positioning the pitot tube point at different distances from the pipe wall.
2. Pitot tube cannot be used for measurement of fluids containing small solid particles as the tube opening may get clogged.
3. Pitot tube is not suitable for measurement of fluids at low velocities i.e. below 5 m/s. Accuracy of pitot tube is less than orifice and venturimeter.
4. It is not suitable for the measurement of highly fluctuating velocities, i.e. highly turbulent flows.

B. Variable Area Flowmeters :

Principle :

In pressure differential meter, the constricted area was kept constant and the pressure differential changes with the velocity of fluid. But if the pressure differential is held constant by adjusting the orifice area then the area of an orifice at any particular instant is a measure of the rate of flow through the orifice. This is the principle of variable area meters.

Various variable area meters include :

(i) Rotameter

(ii) Orifice and Plug meter and

(iii) Gate meters.

(i) Rotameter :

As shown in Fig. 2.12, rotameter consists of a long graduated vertical tube generally made up of glass having a uniform taper, arranged with the smaller section at the bottom. A float moves freely within the tube and is prevented from fouling the side of the tube by means of a series of angled slots cut into the float so that as fluid flows past the float it will be caused to spin. In some forms, float can be prevented from fouling by use of central guide rod.

Fig. 2.12 : Rotameter

When a fluid flows up the tube, it carries with it the float, as the upward force exerted by the fluid is greater than the immersed weight of the float. As the float rises, the area of annulus between the float and tube wall slowly increases, so the upward force due to the fluid velocity decreases. At a certain point all the forces acting on the float are in equilibrium, when the force due to the fluid velocity is exactly balanced by the weight of the float. Rate of flow of fluid can directly be determined by noting the reading on the scale.

Glass tube rotameters can be used for liquid flow rates from 30 ml/sec. to 5 lit/sec. and for gas flow rates from 0.2 ml/sec. to 40 lit./sec. Whereas metal tube rotameters are used for high flow rates upto 120 lit./sec.

Advantages of Rotameter :
- (i) Permanent pressure loss is relatively very low.
- (ii) It is highly versatile and can be used for all kinds of fluids, from heavy viscous or opaque liquids to light gases. It is useful over a wide range of flow rates and at high or low temperatures and pressures.
- (iii) It is relatively simple in construction, and is inexpensive.

But errors may occur while taking the reading due to tendency of float to oscillate.

(ii) Orifice and Plug Meter :

As shown in Fig. 2.13, a tapered plug of such a form that the area of the annular space between the orifice and the plug is proportional to the lift of the plug. Therefore, the height by which the plug rises when a fluid flows past it, is a measure of the rate of flow.

Fig. 2.13 : Orifice and Plug meter

(iii) Gate Meter :

Fig. 2.14 : Variable area gate meter

A gate flowmeter has gate which can be adjusted manually or automatically so that constant pressure drop can be maintained across the orifice. The position of the gate is indicated by a scale which may be calibrated in terms of flow rate.

C. Quantity Flowmeters :

These flowmeters measure the total quantity of fluid flown in a certain time, and average flow rate is determined by dividing the quantity of fluid flown by time. These meters are divided as (i) weighing meters and (ii) volumetric meters.

In weighing meters, the liquid is weighed in weighing tanks and taking into consi-deration density of liquid, volumetric flow rate can be calculated.

Volumetric meters are based on the principle of positive displacement. In this type of meters, as the liquid flows through the meter, it moves a measuring element which seals off the measuring chamber into a number of compartments of definite volume. As the measuring element moves these compartments are successively filled and emptied. Thus, for one cycle of the measuring element, a known quantity of liquid passes from the inlet to the outlet of the meter. The number of cycles of the measuring element are indicated by a pointer moving over a dial. Volumetric meters for liquids are rotating lobe meter and rotating vane meter (Fig. 2.15).

(a) Rotating lobe meter **(b) Rotating vane meter**

Fig. 2.15

For gas flow measurement, the volumetric flowmeters are bellows dry gas meter, water displacement gas meter and rotating lobe gas meter. Bellows gas meter is suitable for low pressure gas whereas rotating lobe meters are suitable for high gas pressure.

D. Other Types :

(i) Electromagnetic Flowmeters :

It is based on Faraday's law of induction i.e. when an electrical conductor moves through a magnetic field in a direction at right angles both to the magnetic field and it's length, an e.m.f. is generated which is given by

$$V = B\, l\, U \text{ volts} \qquad \ldots (29)$$

where   B = magnetic flux density,
          l = length of the conductor,
          U = velocity of the conductor.

Thus, if a conducting fluid is allowed to flow with velocity U along a pipe of internal diameter l and an electromagnetic system directs a magnetic field B across a section of the pipe so that it acts at right angles to the direction of motion of the fluid, an induced voltage V is produced. If the magnetic flux density is constant, the induced voltage will be proportional to the mean flow velocity.

In this flow meter (Fig. 2.16) there is no obstruction to fluid flow and no head loss. It is widely used for fluids containing suspended solids.

(a) Principle of the electromagnetic flowmeter   **(b) Electromagnetic flowmeter**

Fig. 2.16

(ii) Ultrasonic Flowmeters :

These are based on the principle that a linear relationship exists between the apparent velocity of sound in flowing fluid and the velocity of the fluid. Thus, if the direction of the ultrasonic wave is not perpendicular to the flow of fluid then the component of flow velocity in the direction of the ultrasonic wave will alter the sound velocity. It's basic working is shown in Fig. 2.17.

Fig. 2.17 : Single path ultrasonic flowmeter

Ultrasonic flowmeters have many advantages like no head loss, good accuracy. It can be used for conducting as well as non-conducting fluid and also the slurries. But the meters are highly expensive.

(iii) Nuclear Technique :

In nuclear technique method, an radioactive tracer is injected and time taken for the passage of a tracer between two points in a pipeline is recorded using two radiation detectors and suitable recorder.

Now, we will analyse three different conditions of flow of fluids.

1. Fluid flow through pipe (as involved in transfer of solutions or gases through pipe).
2. Fluid past immersed bodies (as involved in sedimentation, suspensions, etc.).
3. Fluid flow through packed beds (as involved in filtration packed fractionating column etc.)

2.3.7 Fluid flow through pipe :

(i) Flow Rate and Velocity Distribution :

The fluid flowing through a pipe may exhibit a laminar or turbulent flow.

(a) Laminar flow in pipe is expressed by *Poiseulli's equation* : Consider the fluid contained in radius r, in a cylinder having radius R. The flow is flowing length l, across pressure drop ΔP. There are two forces acting on the fluid ;

(i) Pressure force which is a driving force and

(ii) Viscous force acting on the wall is opposing the flow.

If flow is steady, pressure force is exactly balanced by the viscous force.

$$\text{Pressure force} = \Delta P \, \pi \, r^2 \quad \ldots (30)$$

$$\text{Viscous force} = \text{shear stress} \propto \text{area over which it acts}$$

$$= \tau \propto 2 \, \pi \, r \, l \quad \ldots (31)$$

But, $\quad$ Shear stress, $\tau = \dfrac{\Delta P r}{2l} \quad \ldots (32)$

This shear stress is proportional to velocity change with distance i.e. $\dfrac{du}{dr}$ (velocity gradient).

$$\tau \propto \dfrac{du}{dr}$$

$$\therefore \quad \tau = \eta \dfrac{du}{dr}$$

where, $\quad \eta$ = dynamic viscosity.

Substituting the value, we get

$$-\dfrac{du}{dr} = \dfrac{\Delta P r}{2 \eta l}$$

As 'u' decreases with increase in r, velocity gradient is given negative sign.

Error!... (33)

Integrating eqn. (33) between limits r to R and u to 0,

$$\int_0^u du = -\frac{\Delta P}{2\eta l} \int_R^r r \cdot dr$$

$$u = \frac{-\Delta P}{2\eta l} \left(\frac{r^2 - R^2}{2}\right)$$

$$\therefore \quad u = \frac{\Delta P}{2\eta l} \left(\frac{R^2 - r^2}{2}\right) \qquad \ldots (34)$$

If this relation is plotted we get velocity distribution across the pipe as shown in Fig. 18. Thus *velocity distribution* is parabolic when fluid is in laminar flow and maximum velocity of fluid in pipe u_{max} i.e. at centre where r = 0, is twice the average velocity in the pipe (u_{avg}).

$$u_{max} = 2 \, (u_{avg}) \text{ for laminar flow.}$$

(a) Laminar flow **(b) Turbulent flow**

Fig. 2.18 : Velocity distribution in pipe

To determine volumetric flow rate across the tube, we will consider a small annular section of tube between r and r + dr, (Fig. 2.19), then

$$Q = u \cdot a$$
$$= u \cdot (2\pi r \cdot dr)$$

Substituting 'u' from equation (34)

$$Q = \frac{\Delta P}{2\eta l} (R^2 - r^2) \cdot \pi r \cdot dr$$

$$= \frac{\Delta P \pi}{2\eta l} (R^2 r - r^3) \cdot dr$$

Total volumetric flow rate can be obtained by integrating above equation between limits r = R and r = 0.

$$\therefore \quad Q = \frac{\Delta P \pi}{2\eta l} \int_0^R (R^2 r - r^3) \, dr$$

$$= \frac{\Delta P \pi}{2\eta l} \left(\frac{R^2 r^2}{2} - \frac{r^4}{4} \right)_0^R$$

$$\therefore \quad Q = \frac{\Delta P \pi R^4}{8 \eta l}$$

Substituting value of π and R = $\frac{d}{2}$ where d is diameter of pipe, we get

$$\boxed{Q = \frac{\Delta P \, d^4}{128 \, \eta l}} \quad \ldots (35)$$

Equation (35) is known as *Poiseulli's equation* which gives volumetric flow rate through a pipe when fluid is flowing in a laminar flow.

(b) Turbulent flow in pipe : As there is increased momentum transfer in turbulent flow as compared to laminar flow the velocity distribution in turbulent flow becomes flatter than the parabolic in laminar flow (Fig. 2.18 (b)). It shows that greater equalisation of velocities occur turbulent flow and velocity gradient is high only near the pipe wall. For turbulent flow, it may be written as, $\boxed{0.8 \, u_{max} = u_{avg}}$ for turbulent flow. Flow may be laminar or turbulent, the velocity at the pipe wall fluid interface is zero. A thin region exists near the pipe wall where velocity gradient is high, this region is known as 'boundary layer'. The boundary in laminar flow shows layer of fluid sliding over one another in a orderly fashion. In turbulent flow, the boundary layer shows distinct regions, a laminar sub-layer next to wall having linear velocity profile. Immediately adjacent to this layer is a buffer layer where turbulent pattern exists slightly, followed by turbulent core with large scale turbulence.

(ii) Energy losses in fluid flow through pipe :

(a) Frictional losses :

When fluid flows over a surface there is friction between the surface and fluid. This friction is considered under two types. The friction due to the tangential force on the smooth surface oriented parallel to the direction of fluid flow is termed as *'skin friction'* or *viscous drag*. When there is hindrance to fluid flow by any means (or any surface) it causes acceleration of fluid in upstream and deceleration in downstream. The friction due to this acceleration and deceleration is called as *'form friction'* or *form drag*. Thus, total frictional loss in Bernoulli's equation is sum of skin friction and form friction.

The frictional losses are related to Reynolds number. It is proportional to the velocity pressure of the fluid.

Thus, frictional force per unit area of pipe wall is given by :

$$\frac{F}{A} = f\frac{\rho u^2}{2} \qquad \ldots (36)$$

where, F = frictional force
A = area over which friction forces act
ρ = density of fluid and
u = velocity of fluid.

f is a coefficient called *friction factor*. Friction factor (f) is a dimensionless number, which indicates the ratio of the total loss of momentum of the fluid to the momentum loss by turbulence or eddy activity.

The energy losses due to friction are given by *Fanning equation*. If we consider a portion dL of a straight horizontal pipe with diameter D, dP is the pressure drop across length dL. (Fig. 2.19) At equilibrium, the friction drag is overcome by pressure force.

Fig. 2.19 : Energy balance over a length of pipe

∴ Pressure force $= dP \propto \dfrac{\pi D^2}{4}$ ... (37)

and Friction force $= \dfrac{F}{A} \propto$ wall area of pipe

$$= f\frac{\rho u^2}{2} \propto \pi D \cdot dL \qquad \ldots (38)$$

If we equate equations (37) and (38)

$$\frac{\pi D^2}{4} \cdot dP = \pi D \cdot dL \left(f\frac{\rho u^2}{2}\right)$$

∴ $$dP = 2f\rho u^2 \cdot \frac{dL}{D}$$

Integrating between limits L_1 and L_2 in which interval pressure energy goes from P_1 and P_2 we get,

$$\int_{P_2}^{P_1} dP = 2f\rho u^2 \int_{L_2}^{L_1} \frac{dL}{D}$$

$$P_1 - P_2 = 2f\rho u^2 \frac{(L_1 - L_2)}{D}$$

Therefore, frictional pressure drop (ΔP_f) is given as

$$\Delta P_f = 2 f \rho u^2 \frac{L}{D} \quad \ldots (39)$$

$$\boxed{\text{Frictional energy loss} = \frac{\Delta P_f}{\rho} = \frac{2 f u^2 L}{D}} \quad \ldots (40)$$

Equation (40) is known as Fanning or Fanning-Darcy equation. It is used to calculate frictional pressure drop when fluid flows through pipe.

In derivation of Poiseulli's equation we have considered shear stress acting on wall and related it to velocity gradient. Here we have considered frictional force and related it to friction factor.

Shear stress per unit area (R) is related to friction factor as $f = \dfrac{R}{\rho u^2}$, then equation (39) becomes

$$\Delta P_f = \frac{4RL}{d}$$

Friction factor (f) in Fanning equation depends on Reynolds number.

$$f \; \alpha \; Re$$

Fig. 2.20 : Friction factors in pipe flow

The logarithmic plot of friction factor as a function of Reynold's number (Fig. 2.20) leads to following conclusions :

(i) The data falls into two distinct curves separated by transition region (where $2100 < Re < 4000$).

(ii) When $Re < 2100$ i.e. flow is laminar, we get linear relationship with equation

$$f = \frac{64}{Re}$$

which shows that friction factor is dependent only on Reynolds number and is not affected by roughness of pipe. This equation is modified Poiseulli's equation. In this condition, due to boundary layer near the wall, the roughness of the wall is completely masked and it acts as a smooth surface.

(iii) At 5000 < Re < 2,00,000 when flow becomes turbulent, equation becomes :

$$f = \frac{0.184}{(Re)^{0.2}}$$

In this region, friction factor is affected by Reynolds number as well as pipe wall roughness as shown in Fig. 2.20.

(iv) At very high values of Re, friction factor is independent of surface roughness.

(Roughness of a pipe is expressed as 'Roughness ratio' which is defined as the ratio of average height of projections which make up the roughness on the wall of the pipe to the pipe diameter i.e. $\frac{e}{a}$).

Thus, once friction factor (f) is known, frictional pressure drop can be determined.

(b) Energy losses in pipe fittings :

In addition to the frictional losses at the pipe wall, liquid encounters loses energy due to bends in the pipe or flow through fittings of varying cross-sections. This loss in energy is not recovered and the energy is dissipated in eddies and additional turbulence and finally lost in the form of heat. These losses occurring due to sudden change in magnitude or direction of flow induced by change in geometry are classified as :

(i) Losses due to sudden contraction or enlargement,

(ii) Losses at entrance or exit, and

(iii) Loss due to pipe curvature.

These energy losses are proportional to velocity pressure of the fluid.

General form of the equation used to calculate these energy losses is :

$$\text{Energy losses due to fitting} = k\frac{u^2}{2}$$

where k is a constant for a particular fitting.

Energy losses at sudden enlargement are given by :

$$F = \frac{(u_1 - u_2)^2}{2\alpha} \qquad \ldots (41)$$

where, u_1 and u_2 are fluid velocities on upstream and downstream side, $\alpha = 1$ for turbulent flow and $\alpha = 0.5$ for laminar flow.

For sudden contraction, energy losses are given by

$$F = k\frac{u_2^2}{2\alpha} \qquad \ldots (42)$$

where, α = 1 for turbulent flow,
α = 0.5 for laminar flow
k = a constant.

Numerical value of k depends on the ratio of pipe diameter D_1 on upstream side and D_2 on downstream side.

$\frac{D_1}{D_2}$	0.1	0.3	0.5	0.7	0.9
k	0.36	0.31	0.22	0.11	0.02

Energy losses in valves and fittings are calculated by Fanning equation :

$$F = \frac{2 f u^2 L}{D}$$

Numerical values of $\frac{L}{D}$ for different fittings and valves are given below :

Fitting/Valve	45° elbow	90° elbow	Gate valve	Globe valve
$\frac{L}{D}$ value	15	32	300	170

Generally, these losses are expressed in terms of equivalent length of pipe i.e. length of straight pipe offering same resistance. In other words, a fictitious length of straight pipe is added to the actual length, such that friction due to fictitious pipe is same as that which would arise from the fitting under consideration e.g. energy loss at 90° elbow is equivalent to a length of pipe equal to forty diameters. The equivalent lengths are calculated in a system for all fittings and valves and they are then added to the actual length of straight pipe, then calculate the total pressure drop using Fanning equation.

2.3.8 Fluid Past Immersed Bodies :

When a solid is moving with the fluid, then the force exerted by the fluid on solid in the direction of flow is known as *'drag'*. This opposing drag force has two components viscous drag and skin drag.

In Fig. 2.21, A is a cylinder with axis perpendicular to the direction of flow. The lines are hypothetical lines drawn tangential at all points to the movement of fluid called 'streamlines'. The streamlines when past the body are split into two parts one passing over the body and below it. This causes crowding of streamlines in the zone above and below the cylinder as shown in regions D and D'. The fluid layer in contact with the solid surface is immobilised when fluid passes over the body. This induces velocity gradient around the body and in turn shear stress is on the surface. This drag or stress due to tangential force on the surface oriented parallel to the flow is *'viscous drag'*.

(a)   (b)

Fig. 2.21 : Flow of a fluid past a cylinder

Similarly, crowding of streamlines in regions D and D' shows increase in velocity and decrease in pressure. On downstream side, there is decrease in velocity and increase in pressure, this causes separation of boundary layer. The region between the breakaway streamlines is known as wake region, where there are eddies and vortices. This acceleration and deceleration causes dissipation of pressure energy, this drag is 'form drag'. At low fluid velocity, viscous drag predominates while at high velocities, form drag predominate.

The relation between this drag force and movement of body in fluid is given by 'Stoke's law'. Let us consider a sphere having diameter d, is moving in fluid. Where, u = velocity of fluid, η = viscosity of fluid, ρ = density of fluid and A_p is projected area of sphere. Drag force acting per unit projected area R, will be contributed by viscous drag if fluid flow is laminar.

$$\therefore \quad R = \rho u^2 \infty \frac{12}{Re'} \quad \ldots (43)$$

where Re' is Reynolds number employing diameter of sphere as linear dimension.

$$\therefore \quad \text{Total drag force} = R \infty \frac{\pi d^2}{4}$$

$$= \rho u^2 \left(\frac{12\,\eta}{\dfrac{d\,u\,\rho}{\eta}}\right) \infty \frac{\pi d^2}{4}$$

$$\text{Total drag force} = 3\,\pi\,\eta\,du$$

This is basic equation of *'Stoke's law'*.

2.3.9 Fluid flow through Packed Beds :

In various operations like filtration, leaching distillation using packed bed involve flow of fluids through bed of solids. This flow is analysed by two approaches :

(i) Poiseulli's approach and

(ii) Kozeny's approach.

(i) Poiseulli's Capillary Model :

This approach has viewed a bed of solid as aggregate of discrete capillaries. Then Poiseulli's equation can be used for determination of volumetric flow rate through the capillary. It will give :

$$Q = \frac{\Delta P d^4}{128\,\eta l} \quad \ldots (44)$$

where, ΔP = pressure drop across the capillary

η = viscosity of the liquid

d = diameter of the capillary

and l = length of the capillary.

But in real, the length of the capillary (l), is greater than the thickness of the bed (L). But this length (l) is proportional to bed thickness (L).

Now equation will become,

$$Q = \frac{\Delta P d^4}{k\eta L}$$

Now if A is the area of bed which contains n capillaries per unit area then Q will be

$$Q = \frac{\Delta P d^4}{k \eta L} \infty\ nA$$

But number of capillaries per unit area (n) and diameter of capillary are not known, so an experimental constant is used and equation now becomes :

$$Q = KA \frac{\Delta P}{\eta L}$$

where, K = Permeability coefficient of the bed = $\frac{d^4 n}{k}$

This is Poiseulli's equation for volumetric flow rate through bed of solid.

This approach is contradicted as the capillaries in the bed cannot be discrete but interconnected with each other.

(ii) Kozeny's Hydraulic Diameter Theory :

In this theory of hydraulic diameter, Kozeny considered porous bed as an assembly of channels of varying cross-section but of definite length. He has viewed the packed bed as made up of channels interconnected in a random manner and resistance to fluid flow depends on the number and dimensions of these channels.

Kozeny has defined hydraulic diameter (δ) of the pore space in a random bed as the voids volume per unit of internal surface given by :

$$\delta = \frac{\text{Void volume}}{\text{Total surface of material forming bed}} = \frac{\epsilon}{S}$$

where,   = porosity of material

∴ $(1 -)$ = volume of solid.

If S_o is specific surface area of material forming bed then,

$$S = S_o (1 -)$$

∴ $$\delta = \frac{\epsilon}{S_o (1 -)}$$

Substitute this value of Poiseulli's equation for flow through channel.

∴ $$Q = \frac{\Delta P \delta^4}{k \eta L}$$

From continuity equation Q = ua. Area of the channel is given by $k'\delta^2$.

∴ Mean velocity through channel $u' = \dfrac{Q}{k'\delta^2} = \dfrac{\Delta P \delta^2}{kk' \eta L}$

If we consider $k'' = kk'$

∴ $$u' = \frac{\Delta P \delta^2}{k'' \eta L}$$

where, L is thickness of bed.

The velocity when averaged over the entire area of bed, it gives lower value of actual velocity. This velocity (u) is given by equation

$$u' = \frac{u}{\epsilon} \quad \text{or} \quad u = u'\epsilon$$

Substituting this value in equation

$$u = \frac{\Delta P\, \delta^2}{k''\, \eta\, L}$$

Substituting value of δ in the above equation

$$\therefore \quad u = \frac{\Delta P}{k''\, \eta\, L} \cdot \frac{\epsilon^2}{S_0^2\,(1-\epsilon)^2}$$

$$\therefore \quad u = \frac{\Delta P\, \epsilon^3}{k''\, \eta L\, S_0^2\,(1-\epsilon)^2}$$

Constant k" has value between 5 ± 0.5.

Since Q = uA, where A is area of bed,

$$Q = \frac{\Delta P A}{\eta L} \cdot \frac{\epsilon^3}{5\, S_0^2\,(1-\epsilon)^2}$$

or $\therefore$

$$Q = \frac{K A\, \Delta P}{\eta L}$$

where

$$K = \frac{\epsilon^3}{5\, S_0^2(1-\epsilon)^2} \quad \text{is permeability coefficient.} \quad \ldots (45)$$

Equation (45) is known as Kozeny's equation. It is similar to Poiseulli's equation with only difference in permeability coefficient Kozeny's equation take into consideration, porosity of bed and specific surface area of material. Therefore, it can explain the effect of size, shape and porosity of flow of fluids through packed bed which is not possible by Poiseulli's equation.

***

MANUAL CORRECTIONS

The pressure of fluid varies with depth. If we consider the fluid at depth Z below the surface and A as the area ; the volume of fluid will be ZA. Therefore, force exerted will be ZA ρ g. But total force is sum of the force exerted on the surface of the liquid and force of the liquid.

$$\therefore \quad \text{Total force} = A P_a + Z A \rho g$$

where, P_a is the pressure at the surface (atmospheric pressure).

$$\therefore \quad \text{Total pressure} = \frac{\text{Total force}}{A}$$
$$= P_a + Z \rho g \qquad \ldots (1)$$

Fig. 2.2

fluid A and fluid B respectively, Z_1 and Z_2 are heights of liquid columns in two arms and

... (8)

gauge

Fig. 2.4 : Bourdon tube gauge

region, the flow is either turbulent or laminar. Depending on the conditions it alternate

Reynolds claimed that the fluid flow changes with the change in these forces. The type of

2.3.2 Significance of Reynolds Number :

u_1 be cross-sectional area of pipe, density and velocity of fluid at point 1. Similarly, a_2, ρ_2 and u_2 denote same parameters at point 2. The material balance across the pipe between point 1 and

This is known as *continuity equation* for liquids; obtained for material balance of fluid flow.

u_a

$$\boxed{Z_a + \frac{u_a^2}{2g} + \frac{P_A}{\rho g} + \frac{W}{g} - \frac{F}{g} = Z_b + \frac{u_b^2}{2g} + \frac{P_B}{\rho g}} \qquad \ldots (17)$$

through

(i) For gas flow rate measurement, the plate is placed with the small hole below the orifice so that condensate will pass through this hole.

Pharmaceutical Engineering — Flow of Fluids

constricts the fluid and the diffuser carries out gradual expansion thereby reducing loss of

Main advantage of venturi meter is gradual constriction and expansion of fluid reduces the head loss considerably in a venturi meter, therefore, power loss is less with the flow meter. But it is relatively expensive and difficult to install.

meter.

where   B = magnetic flux density,
         l = length of the conductor,
         U = velocity of the conductor.

If flow is steady, pressure force is exactly balanced by the viscous force.

Substituting 'u' from equation (34)

Substituting value of π and $R = \dfrac{d}{2}$ where d is diameter of pipe, we get

(Fig. 2.19) At equilibrium, the friction drag is overcome by pressure force.

Therefore, frictional pressure drop (ΔP_f) is given as

which shows that friction factor is dependent only on Reynolds number and is not affected by roughness of pipe. This equation is modified Poiseulli's equation. In this condition, due to boundary layer near the wall, the roughness of the wall is completely masked and it acts as a smooth surface.

k = a constant.

Poiseulli's

Poiseulli's equation can be used for determination of volumetric flow rate through the

Now if A is the area of bed which contains n capillaries per unit area then Q will be

Equation (45) is known as Kozeny's equation. It is similar to Poiseulli's equation with

NEW MANUAL CORRECTIONS

CH.2

Example 2.1 : Calculate the greatest gauge and absolute pressure in a spherical tank of 5 m

Example 2.2 : Calculate head of water equivalent to standard atmospheric pressure.

Reynolds Number, $\quad Re = \dfrac{\text{Inertial force}}{\text{Viscous force}} = \dfrac{\rho u^2 D}{u\eta}$

Error! ... (9)

where,
- D = pipe diameter,
- u = velocity of fluid,
- η = viscosity of liquid and
- ρ = density of fluid.

Ex. 2.3 : Calculate the power required to pump castor oil from a vessel at ground level to a

CH. 3

$$(Nu) = 0.023 \, (Pr)^{0.4} \, (Re)^{0.8} \qquad \ldots (24)$$

CH. 5

Soft, weak

5.4.5 Edge and End Runner Mill :

CH. 6

Screen Cloth   Centre time down bolt   Motor cover plate   Upper weight   Clamp
Oversize discharge   Table assembly   Undersize discharge   Springs   Base   Motor
Angle lead graduated adjustment   Lower weight

Fine material cut   Observation ports   Feed   Perforated plate   Coarse material out

Fig. 6.14 : Rake Classifier

Feed slurry   Wash liquor   Liquids discharge   Solids discharge

Fig. 6.24 : Horizontal bowl centrifuge

CH. 7

Fig. 7.5 : Effect of Filter aid concentration

Fig. 7.7 : Filter Press   **Fig. 7.7 : Fiter Press**

Projections
with give the
required spacing

Fig. 7.16 : Reverse Osmosis and Ultrafiltration

MANUAL CORRECTIONS
CH. 2

Fig. 2.6 : Pressure energy

Fig. 2.8 : Pressure differential

MANUAL CORRECTION

Fluid   Fluid

(i) It enables the product to be presented in the form, suitable for subsequent processing or marketing. For example, tablet granules are dried to the extent suitable for further compression; liquid extracts are dried to a dry form.

Spray drying is a one step continuous drying process which involves transformation of feed from a fluid state into a dried particulate form by spraying the feed into a hot drying medium. The feed may be either a solution, suspension or paste. The feed is atomized into a spray and contact between the spray and drying medium takes place resulting in moisture evaporation. This is continued until a dried product is obtained.

Discharge pipe for
air and product

(b) Pressure Atomizer : e.g. Centrifugal pressure nozzle. The pressure nozzle is based

(b) Pre freezing to solidify the water : The aqueous solutions packed in vials, ampoules or bottles are cooled by using cold shelves (around $-50\ ^\circ C$), alcohol baths, (around $-50\ ^\circ C$) or liquid nitrogen bath ($-195\ ^\circ C$). Normal cooling rates in pre-freezing stage is around 1 to 3 $^\circ K/min$. Thickness of the frozen material affects the rate of drying, thinner is the layer, higher is the drying rate. The thickness is usually maintained between 1/2 to 3/4 inch. During this stage cabinet is maintained at low temperature and atmospheric pressure.

In nature metals are present in the form of their oxides, sulphides, hydroxides etc. By different processes, metals are extracted from the ores. Process of extraction increases energy of the metal. This high energy state has tendency to get transformed into a low energy form, such as oxides of the metals. This causes corrosion of the metal. Therefore, corrosion may be defined as *unintentional destruction in part or completely of a metal due to chemical or electrochemical reactions with the environment.*

As shown in Fig. 9.17 (a), when solvent MIK is added to a mixture of acetone and water, the composition of the resulting mixture lies on a straight line between the point for pure solvent and the point for the original binary mixture. When sufficient solvent is added such that the overall composition falls under the dome-shaped curve, the mixture separates into two phases. The points representing the phase compositions can be joined by straight tie lines. The tie line passes through the overall mixture composition (M) which separates into two phases (C) and (D). In the Fig. 9.17 (a), line ACE shows the compositions of MIK layer i.e. extract, and line BDE shows composition of water layer i.e. raffinate. As the proportion of solute i.e. acetone in the mixture increases, the compositions of the extract and raffinate layer approach each other and become equal at point E called 'plait point'.

As feed rate to the cyclone increases, there is improvement in efficiency by improving centrifugal force acting on the particles. Increase in feed rate or pressure drop, increases centrifugal force on the particle and finer particles are carried to underflow i.e. d_{50} is decreased and efficiency increases. Increase in density and viscosity of the slurry, hinders settling and sharpness of separation decreases. Flat coarse particles also report in the overflow, thus shape of particle is also important.

CHAPTER 3

HEAT TRANSFER

3.1 INTRODUCTION

Heat transfer is a dynamic process in which heat is transferred spontaneously from a region of higher temperature to a region of lower temperature, e.g. if heat is added to a metal vessel which contains liquid or vapour, the molecules of the metal vibrate faster. These vibrating molecules strike the fluid molecules. In this way, the heat energy is transferred to a liquid or vapour. Now, if the liquid or vapour inside a vessel is hotter than the metal of the vessel, the faster moving fluid molecules strike the metal molecules and make them vibrating faster. In this way, the heat energy is transferred from more energetic molecules to those with less energy. Therefore, substances always tend to equalize in temperature if they are in contact.

3.2 MECHANISMS OF HEAT TRANSFER

Heat is transferred by three mechanisms :

(i)   Conduction

(ii) Convection and

(iii) Radiation.

(i) Conduction : When a solid is heated, the vibrational energy of the heated molecules is transferred to their neighbouring molecules by the movement of free electrons. Solid metals are good conductors, whereas, non-metals and liquids are poor conductors where conduction generally takes place by transport of individual molecules along the temperature gradient. Gases or vapours are the worst conductors of all, where conduction occurs by the random motion of the molecules. Thus heat is diffused from hotter regions to colder ones.

(ii) Convection : When a liquid or vapour is in contact with hotter metal, the fluid molecules alongside the metal get speeded up almost instantly, although, they transfer the momentum to their neighbours slowly. The layer of more active molecules expands and its density becomes less than other molecules. This hot layer rises and a cooler fluid flows in, to replace it and is in turn brought into contact with the hot surface. This movement of group of molecules continues. The movement of hot and cooler molecules in group is known as *convection*. When this movement occurs due to difference in density of molecules, it is known as *natural convection* and as the motion continues to give continuous flow of molecules in the liquid, it is known as natural convection currents. The convection currents if set with the help of an external energy supplying device as pumps or agitator then it is called as *forced convection*. Forced convection is independent of density difference in two regions.

(iii) Radiation : Radiation is the transfer of heat energy by electromagnetic waves. All bodies with a temperature above absolute zero radiate heat in the form of electromagnetic waves. The radiation emitted by any material is independent of that being emitted by other material in sight, or in contact with it. Radiation heat transfer is important to be considered mainly at very high or very low temperatures, because in other conditions, it's effect is blanketed by other two mechanisms.

3.3 HEAT TRANSFER BY CONDUCTION

Heat transfer by conduction is considered under following categories :

(i) Fourier's law and thermal conductivity.

(ii) Steady state heat transfer.

(iii) Unsteady state heat transfer.

3.3.1 Fourier's Law

The rate of heat transfer depends upon the differences in temperature between the bodies, the greater the difference in temperature, the higher is the rate of heat transfer. Thus, temperature difference acts as a driving force for heat transfer. The medium through which heat transfers from one body to another offers certain resistance to the heat flow. Thus, rate of heat transfer can be written as,

$$\text{Rate of Heat Transfer} = \frac{\text{Temperature difference}}{\text{Resistance of the medium}}$$

This concept is expressed by Fourier's law which states that *'rate of heat transfer across a surface is proportional to the temperature gradient at the surface'*.

$$\frac{dQ}{d\theta} \; \alpha \; \frac{dt}{dx}$$

Thus, if A is the area normal to the heat flow then,

$$\frac{dQ}{d\theta} = -kA\frac{dt}{dx} \qquad \ldots (1)$$

where, $\frac{dQ}{d\theta}$ = Rate of heat transfer

A = Area of cross-section of heat flow path

$\frac{dt}{dx}$ = Temperature gradient i.e. rate of change of temperature per unit path length.

k = Thermal conductivity of the medium.

Equation (1) is known as Fourier's equation. The negative sign indicates that the heat flow occurs from hot to cold region.

Thermal conductivity : In Fourier's equation, k is a proportionality constant which indicates the resistance per unit flow path and is independent of temperature gradient. The numerical value of it depends upon the material of which the body is made and temperature. But over a small temperature range, change in k value is negligible and can be considered as constant. If temperature range is large, then k is related by equation :

$$k = a + bT \qquad \ldots (2)$$

where, a and b are constants.

At a given temperature, thermal conductivity is a function of bulk density of material. Thermal conductivity is expressed in units as : $BTU/ft^2 - h - (°F/ft)$; $Watt / m - °C$ or $J\ m^{-1}\ s^{-1}\ °C^{-1}$.

Values of thermal conductivity for some materials are given in Table 3.1.

Table 3.1 : Thermal conductivities (B.T.U. / ft^2 hr (°F/ft))

Material	Temp °C	k	Material	Temp °C	k
Solids			**Liquids :**		
Metals :			Mercury	0	4.8
1. Silver	100	238	Ethyl ether	40	0.080
2. Copper	100	218	Water	100	0.39
3. Aluminium	100	19			
4. Iron (cast)	100	30			
5. Mild steel	100	26			
6. Stainless steel (304)	100	218	**Gases :**		
Non-Metals :			Air	100	0.018
1. Carbon (graphite)	50	80	Steam	100	0.0136
2. Glass	50	0.63	Nitrogen	100	0.018
3. Glass wool	100	0.036	Carbon dioxide	100	0.013
Ice	0°	1.2	Hydrogen	100	0.124

3.3.2 Steady-State Heat Transfer :

When rate of heat transfer remains constant and is unaffected by time, then it is termed as steady-state heat transfer. For such conditions, $\frac{dQ}{d\theta}$ in Fourier's equation is constant called as a. Thus, Fourier's equation for steady state heat transfer can be written as :

$$\frac{Q}{\theta} = q = -kA \frac{dt}{dx} \qquad \ldots (3)$$

Fig. 3.1 : Heat conduction through a slab

Thus, if we consider a slab of a material (Fig. 3.1) of which two faces have temperatures t_1 and t_2. If t_1 is greater, heat flows from higher temperature t_1 to other face having temperature t_2. If x is the thickness of the slab then by Fourier's equation, rate of heat transfer is given as :

$$q = kA\frac{(t_1 - t_2)}{x}$$

$$q = \left(\frac{k}{x}\right) A \, \Delta t \quad \ldots (4)$$

But many times, heat flows through several consecutive layers of different materials (Fig. 3.2) ; in such condition equation (4) has to be applied for every layer separately. Thus if steady-state condition exists i.e. the same quantity of heat per unit time passes through each layer then,

$$q = A_1 \, \Delta t_1 \, \frac{k_1}{x_1} = A_2 \, \Delta t_2 \, \frac{k_2}{x_2}$$

$$= A_3 \, \Delta t_3 \, \frac{k_3}{x_3}$$

Fig. 3.2 : Heat Transfer through series of slabs

If cross-sectional areas of the layers are same

i.e. $\qquad A_1 = A_2 = A_3 = \ldots = A$

then, $q = A\,\Delta t_1 \dfrac{k_1}{x_1}$

$\qquad\qquad = A\,\Delta t_2 \dfrac{k_2}{x_2}$

$\qquad\qquad = A\,\Delta t_3 \dfrac{k_3}{x_3} \ldots$

$\therefore \qquad q\left(\dfrac{x_1}{k_1}\right) = A\,\Delta t_1$

$\qquad\qquad A\,\Delta t_2 = q\left(\dfrac{x_2}{k_2}\right)$

and $\qquad A\,\Delta t_3 = q\left(\dfrac{x_3}{k_3}\right) \ldots$

$\therefore \quad A\,\Delta t_1 + A\,\Delta t_2 + A\,\Delta t_3 + \ldots = q\left(\dfrac{x_1}{k_1}\right) + q\left(\dfrac{x_2}{k_2}\right) + q\left(\dfrac{x_3}{k_3}\right) + \ldots$

Sum of the temperature gradients across each layer is equal to the difference in temperature between inside and outside surface. i.e.

$\qquad \Delta t_1 + \Delta t_2 + \Delta t_3 + \ldots = \Delta t$

Thermal conductivity per unit length is conductance (C). Therefore, $\dfrac{k_1}{x_1}$ is the conductance C_1 of first layer, if we say for all the subsequent layers then,

$$\dfrac{x_1}{k_1} + \dfrac{x_2}{k_2} + \dfrac{x_3}{k_3} = \dfrac{1}{C_1} + \dfrac{1}{C_2} + \dfrac{1}{C_3} + \ldots$$

$$= \dfrac{1}{U}$$

where, U is overall conductance for combined layers.

$\therefore \qquad A\,\Delta t = q\left(\dfrac{1}{U}\right)$

$\qquad\qquad q = UA\,\Delta t \qquad\qquad \ldots (5)$

Equation (5), gives the heat flow through the combination of layers and U is called as overall heat transfer coefficient.

Heat Transfer in Pipes and Tubes :

In the heat exchangers and pharmaceutical equipments, heat transfer takes place across a pipe or tube. In such cases for tubes and pipes, area values change. Therefore, it is important to determine the value of A and thickness of pipe. If we consider a pipe having length l, with internal radius r_1 and r_2 as external radius then area ($2\pi r l$) will have to be determined as per the thickness of wall.

(i) For thin walled pipes i.e where $\frac{r_2}{r_1} < 1.5$

then mean radius $r_m = \frac{r_1 + r_2}{2}$

$\therefore \quad A = 2\pi \left(\frac{r_1 + r_2}{2}\right) l$

By substituting value of A in equation (5), we get

$\therefore \quad q = k\, 2\pi \left(\frac{r_1 + r_2}{2}\right) l\, \frac{\Delta t}{r_2 - r_1}$ ... (6)

(ii) For thick walled pipes, heat transfer area is calculated using logarithmic mean radius (r_m).

$$r_m = \frac{r_2 - r_1}{\ln\left(\frac{r_2}{r_1}\right)}$$

$\therefore \quad q = k\, 2\pi \left(\frac{r_2 - r_1}{\ln\left(\frac{r_2}{r_1}\right)}\right) l\, \frac{\Delta t}{r_2 - r_1}$

$$= \frac{2\pi\, k\, l\, \Delta t}{\ln\left(\frac{r_2}{r_1}\right)}$$ ... (7)

Example 3.1 : Calculate the rate of heat loss for a red brick wall of length 10 m, height 5 m and thickness 0.25 m. The temperature of inner surface is 105 °C and of the outer surface is 45 °C. The thermal conductivity of red brick is 0.7 W/m.°C.

Solution :

$$Q = \frac{k\, A\, (T_1 - T_2)}{x}$$

$A = 10 \times 5 = 50\ m^2$; $k = 0.7\ W/m\ °C$, $x = 0.25\ m$

$T_1 = 105\ °C$ and $T_2 = 45\ °C$

$\therefore \quad Q = \frac{0.7 \times 50\,(105 - 45)}{0.25} = 8400\ W\ \text{or}\ 8.4\ kW$

Example 3.2 : A cold store has a wall comprising of 10 cm of brick on outside, then 10 cm of concrete and then 10 cm of cork. The mean temperature within the store is maintained at – 20 °C and mean temperature of the outside surface of the wall is 15 °C. Calculate the rate of heat transfer through the wall and the temperature at the interface between cork and concrete. Thermal conductivities for brick, concrete and cork are 0.7, 0.75 and 0.043 W/m °C. Area of wall is 1 m².

Solution : $q = U A \Delta t$

First calculate value of U.

$$\frac{1}{U} = \frac{x_1}{k_1} + \frac{x_2}{k_2} + \frac{x_3}{k_3}$$

$$= \frac{0.1}{0.7} + \frac{0.1}{0.75} + \frac{0.1}{0.043} = 2.6$$

$$U = 0.385 \text{ W/m}^2 \text{ K}$$
$$\Delta t = 15 - (-20) = 35 \,°C \text{ and } A = 1 \text{ m}^2$$
$$q = U A \Delta T$$
$$q = 0.385 \times 1 \times 35$$
$$= 13.475 \text{ W}$$

For cork wall ; $\quad q = k_3 \dfrac{A_3 \, \Delta t_3}{x_3}$

$$A_3 = 1 \text{ m}^2$$
$$k_3 = 0.043 \text{ W/m }°C, \quad x_3 = 0.1 \text{ m}$$

and $\quad q = 13.475 \text{ J}$

∴ $\quad 13.475 = \dfrac{1 \times \Delta t_3 \times 0.043}{0.1}$

∴ $\quad \Delta t_3 = 31.34 \,°C$

31.34 °C is the difference in temperature between inner wall surface and concrete-cork interface, (inner wall temperature is – 20°C).

∴ $\quad 31.34 = $ (temperature of cork-concrete interface) $- (-20)$

∴ Temperature of cork-concrete interface $= 11.34 \,°C$.

Example 3.3 : Calculate heat flow rate per unit length of cylindrical pipe with inner diameter 2 cm and outer diameter 4 cm. The outer surface temperature is 100 °C and the inner surface temperature is 70°C. Thermal conductivity of the pipe material is 0.56 W/m °C.

Solution : Given : $r_1 = 1$ cm, $r_2 = 4$ cm ∴ $\dfrac{r_2}{r_1} = 2$ as $\dfrac{r_2}{r_1} > 1.5$ we must use logarithmic mean radius. $k = 0.56$ W/m °C, $T_2 = 100$ °C ; $T_1 = 70$ °C and $l = 1$.

$$Q = \dfrac{2 \pi k \, l \, \Delta t}{\ln \left(\dfrac{r_2}{r_1} \right)}$$

$$= \dfrac{2 \times 3.14 \times 0.56 \times 1 \times 30}{\ln (2)} = -157.7 \text{ W/m}$$

This flow rate should be given negative sign to indicate the flow radially inwards.

3.3.3 Unsteady State Heat Transfer :

In most of the pharmaceutical systems, temperature changes with time and heat transfer in such systems is unsteady state heat transfer. Heating and cooling of pharmaceuticals during sterilisation is a best example of unsteady heat transfer. Analysis of unsteady-state heat transfer is more complex, since an additional variable time enters into the rate equation. Unsteady state heat transfer analysis involves complicated mathematical calculations including solving Fourier's equation written in terms of partial differentials in three dimensions but it is out of reach of this book.

3.4 RADIATION HEAT TRANSFER

In radiation heat transfer, heat energy is transferred in the form of electromagnetic waves. It can occur in vacuum ; and is independent of temperature and geometry of the surface emitting or absorbing it. Emission of energy will occur when an electron from a high energy orbit jumps to a lower energy orbit, and the energy released from it has all properties of electromagnetic waves. These waves upon striking a receiver, the photons travel into it until they strike an electron or nucleus that is susceptible to the energy level of the photon. This collision results in an increase in the energy of receiver. In solids due to dense nature, radiation is usually absorbed very close to the surface, whereas penetration is more in liquids and it is still higher in gases.

Any body above absolute zero temperature emits radiations. The radiation that result only due to temperature is called *thermal radiation*. A part of incident radiation is absorbed by the body, a part is reflected and a part is transmitted. The absorbed radiation is transformed into heat. The proportion of the incident energy that is absorbed, reflected and transmitted depend on the properties of the receiver and to some extent wavelength of radiation and temperature of receiver. A *black body* is one that converts all the incident radiation into heat and emits all thermal energy as radiation.

Thus, we can state,

$$\alpha + r + \tau = 1 \qquad \ldots(18)$$

where
- α = Absorptivity, fraction of incident radiation that is absorbed.
- r = Reflectivity, fraction of incident radiation that is reflected.
- τ = Transmissivity, fraction of incident radiation that is transmitted.

For most of the solids transmissivity is zero, therefore equation (8) reduces to

$$\alpha + r = 1$$

whereas for a black body absorptivity is unity ($\alpha = 1$).

The radiation heat transfer is based on two basic laws :
(i) Kirchoff's law and
(ii) Stefan-Boltzmann law.

3.4.1 Kirchoff's law :

Emissive power of a body, E, is the radiant energy emitted from unit area in unit time. Kirchoff's law establishes a relationship between the emissive power of a surface to its absorptivity.

If a small body is placed inside a large evacuated enclosure with wall temperature T, the heat will be exchanged between the body and the enclosure until equilibrium is established, i.e. enclosure wall and body will have the same temperature. Then body will emit as much energy as it absorbs. Now, if E is the emissive power of the body, α is its absorptivity and G is the rate at which the energy falls from the wall on the body ; then energy balance at this equilibrium state can be written as

$$G\alpha = E$$

$$\therefore \quad G = \frac{E}{\alpha} \qquad \ldots (9)$$

Rate of energy fall G is a function of temperature T, and geometrical arrangement of both surfaces. But if the body is very small as compared to the enclosure and its effect upon the irradiation field of the enclosure is negligible. Hence, G will remain constant at temperature. This is stated by Kirchoff's law. It states that *"the ratio of emissive power to the absorptivity is same for all bodies in thermal equilibrium"*. Thus, for two bodies at same temperature,

$$\frac{E_1}{\alpha_1} = \frac{E_2}{\alpha_2} \qquad \ldots (10)$$

where, E_1 and E_2 = Emissive powers of two bodies

α_1 and α_2 = Absorptivities of two bodies.

For black bodies $\alpha = 1$, then according to Kirchoff's law, (where E_b is emissive power of black body)

$$\frac{E_b}{1} = \frac{E}{\alpha}$$

$$\therefore \quad \alpha = \frac{E}{E_b} \qquad \ldots (11)$$

As black body is a perfect radiator, it is used as for comparison of emissive powers. The ratio of emissive power (E) of a surface to the emissive power (E_b) of a perfectly black body at the same temperature is known as emissivity (ε) of the surface.

$$\varepsilon = \frac{E}{E_b} \qquad \ldots (12)$$

Therefore, emissivity of a body is equal to absorptivity, at thermal equilibrium.

Although, emissive power of a surface varies with the wavelength, for certain materials it is a constant fraction of the emissive power of a perfectly black body (E_b) i.e. $\frac{E}{E_b}$ is constant. Such materials which have constant emissivity are known as *"grey bodies"*. Thus for grey bodies it is not necessary that the two bodies should be at thermal equilibrium to apply Kirchoff's law.

3.4.2 Stefan – Boltzmann law :

Stefan-Boltzmann law states that *"emissive power of a black body is proportional to the fourth power of the absolute temperature (T) "*.

$$E_b = \sigma T^4 \qquad \ldots (13)$$

where, σ is Stefan-Boltzmann constant, it's numerical value is $5.67 \infty 10^{-8}$ W/m^2 – K^4.

As we know, emissive power is radiant energy, emitted from unit area in unit time. Therefore, a black body of area A and emissive power E emits energy at a rate E A. Therefore, heat emitted per unit time (Q) is written as,

$$Q = \sigma AT^4 \qquad \ldots (14)$$

As we know, $\quad \varepsilon = \dfrac{E}{E_b}$

Thus for a body which is not perfectly black,

$$Q = \varepsilon \sigma A T^4 \qquad \ldots (15)$$

where ε = emissivity.

Consider a black body with surface area A at an absolute temperature T_1, exchanging radiation with another black body at temperature T_2. Then rate of heat exchange will be

$$Q = \sigma A \left(T_1^4 - T_2^4\right) \qquad \ldots (16)$$

For heat transfer between grey and black bodies :

$$Q = \sigma A \varepsilon \left(T_1^4 - T_2^4\right) \qquad \ldots (17)$$

A correction factor is generally introduced to take into account the geometry and orientation of two black bodies exchanging radiations. This factor (F) is known as *view factor*.

$$Q = \sigma A \varepsilon F \left(T_1^4 - T_2^4\right) \qquad \ldots (18)$$

Example 3.4 : Calculate the heat radiated per unit area from radiator which behaves like a black body and operates at the temperature of 55 °C.

Solution :
$$q = \frac{Q}{A} = \sigma T^4$$
$$= 5.67 \times 10^{-8} (328)^4$$
$$= 0.66 \text{ kW/m}^2$$

3.5 CONVECTION HEAT TRANSFER

Convection is a mode of heat transfer between a surface and fluid moving over it. It involves movement of group of molecules, which transfer energy. It is restricted to liquids and gases as movement of group of molecules is not possible with solids. There are two types of convection heat transfer :

(a) Natural convection,
(b) Forced convection.

(a) Natural convection : In convection heat transfer, when the movement of group of molecules occur due to change in density resulting from temperature gradient, it is known as *free* or *natural convection*. The fluid molecules in the immediate vicinity of the hot object become warmer than the bulk of the fluid causing local change of density. The warmer fluid will be replaced by the cooler fluid generating the convection currents. These currents start when body forces like gravitational, centrifugal, electrostatic etc. act on fluid in which
there are density gradients. The force which induces these convection currents is called as *buoyancy force,* which is due to the presence of a density gradient within the fluid and a body force.

(b) Forced convection : When a fluid is forced past a solid body and heat is transferred between the fluid and the body, it is called *forced convection* heat transfer. In pharmaceutical industry, forced convection is involved during drying in ovens, fluidized bed dryers etc. In forced convection, fluid surrounding the surface is constantly replaced, therefore rate of heat transfer are higher than for natural convection.

Rate of heat transfer by convection is given by the equation

$$q = h_c A (t_1 - t_2) \qquad \ldots (19)$$

where, h_c is convective heat transfer coefficient or surface heat transfer coefficient.

3.5.1 Dimensional Analysis :

The convention heat transfer cannot be analysed by simple theoretical calculations because it involves many variables. The effects of these variables on heat transfer has to be determined, and relation between the variables is established by dimensional analysis.

In natural convection, heat transfer rates depend on variables like viscosity of fluid (η), thermal conductivity (k), density (ρ), specific heat (C_p), temperature difference between the surface and the bulk of the fluid (Δt) and the buoyancy force. Buoyancy forces depend on coefficient of thermal expansion (β), gravitational acceleration (g), convection heat transfer coefficient (h_c) and length dimensions (l or D).

Taking into consideration these variables, dimensionless numbers are selected for convection heat transfer. These dimensionless numbers are as follows :

Prandtl number : $\quad Pr = \dfrac{C_p \eta}{k}$

Nusselt number : $\quad Nu = \dfrac{h_c D}{k}$

Grashof number : $\quad Gr = \dfrac{D^3 \rho^2 g \beta \Delta t}{\eta^2}$

These dimensionless numbers are correlated by a power equation for natural convection as :

$$(Nu) = K (Pr)^k (Gr)^m \left(\dfrac{L}{D}\right)^n \qquad \ldots (20)$$

where, K, k, m and n are constants which vary with conditions.

e.g. If the natural convection is taking place about a vertical cylinder then

$$(Nu) = 0.53 (Pr.\ Gr.)^{0.25} \qquad \ldots (21)$$

and $\quad (Nu) = 0.12 (Pr.\ Gr.)^{0.33} \qquad \ldots (22)$

Equation (21) is observed when product of Prandtl and Grashof numbers has value between 10^4 and 10^9 and equation (22) when product is between 10^9 and 10^{12}.

In forced convection, fluid is forced past over a surface by a pump or an agitator. At low fluid velocities rates of natural convection are comparable to those of forced convection heat transfer. In natural convection, Grashof number has significant value whereas Reynold's number, a dimensionless number related to fluid dynamics is used for forced convection, heat transfer. Correlation of the dimensionless numbers is as follows :

$$(Nu) = K (Pr)^x (Re)^z$$

where, K, x and z are constants which change as per the conditions.

e.g. For turbulent flow of a low velocity fluid through pipe the correlation equation becomes :

$$(Nu) = 0.023 (Pr)^{0.4} (Re)^{0.8} \qquad \ldots (24)$$

where, x is 0.4 for heating and 0.3 for cooling.

The correlations of dimensionless numbers in heat transfer are given in Table 3.2.

Table 3.2 : Correlations in Heat Transfer

	Correlation	Condition
Natural Convection		
1. About vertical cylinder	$(Nu) = 0.53 \, (Pr. \, Gr.)^{0.25}$	$10^4 < (Pr. \, Gr.) < 10^9$
	$(Nu) = 0.12 \, (Pr. \, Gr.)^{0.33}$	$10^9 < (Pr. \, Gr.) < 10^{12}$
2. About horizontal cylinder	$(Nu) = 0.54 \, (Pr. \, Gr.)^{0.25}$	$10^3 < (Pr. \, Gr.) < 10^9$
Forced Convection		
1. Heating & cooling inside tubes	$(Nu) = 4$	Laminar flow, long tubes and moderate Δt.
	$(Nu) = 0.023 \, (Re)^{0.8} \, (Pr)^{0.4}$	$(Re) > 2100$ and $(Pr) > 0.5$ (for liquids)
	$(Nu) = 0.02 \, (Re)^{0.8}$	For gases where (Pr) is constant at 0.75
2. Heating or cooling over plane surface	$(Nu) = 0.036 \, (Re)^{0.8} \, (Pr)^{0.33}$	$Re > 20,000$
3. Heating and cooling outside tubes	$(Nu) = 0.86 \, (Re)^{0.43} \, (Pr)^{0.3}$	$1 < (Re) < 200$
	$(Nu) = 0.23 \, (Re)^{0.6} \, (Pr)^{0.3}$	For high to moderate Re values

Example 3.5 : Calculate heat transfer coefficient for a laminar fully developed fluid (k = 0.175 W/m °C) inside a 6 mm inside diameter tube, under uniform wall temperature boundary conditions and moderate temperature drop.

Solution : As flow is laminar in tube with moderate Δt form table 3.2, we can select the equation as :

$$(Nu) = 4$$

$$\therefore \quad \frac{hD}{k} = (Nu) = 4$$

$$\therefore \quad h = \frac{4k}{D} = \frac{4 \infty 0.175}{0.006}$$

$$= 116.66 \text{ W/m}^2 \text{ °C}.$$

Example 3.6 : Water is flowing at 0.15 m s^{-1} across a 7.5 cm diameter sausage at 75 °C. If the bulk water temperature is 25 °C, estimate the heat transfer coefficient.

Solution : As the liquid is flowing through sausage (heating and cooling outside the tube), for forced convection, fluid properties are evaluated at the mean film temperature which is the arithmetic mean temperature between the temperature of the tube wall and temperature of the bulk fluid.

Equation selected is :
$$Nu = 0.23\,(Re)^{0.6}\,(Pr)^{0.3}$$
$$\text{Mean temperature} = (75 + 25)/2 = 50\,°C$$

Properties of water at 50 °C are as follows :

C_p = 4.186 kJ/kg

k = 0.64 W/m °C

η = 5.6 × 10^{-4} Ns/m²

ρ = 1000 kg/m³.

$$Re = \frac{Du\rho}{\eta} = \frac{0.075 \times 0.15 \times 1000}{5.6 \times 10^{-4}} = 2 \times 10^4$$

$$(Re)^{0.6} = (2 \times 10^4)^{0.6} = 380.97$$

$$(Pr) = \frac{C_p\,\eta}{k} = \frac{4.186 \times 5.6 \times 10^{-4}}{0.64} = 3.66 \times 10^{-3}$$

∴
$$(Pr)^{0.3} = (3.66 \times 10^{-3})^{0.3} = 0.1858$$

$$(Nu) = 0.23\,(Re)^{0.6}\,(Pr)^{0.3} = 16.25 = \frac{hD}{k}$$

$$h = \frac{0.64 \times 16.25}{0.075} = 138.66\ W/m^2\,°C.$$

3.6 OVERALL HEAT TRANSFER COEFFICIENTS

Overall heat transfer coefficient is obtained by summation of heat transfer coefficients for conduction, convection and radiation. Generally, radiation coefficient is combined with convective heat transfer coefficient to get overall surface transfer coefficient.

∴
$$h_s = h_c + h_r \qquad \ldots (25)$$

where h_s is overall surface transfer coefficient, h_c and h_r are convective and radiation transfer coefficients respectively.

The overall heat transfer coefficient (U) for a solid wall with two fluid layers on either sides will be given by :

$$\frac{1}{U} = \frac{1}{\dfrac{1}{(h_s)_1} + \dfrac{x}{k} + \dfrac{1}{(h_s)_2}} \qquad \ldots (26)$$

where k is thermal conductivity of wall material and x is wall thickness, $(h_s)_1$ and $(h_s)_2$ are overall surface coefficients (film coefficient) of two fluids.

3.7 HEAT TRANSFER BETWEEN FLUID AND SOLID BOUNDARY

At fluid and solid boundary heat transfer takes place by both the mechanisms, conduction and convection. as shown in Fig. 3.3. A metal wall separates the warm fluid on left side from the cold fluid on the right. The fluids are moving in turbulent motion and temperatures at different locations are shown by t_1, t_2, t_3, t_4, t_5 and t_6. As discussed in chapter (Flow of Fluids), the turbulent flow shows three zones (i) Laminar sub-layer, (ii) Buffer layer and (iii) Turbulent zone.

Fig. 3.3 : Heat transfer between fluid and solid boundary

The laminar sub-layer on both sides are shown by $A_1 A_2$ and $B_1 B_2$. In the laminar sub-layer, the velocity gradient is maximum and the fluid mixing is almost zero, hence heat flows by conduction. But thermal conductivity of fluids is very low, therefore, due to high resistance it shows large temperature gradient of $(t_2 - t_3)$ and $(t_4 - t_5)$ on either side.

In the buffer zone, there is rapid change in velocity gradient as well as temperature gradient. In this region, conduction and convection is in combination. In the turbulent zone and bulk of the fluid, the velocity gradient is small and similarly the temperature gradient is also very small. Here turbulent mixing causes convective heat transfer.

As the thermal conductivity of metal wall is high there is no significant drop in temperature as shown by $t_3 - t_4$.

Thus, major resistance to heat flow will be from laminar sub-layer. Thickness of this layer depends on physical properties of fluid, nature of the surface and flow conditions. Higher is the thickness of the layer, higher is the resistance.

To calculate the rate of heat transfer, we have to take into consideration, resistance of layer on warm side, and cold side and resistance of metal wall. For the calculation of heat transfer through fluid film the thickness (x_1 and x_2) is taken slightly greater than the laminar sub-layer thickness because, there is some resistance to heat transfer in the buffer zone. Thus, x_1 is a thickness of a fictitious layer or film giving same resistance to heat transfer as the complex turbulent and laminar regions on warm side near the wall.

$$\therefore \quad Q = \frac{k}{x_1} A (t_1 - t_3) \quad \ldots (27)$$

$$= h_1 A (t_1 - t_3)$$

where k is thermal conductivity of fluid and h_1 is film transfer coefficient.

$$\therefore \quad (t_1 - t_3) = \frac{Q}{h_1 A} \qquad \ldots (28)$$

Similarly, on cold side,

$$(t_4 - t_6) = \frac{Q}{h_2 A}$$

Heat transfer through wall is given by,

$$Q = \frac{k_w}{x_w} A (t_3 - t_4) \qquad \ldots (29)$$

$$\therefore \quad t_3 - t_4 = \frac{Q}{A \frac{k_w}{x_w}} \qquad \ldots (30)$$

Total temperature gradient $(t_1 - t_6)$ can be obtained as

$$(t_1 - t_6) = \frac{Q}{A} \left(\frac{1}{h_1} + \frac{x_w}{k_w} + \frac{1}{h_2} \right)$$

$$\therefore \quad Q = \frac{A(t_1 - t_6)}{\left(\frac{1}{h_1} + \frac{x_w}{k_w} + \frac{1}{h_2} \right)} \qquad \ldots (31)$$

where, $\dfrac{1}{\frac{1}{h_1} + \frac{x_w}{k_w} + \frac{1}{h_2}}$ is called overall heat transfer coefficient U, therefore equation (31) now becomes

$$Q = UA \, \Delta T. \qquad \ldots (32)$$

3.8 HEAT TRANSFER TO BOILING LIQUIDS

Boiling is a convection heat transfer process which involves change in phase from liquid to vapour. Boiling may occur when a liquid is in contact with a surface maintained at temperature greater than the saturation temperature of the liquid. The boiling process depends upon the nature of the surface, thermophysical properties of the liquid and vapour bubble dynamics. We will discuss boiling process as :

(a) Pool boiling

(b) Boiling inside a vertical tube

(c) Boiling with forced circulation.

3.8.1 Pool Boiling :

If heat is added to a liquid from a submerged solid surface (e.g. heater), the boiling is called as *'pool boiling'*. In this process, the vapour produced form bubbles which grow and subsequently detach themselves from the surface, rising to the free surface due to buoyancy effects.

The heat transfer changes with the change in temperature difference between the surface and boiling liquid (ΔT). The heat flux versus ΔT is shown in Fig. 3.4. In the initial zone (AB) when ΔT is very small, natural convection currents are observed and heat flux increases. Evaporation is taking place at this ΔT. Heat transfer coefficient (h) also increases.

Fig. 3.4 : Pool boiling

Next zone (BC) is called *nucleate boiling region*, where ΔT is further increased. In this region, bubbles are formed continuously and rise to liquid surface resulting in rapid evaporation. At point C, heat flux is maximum, ΔT at this point is known as *critical temperature drop*.

As ΔT increases further, there is decrease in the heat flux as shown by CD, this is *film boiling* region. In this region, bubbles are formed so rapidly that they blanket the heating surface with vapour film. Now heat is transferred through this vapour film by conduction. As thermal conductivity of vapour film is very low, heat flux decreases.

After point D we can again observe increase in heat flux as at those large values of ΔT between DE (ΔT = 10^3 to 10^4), heat is lost by the surface due to radiation.

Thus from the above discussion, it is clear that heat flux and heat transfer coefficients are high in the nucleate boiling region. Therefore, the equipments involved with boiling liquids should be maintained in nucleate boiling region. Temperature of heating surface at critical temperature drop is so high that it may even cause melting of heating element, hence known as *burnout point*. Therefore, the equipment should be operated below this point.

3.8.2 Boiling Inside a Vertical Tube :

This commonly occurs in evaporators and other heat exchangers. The mechanism and hydrodynamics of boiling inside the tube is complex than in pool boiling, because the bubble growth and separation are strongly affected by the velocity of fluid.

As shown in Fig. 3.5, in a tube with low levels of liquid there are different patterns of boiling. Near the base of the tube, boiling of the liquid is suppressed by liquid column above. Heat transfer in this region takes place by natural convection. Above this height, the bubbles are formed, grow and are carried into the liquid over length of the tube, this is called as *bubbly region*. Heat transfer coefficients show significant increase in this region. As the volume occupied by the bubbles increases, the individual bubbles coalesce and form plug. This is called as *plug* or *slug flow region*. As the vapours coalesce, the escape is hindered and both liquid and vapour move upwards at an increasing speed. The vapour velocity is much higher than that of the liquid causing separation of two phases. This forms an annular film of the liquid dragged upwards by a core of high velocity vapour. This is called *annular flow*. Heat transfer coefficient remains high as long as the liquid film wets the wall. The film then thins and tend to break to give droplets then termed as *mist flow*. As the film is evaporated, dry spots appear on the tube and heat transfer coefficient drops significantly.

Fig. 3.5 : Boiling inside a vertical tube

3.8.3 Boiling with Forced Circulation :

Boiling in an agitated vessel where the movement of fluid is caused by other than those by boiling. The heat transfer coefficients in this type of the boiling depend on the properties of liquid and the agitation used. But these coefficients are higher than that in pool boiling.

3.9 HEAT TRANSFER FROM CONDENSING VAPOURS

Whenever hot vapours come in contact with a surface at a lower temperature, condensation occurs. It is the process exactly reverse that of the boiling. There are two types by which condensation may occur.

(i) Film–wise condensation.

(ii) Drop–wise condensation.

In *film–wise condensation,* the condensate wets the surface forming a continuous film over the entire surface. It generally occurs on clean, uncontaminated surface. The latent heat liberated during condensation is transferred through the film to the surface by condensation. Thermal gradient exists in the film and acts as a resistance to heat transfer.

In *drop–wise condensation,* the vapour condenses into small droplets of various sizes which may grow in size or coalesce with neighbouring droplets and eventually roll off the surface under the influence of gravity. During drop–wise condensation, a large portion of the area of condensing surface remain directly exposed to vapour, therefore, rates of heat transfer are around five to ten times greater than film–wise condensation. Due to these, high heat transfer rates drop–wise condensation is preferred over film–wise condensation but drop–wise condensation is very difficult to achieve and maintain for prolonged period of time. Some additives can be added to favour dropwise condensation e.g. oleic acid, but is not possible commercially. Therefore, in industrial equipments film–wise condensation occurs. The film generally shows laminar or turbulent flow. The heat transfer is naturally greater when it is in turbulent flow.

If the condensing vapour contains some non-condensable gases like air, the heat transfer coefficient is reduced significantly. Presence of few percent by volume of air in the steam reduces heat transfer by around fifty percent. This is due to the fact that on condensation of vapour, the non-condensable gas is left at the surface. These non-condensable gases near the surface act as a thermal resistance to the condensation process. Therefore, in heat exchange equipments like evaporators, the vent valve is provided to remove non-condensable gases.

Thus presence of condensate and non-condensable gases near the heat transfer area decrease the rate of heat transfer. Therefore, condensate and non-condensable gases should be removed as early as possible from the heat exchanger, it is discussed in details in heat exchangers.

3.10 HEAT EXCHANGERS

Heat exchangers are the devices used for exchange of heat between two fluids that are at different temperatures. Heat exchangers are classified on the type of fluid flow arrangement and on method of heat transfer.

On the basis of fluid flow or the relative direction of the hot and cold fluids, their types are :

(i)   Parallel flow Heat Exchanger,

(ii)   Counter flow Heat Exchanger, and

(iii)   Cross flow Heat Exchanger.

In the parallel flow heat exchanger [Fig. 3.6 (a)], the fluid streams enter at one end, flow through in the same direction and leave at the other end. In counter flow type [Fig. 3.6 (b)], the fluids move in parallel but in opposite directions. In a cross-flow type, one fluid moves through the heat exchanger at right angles to the flow path of the other fluid [Fig. 3.6 (c)].

(a) Parallel flow   (b) Counter flow

(c) Cross flow

Fig. 3.6 : Fluid flow arrangement in heat exchangers

3.10.1 Heat Transfer in Heat Exchangers :

If flow rates and inlet and outlet temperatures are maintained same for all the three types, then heat transfer area required for these types are significantly different. A parallel flow heat exchanger requires maximum heat transfer area, a counter-flow heat exchanger requires the minimum area whereas, a cross-flow heat exchanger requires an area between two extremes. Therefore, counter flow arrangements are preferred over parallel flow type.

In the parallel flow as well as in the counter flow, the rate of heat transfer is given as :

$$Q = U A \Delta T_m \qquad \ldots (33)$$

where, U = overall heat transfer coefficient

A = the area of heat transfer.

and ΔT_m = the mean temperature difference across the heat exchanger.

Mean temperature difference is used because the temperature difference ΔT between the hot and cold fluids varies with position in the heat exchanger. Fig. 3.7 shows the change in temperature drop with distance in parallel flow and counter flow.

(a) Parallel flow **(b) Counter flow**

Fig. 3.7 : Temperature drop changes in heat exchangers

In the above Fig.3.7

T_{hi} = Temperature of hot fluid at inlet
T_{ho} = Temperature of hot fluid at outlet
T_{ci} = Temperature of cold fluid at inlet
T_{co} = Temperature of cold fluid at outlet.

Mean temperature drop for these heat exchangers is calculated by Logarithmic Mean Temperature Difference (LMTD) method of analysis. The ΔT_m in both cases are given below :

For Parallel Flow

$$\Delta T_m = \frac{\Delta T_i - \Delta T_o}{\ln(\Delta T_i/\Delta T_o)} \qquad \ldots (34)$$

where, $\Delta T_i = T_{hi} - T_{ci}$

$\Delta T_{oc} = T_{ho} - T_{co}$

For Counter Flow

$$\Delta T_m = \frac{\Delta T_i - \Delta T_o}{\ln(\Delta T_i/\Delta T_o)} \qquad \ldots (35)$$

Although equation is same as that for parallel flow, values of ΔT_i and ΔT_o are different. For counter flow,

$\Delta T_i = T_{hi} - T_{co}$

$\Delta T_o = T_{ho} - T_{ci}$

3.10.2 Scaling :

Many times, the surfaces of the heat exchanger get coated with the deposits and scales which cause decline in the performance of the exchanger. The deposits and scales are formed due to impurities in fluids, chemical reaction between the fluid and the wall material, rust formation etc. Therefore, in heat exchangers use of hard water should be avoided. The effect of the scales and deposits is usually represented by a *fouling factor*. Fouling factor is a resistance, which should be added to the other thermal resistances for the calculation of overall heat transfer coefficient.

3.10.3 Types of Heat exchangers :

On the basis of transfer of heat, heat exchangers are classified as : direct transfer type, storage type and direct contact type.

In *direct transfer type* heat exchanger, the cold and hot fluids flow simultaneously through the device and heat is transferred through a wall separating the fluids.

In *storage type* heat exchanger, the heat transfer from the hot fluid to the cold fluid occurs through a coupling medium in the form of a porous solid matrix. The hot and cold fluid, flow alternately through the matrix, the hot fluid storing heat in it and cold fluid extracting from it. It is not commonly used in pharmaceutical industry.

A *direct contact type* of heat exchanger is one in which the two fluids are not separated e.g. for heat transfer between gas and liquid, gas is bubbled through the liquid or liquid is sprayed in the gas. This type will be discussed in airconditioning chapter.

Direct transfer type heat exchangers are widely used. The two important types are :

(i) Tubular Heat Exchangers and

(ii) Plate Heat Exchanger.

Tubular Heat Exchangers :

Tubular heat exchanger consists of circular tubes, one fluid flows inside the tube and the other on the outside. The heat transfer takes place across the wall of the tube.

Tubular heat exchangers are further classified as :
(i) Concentric tube or double pipe
(ii) Shell and tube.

In *concentric tube heat exchanger* [Fig. 3.8 (a)], one fluid flows through the inner tube, while the other flows through the annular space between the two tubes. The heat transfer takes place across the wall of the inner tube. Simultaneous flow of two fluids occurs in the heat exchanger. There are no moving parts.

(a) Concentric tube

(b) Shell and Tube

Fig. 3.8 : Tubular heat exchangers

A *shell and tube heat exchanger* consists of a bundle of round tubes packed together inside a cylindrical shell. One fluid flows inside the tubes, called as tube fluid and the other on the outside called shell fluid. Baffles may be provided on the shell side to prevent stagnation of the shell side fluid and promote better heat transfer.

The shell tube heat exchanger offers many advantages :
(i) It can be designed over a wide range of capacity.
(ii) The tubes are replaceable and can be cleaned easily.
(iii) High heat transfer area is available per unit volume of the exchanger between 100 to 500 m^2/m^3.

It can be modified to Double pass arrangement as shown in Fig. 3.9

Fig. 3.9 : Double pass heat exchanger

This modification increases overall effectiveness of the heat exchanger.

Plate Heat Exchangers :

The plate heat exchangers are classified into two types :
(i) Flat plate type
(ii) Spiral plate type.

Fig. 3.10 : Flat plate heat exchanger

The *flat plate heat exchanger* consists of a series of rectangular thin gauge metal plates which are clamped together to form narrow parallel plate channels. Grooves are provided along the periphery of the plates so as to adjust the gasket. Each plate has holes at the corners for the flow of fluid. The plates are arranged in parallel with each other in groups known as 'passes'. The number of plates in each pass depend upon the volumes of liquids to be handled. The flow pattern which may occur in flat plate exchanger is shown in Fig. 3.10.

Advantages of flat plate exchanger :
(i) The corrugations on the surface of the plate increases rigidity of plate, at the same time creates turbulence in fluid flow which helps in better heat transfer.

(ii) The heat transfer area per unit volume is around 100 to 200 m²/m³.
(iii) Mechanical cleaning of both the sides of the heating surfaces is possible.
(iv) It gives high degree of bacteriological cleanliness which is desirable in pharmaceutical industry.

The *spiral plate heat exchanger* consists of a continuous sheet of metal formed into a double spiral, one within the other, by winding on a special type of mandrel. This spiral body is closed at both ends by covers when the unit is in operation (Fig. 3.11)

Fig. 3.11 : Spiral plate heat exchanger

Advantages of Spiral type heat exchanger :

(i) It can be used for liquid-liquid as well as vapour-liquid heat transfer (flat plate is suitable only for liquid-liquid heat transfer).

(ii) During liquid-liquid heat transfer, complete counter-current flow pattern is maintained. Thus high heat transfer coefficients are maintained.

(iii) The spiral can be removed for cleaning, hence we get access to both sides of the heat transfer surface.

Applications of Plate Heat Exchangers :

Plate heat exchangers are widely used in the fine chemical, pharmaceutical and cosmetic industries.

(i) Antibiotic manufacture : In penicillin production, drug is extracted with solvents like amyl or butyl acetate, or methyl iso-butyl ketone. The solvent is recovered by passing the feed through plate heat exchanger.

Corn steep liquor, a commonly used medium for antibiotic production is sterilised using plate heat exchanger.

(ii) Pasteurisation : Plate exchangers are used in pasteurisation of gelatin liquors. In the process of pasteurisation, energy can be saved by manipulation of flow of the liquor and water. Exchanger is divided into three sections. In first section, there is contact between raw liquor (which is to be pasteurised) and a hot pasteurised liquor. This contact preheats the raw liquor and cools the pasteurised liquor to a great extent. This saves around 75% energy. The preheated liquor passes to second section where it comes in contact with hot water and remains there till pasteurisation is complete. After pasteurisation, this hot liquor passes to first section to transfer heat to fresh raw liquor. From first section this pasteurised liquor passes to third section where it is completely cooled by cold water.

(iii) Perfumes and cosmetics : The chemicals used in perfume and cosmetic manufacture include benzene, acetic anhydride, acetaldehyde, glycols, isopropyl alcohols, ethyl and methyl alcohol, amyl acetate, butyl acetate etc. All these chemicals are successfully handled by spiral heat exchanger for their heating, cooling and condensation.

3.11 REMOVAL OF CONDENSATE

Accumulation of condensate in the space for heating medium (steam) reduces heat transfer. Similarly, non-condensable gases present in the steam or entering through the leaks decrease heat transfer rate significantly. Therefore, it is necessary to remove the condensate as soon as it is formed and also the non-condensable gases like air, CO_2 and hydrogen. Steam traps are the devices used for this purpose.

3.11.1 Steam Traps :

A steam trap is a simple device which opens in the presence of condensate and/or non-condensable gases and closes in the presence of steam.

The steam traps are categorised as follows :

(A) Mechanical Traps

(B) Thermostatic Traps

(C) Thermodynamic Traps.

(A) Mechanical Traps : These traps detect the presence of condensate on the basis of difference in density of steam and condensate e.g. Inverted bucket traps and float and thermostatic (F & T) traps.

Fig. 3.12 : Float and thermostatic trap

The *float and thermostatic trap* consists of a chamber, a float and a valve (Fig. 3.12).

The condensate flows into the chamber, where it raises a float. The float is directly attached to the discharge valve so that higher is the level of condensate, the more the valve opens. But the discharge valve is always submerged in condensate, so it is impossible for it to discharge non-condensable gas. Hence a thermostatically controlled valve is fitted in the vapour space above the condensate level. This valve remains closed at steam temperature and opens when the temperature in the vapour space drops below the saturation temperature of the steam. This trap discharges condensate continuously.

Fig. 3.13 : Inverted bucket traps

Inverted bucket trap consists of an inverted cylinder or bucket open at the bottom end- connected directly to the condensate discharge valve mechanism, as shown in Fig. 3.13. The open end of the bucket is sealed with a pool of condensate at the bottom of the chamber. When the bucket is filled with steam, due to buoyancy it rises and discharge valve will get closed. When condensate floods the bucket, its buoyancy decreases and it sinks, this causes the valve to open. A weep hole at the top of the bucket provides a fixed bleed rate for removal of air and other non-condensable gases. It also provides a continuous bleed of steam trapped in the bucket. It removes condensate intermittently, one bucket at a time.

(B) Thermostatic Traps : It operates on the principle that steam is hotter than its condensate or steam containing non-condensable gases. Thus, a thermostatic trap opens its discharge valve when temperature is lower and remains closed at high temperature.

The *balanced pressure thermostatic trap* is shown in Fig. 3.14. The trap automatically changes its opening temperature with changes in the steam pressure. The bellows is subjected to the system pressure and temperature, so the boiling point of the material in the bellows increases as the surrounding steam pressure increases. Thus, the trap is actuated by boiling liquid and the resultant expansion of a sealed liquid-filled, flexible bellows.

Fig. 3.14 : Balanced Pressure Trap

Bimetallic trap consists of a bimetal plate which bends with temperature change. At the temperature of steam, bimetal plate bends and closes the discharge valve.

Fig. 3.15 : Bimetallic trap

(C) Thermodynamic Traps : These traps use the velocity and pressure of flash steam to open and close the discharge valve.

Fig. 3.16 : Thermodynamic trap

In a thermodynamic trap (Fig. 3.16), a flat coin-size disc lies on a flat seat and covers both inlet and discharge orifices. When cool condensate flows through the orifice, it lifts the disc, and flows over the seat to the discharge orifice. When a condensate near the steam temperature flows under the disc, this high velocity flash steam creates a low pressure area on the bottom of the disc, this low pressure between the disc and the seat, combined with a pressure increase above the disc during flow, forces the disc down onto the seat and seals the orifices. When the steam pressure exerts its upward force on the disc over inlet orifice, the disc remains closed until the flash steam above the disc condenses and loses its force. When the downward pressure on the disc is relieved, the disc lifts only long enough to discharge fresh condensate, produce new flash steam, and again force the disc back onto the seat, sealing the orifices before live steam is lost.

***

MANUAL CORRECTIONS
CH. 3
119   9.4

as q.

Fig. 3.2 : Heat Transfer through series of slabs

... (8)

If a small body is placed inside a large evacuated enclosure with wall temperature T, the

Example 3.4 : Calculate the heat radiated per unit area from radiator which behaves like a black body and operates at the temperature of 55 °C.

transfer. In natural convection, Grashof number has significant value whereas Reynold's

... (23)   from

(b) Counter flow

like amyl or butyl acetate, or methyl iso-butyl ketone. The solvent is recovered by passing the

the disc, this low pressure between the disc and the seat, combined with a pressure increase

CH. 4

where P_{A_1} and P_{A_2} are partial pressures of A at distances X_1 and X_2. Similar equation can be written for counter diffusion of B.

Mass transfer coefficient k_g is expressed by unit cm/sec. We know $C_A = \dfrac{P_A}{RT}$, therefore

where C_{A_i} and C_{A_b} are concentrations of A on either side of the film. Similar equation can be

Danckwert contradicted the assumption by Higbie, that each eddy has gets equal exposure

LABELLING

Hot liquid in	Cold liquid out	Hot liquid out	Cold liquid in	Gasket
Thermostatic vent	Float	Condensate valve		
Weep hole	Bucket	Condensate valve	Bellows	Condensate valve

Bimetal plate   Condensate valve   Condensate Discharge Oriface   Disc

Manual corretions

the greater the difference in temperature, the higher is the rate of heat transfer. Thus,

$$q = A_1 \Delta t_1 \frac{k_1}{x_1} = A_2 \Delta t_2 \frac{k_2}{x_2} = A_3 \Delta t_3 \frac{k_3}{x_3}$$

Equation (5), gives the heat flow through the combination of layers and U is called as overall heat transfer coefficient.

internal radius r_1 and r_2 as external radius then area ($2\pi r l$) will have to be determined as per the thickness of wall.

(i) For thin walled pipes i.e where $\frac{r_2}{r_1} < 1.5$

then mean radius $\quad r_m = \frac{r_1 + r_2}{2}$

∴ $\quad A = 2\pi \left(\frac{r_1 + r_2}{2}\right) l$

By substituting value of A in equation (5), we get

∴ $\quad q = k \, 2\pi \left(\frac{r_1 + r_2}{2}\right) l \, \frac{\Delta t}{r_2 - r_1}$ ... (6)

(ii) For thick walled pipes, heat transfer area is calculated using logarithmic mean radius (r_m).

q q q

3.3.3 Unsteady State Heat Transfer :

In most of the pharmaceutical systems, temperature changes with time and heat transfer in such systems is unsteady state heat transfer. Heating and cooling of pharmaceuticals during sterilisation is a best example of unsteady heat transfer. Analysis of unsteady-state heat transfer is more complex, since an additional variable time enters into the rate equation. Unsteady state heat transfer analysis involves complicated mathematical calculations including solving Fourier's equation written in terms of partial differentials in three dimensions but it is out of reach of this book.

3.8.2 Boiling Inside a Vertical Tube :
3.8.1 Pool Boiling :
3.8.3 Boiling with Forced Circulation :

MASS TRANSFER

4.1 INTRODUCTION

Mass transfer is the complex phenomenon occurring frequently in almost all unit operations. Extraction, humidification are the operations involving transfer of solute and water molecules respectively. Evaporation, drying and distillation are the operations which involve simultaneous heat transfer and mass transfer.

Mass transfer can occur through different mechanisms such as, molecular diffusion, convection or bulk flow, and turbulent mixing. To understand the various mechanisms, molecular diffusion is discussed in details for gases and liquids, followed by turbulent mixing in single phase, and various theories for interfacial mass transfer.

4.2 MOLECULAR DIFFUSION

4.2.1 Molecular diffusion in gases :

Fig. 4.1 : Molecular diffusion of gases A and B

Molecular diffusion is the main mechanism of mass transfer in fluids under stagnant condition or moving in laminar flow. Consider that, two gases A and B are present in two chambers (Fig. 4.1). The partition forming two chambers is removed, then molecules of A will move towards B and B towards region of A. If we check concentration of A with distance towards chamber B or B towards A, the variation in concentration of the component with distance in the system is known as concentration gradient. The movement of molecules of A or B is taking place due to concentration gradient, is called molecular diffusion. Fick's law states *that the rate of diffusion (N_A) is proportional to concentration gradient* $\frac{dC_A}{dX}$ *existing across the direction of movement of A.* The Fick's law may be written as :

$$N_A \; \alpha \; -\frac{dC_A}{dX} \quad \text{(negative sign, as concentration decreases with distance)}$$

$$\therefore \quad N_A = -D_{AB} \frac{dC_A}{dX} \quad \ldots (1)$$

For molecules of gas B moving from chamber B to A, we can write

$$N_B = -D_{BA} \frac{dC_B}{dX} \quad \ldots (2)$$

where, D_{AB} and D_{BA} denote diffusivity of A in B and B in A respectively expressed as cm²/sec. N_A and N_B are rate of diffusion of A and B respectively, expressed as gm. moles/cm²/ sec.

The two important conditions which may occur in gaseous mass transfer are :

(a) Equimolecular counter diffusion :

Consider, over a small element dX in the system, if molecular diffusion is the only mechanism of mass transfer then,

$$N_A = -N_B \quad \ldots (3)$$

i.e. rates of diffusion of A and B are equal and opposite. Consider, dP_A and dP_B are changes in partial pressures of A and B over the element dX. As we have assumed that there is no bulk flow, i.e. total pressure across the element is same then we can say $\frac{dP_A}{dX}$ is equal to $\frac{dP_B}{dX}$.

For an ideal gas,

$$P_A V = n_A RT$$

where, P_A and n_A are partial vapour pressure and number of moles in volume V at temperature T. R is gas constant. Molar concentration of gas (C_A) is n_A divided by volume, therefore,

$$P_A = C_A RT$$

$$\therefore \quad C_A = \frac{P_A}{RT} \quad \ldots (4)$$

Substituting in equation 1, we get,

$$N_A = -\frac{D_{AB}}{RT} \frac{dP_A}{dX} \quad \ldots (5)$$

Similarly, for gas B,

$$N_B = -\frac{D_{BA}}{RT} \frac{dP_B}{dX} \quad \ldots (6)$$

But for equimolecular counter diffusion $N_A = -N_B$, therefore,

$$N_A = \frac{D_{AB}}{RT}\frac{dP_A}{dX} = -\frac{D_{BA}}{RT}\frac{dP_B}{dX} \qquad \ldots (7)$$

Therefore, $D_{BA} = D_{BA} = D$. The equation for equimolecular counter diffusion for A can be obtained as,

$$N_A = \frac{D}{RT}\int_{X_1}^{X_2}\frac{dP_A}{dX}$$

$$N_A = \frac{D}{RT}\frac{P_{A_2} - P_{A_1}}{X_2 - X_1} \qquad \ldots (8)$$

where P_{A_1} and P_{A_2} are partial pressures of A at distances X_1 and X_2. Similar equation can be written for counter diffusion of B.

(b) Diffusion through a stationary, non-diffusing gas :

In case of movement of molecules from liquid surface or film on drying solids, occurs to a non-diffusing gas (atmospheric gas). Suppose, molecule A is moving from surface to atmosphere due to gradient in partial pressure $\frac{dP_A}{dx}$, but as B is not moving towards the surface, the bulk flow (convective transfer) must be taking place away from surface in such cases. Therefore, rate of mass transfer of A takes place by molecular diffusion and bulk flow.

4.2.2 Molecular diffusion in liquids :

According to Fick's law, for diffusion in liquids we can write,

$$N_A = -D\frac{dC_A}{dX} \qquad \ldots (9)$$

Similarly, for equimolal counter diffusion it will be :

$$N_A = -D\frac{C_{A_2} - C_{A_1}}{X_2 - X_1} \qquad \ldots (10)$$

where, C_{A_1} and C_{A_2} are concentration of A at points X_1 and X_2 respectively. The diffusivities of liquids are much less than diffusivities of gases (nearly by a factor of 10^4) e.g. diffusivity of gaseous ethanol in air is 0.119 cm²/sec, whereas diffusivity of liquid ethanol in water is $1 \infty 10^{-5}$ cm²/sec.

The molecular diffusion of liquids across a stagnant liquid is complex and not used frequently, therefore is not considered here.

4.3 MASS TRANSFER IN TURBULENT AND LAMINAR FLOW

Single phase mass transfer in turbulent and laminar flow is explained by boundary layer or film theory.

When fluid flows, there is formation of a boundary layer adjacent to the surface over which it flows. Now we will consider two regions, boundary layer and bulk. If bulk of fluid is flowing in laminar fashion, then rate of mass transfer in such fluid is given by molecular diffusion equation discussed above.

If fluid bulk shows turbulent flow, then rate of mass transfer is dependent on transfer rate across the boundary layer. The boundary layer consists of three sub-layers viz. laminar sub-layer adjacent to surface, buffer or transient sub-layer and turbulent region towards the bulk of fluid. In the turbulent region, the macroscopic packets of fluid or eddies move under inertial forces causing mass transfer. The rate of mass transfer is high and concentration gradient is low. In the buffer layer combination of eddy diffusion and molecular diffusion is responsible for mass transfer. Molecular diffusion is the only mechanism of mass transfer in the laminar sub-layer. In this region, concentration gradient is high and rate of mass transfer is low. Thickness of laminar sub-layer decreases with increase in the turbulence in the fluid. The rate of mass transfer in this case of boundary layer and bulk in turbulent flow, is dependent on the resistance given by the boundary layer. The rate of mass transfer can be estimated by considering a film which offers the resistance equivalent to the three sub-layers of boundary layer.

Consider a gas flows over a surface and equimolar counter diffusion occurs. A moves away from surface and B towards the surface (Fig. 4.2).

Fig. 4.2 : Boundary layer – Mass Transfer

Let P_{A_i} be the partial pressure of A at the surface which decreases sharply to P_{A_l} at the end of laminar sub-layer of thickness X. P_{A_b} is the partial pressure of A at the edge of boundary layer. It can be seen that partial pressure decrease in the laminar sub-layer is very fast and is very slow after that. It is because molecular diffusion is the only mechanism in the laminar sub-layer. If we consider molecular diffusion as the only mechanism further also then partial pressure P_{A_b} would have reached at distance X' only, instead of boundary layer edge. Therefore, we can say a film of thickness X' gives resistance equivalent to the boundary layer. The concentration gradient can now be written as $\dfrac{P_{A_i} - P_{A_b}}{X'}$. Then according to Fick's law for diffusion,

$$N_A = \frac{D}{RT} \frac{P_{A_i} - P_{A_b}}{X'} \quad \ldots (11)$$

X' is not known, therefore a constant k_g known as mass transfer coefficient is introduced which is diffusivity per unit length. Now equation becomes,

$$N_A = \frac{k_g}{RT} (P_{A_i} - P_{A_b}) \quad \ldots (12)$$

Mass transfer coefficient k_g is expressed by unit cm/sec. We know $C_A = \frac{P_A}{RT}$, therefore

$$N_A = k_g (C_{A_i} - C_{A_b}) \quad \ldots (13)$$

where C_{A_i} and C_{A_b} are concentrations of A on either side of the film. Similar equation can be written for liquid also with mass transfer coefficient k_l.

The mass transfer coefficient is dependent on diffusivity of the molecule and thickness of laminar sub-layer.

Dimensional analysis of mass transfer analogus to heat transfer, correlates it to dependence on Reynolds number (Re) and Schmidt number (Sc).

$$\frac{kd}{D} = \text{constant} \propto (Re)^q (S_E)^r \quad \ldots (14)$$

where, k and D are mass transfer coefficient and diffusivity of molecule respectively, d is a dimension related to geometry of the system. Schmidt number is analogus to Prandtl number in heat transfer, it is ratio of molecular diffusivity of momentum to molecular diffusivity given by $\frac{\eta}{\rho D}$.

4.4 INTERPHASE MASS TRANSFER

We have discussed single phase mass transfer, but frequently we have to deal with two phase mass transfer e.g. distillation, liquid-liquid extraction. The phenomenon of mass transfer across interface of two phases was studied by many workers and various models or theories have been proposed to explain it. The important theories are discussed below :

4.4.1 Two Film Theory :

This theory has been developed by Nernst, Lewis and Whitman. The theory postulates that two non-turbulent fictitious films are present on either side of the interface between the phases. The mass transfer across these films occurs purely by molecular diffusion. Interface does not offer any resistance to mass transfer, therefore, total resistance for mass transfer is summation of resistances of two films.

Consider that solute A is transferred from gas phase to the liquid. This will involve diffusional transfer of A across the two films adjacent to the interface (Fig. 4.3).

Fig. 4.3 : Interfacial mass transfer

Let, P_{A_g} = Partial pressure of A in bulk of gas

P_{A_i} = Partial pressure of A in gas at the interface

C_{A_i} = Concentration of A in liquid at interface

C_{A_l} = Concentration of A in the bulk of liquid.

k_g and k_l are mass transfer coefficients of individual films of gas and liquid respectively.

But it is difficult to know P_{A_i} and C_{A_i}. Hence concept of overall mass transfer coefficient is used. Consider,

P_{A_e} = the gas phase partial pressure of A which is in equilibrium with concentration of A in bulk of liquid (C_{A_l}) and,

C_{A_e} = Concentration of A in the liquid phase which is in equilibrium with partial pressure of A bulk of gas $\left(P^b_{A_g}\right)$

K_G and K_L are overall mass transfer coefficients. Then applying Fick's law,

$$N_A = K_G \left(P_{A_g} - P_{A_e}\right) \quad \ldots (15)$$

or

$$N_A = K_L \left(C_{A_e} - C_{A_l}\right) \quad \ldots (16)$$

The equilibrium between two phases is expressed by following equation,

$$P_A = H C_A + b \quad \ldots (17)$$

where H and b are constants.

By considering individual film transfer equations (12) and (13) and overall mass transfer equations (15) and (16) and equilibrium equation (17), following relationship can be developed between overall and individual phase mass transfer coefficients.

$$\frac{1}{K_G} = \frac{1}{k_g} + \frac{H}{k_l} \quad \ldots (18)$$

$$\frac{1}{K_L} = \frac{1}{HK_G} = \frac{1}{Hk_g} + \frac{1}{k_l} \quad \ldots (19)$$

If H is very large i.e. A is less soluble in the liquid, then $K_G \approx \frac{k_l}{H}$ and process becomes liquid phase controlled.

If H is very low i.e. A is highly soluble in the liquid, then $K_G \approx k_g$ and process is gas phase controlled.

According to this theory, mass transfer is directly proportional to molecular diffusivity of solute in the phase into which it is going and inversely proportional to thickness of films.

4.4.2 Penetration Theory :

Higbie proposed penetration theory to explain mass transfer considering unsteady-state at interface. According to this theory, fluid eddies travel from bulk to interface by convection, and remain there for a equal but limited period of time. When the eddy is at interface, the solute moves into it by molecular diffusion and gets penetrated into the bulk when eddy moves to the bulk. The theory suggests that rate of mass transfer is proportional to square root of molecular diffusivity and inversely proportional to the exposure time of eddy at interface.

4.4.3 Surface Renewal Theory :

Danckwert contradicted the assumption by Higbie, that each eddy gets equal exposure period at the interface and proposed surface renewal theory. According to this theory, the turbulence in the bulk phase is extended to the interface i.e. there is continuous renewal of interface by fresh eddies, which have composition that of the bulk. The turbulent eddies remain at the interface for time varying from zero to infinity, and then taken back into the bulk phase by convection currents. Thus at any instant the interface consists of eddies having different ages. According to this Danckwert's theory, also rate of mass transfer is proportional to square root of molecular diffusivity.

***

MANUAL CORRECTIONS
CH. 4

where P_{A_1} and P_{A_2} are partial pressures of A at distances X_1 and X_2. Similar equation can be written for counter diffusion of B.

Mass transfer coefficient k_g is expressed by unit cm/sec. We know $C_A = \frac{P_A}{RT}$, therefore

where C_{A_i} and C_{A_b} are concentrations of A on either side of the film. Similar equation can be

Danckwert contradicted the assumption by Higbie, that each eddy has gets equal exposure

CHAPTER 5

SIZE REDUCTION

5.1 INTRODUCTION

Size reduction is an important unit operation in pharmacy. Generally raw materials often present in sizes that are too large to be used and therefore they must be reduced in size. Size reduction includes crushing, grinding, pulverizing, shredding, cutting etc.

Significance of Size reduction in Pharmacy :

1. Size reduction leads to increase in surface area. The rate of chemical reactions is highly influenced by surface area. Hence chemical reaction can be carried out faster. The process of dissolution of particle and in turn its absorption from gastrointestinal tract was found to increase several fold due to fine size e.g. griseofulvin when administered in its micronized form shows around five times better absorption.

2. The process of diffusion of active ingredient from solid to liquid in the leaching process is dependent on particle size. The rate of extraction is high at low particle size.

3. Size reduction with some controls produces particles in the narrow size range, which is most essential during mixing of powder. Narrow particle size range reduces segregation giving uniform powder.

4. Many formulations require fine size particles e.g. lipsticks require the particles size control well down 2 µm for better quality.

But particle size reduction may also cause increase in the rate of degradation reactions, dusting problems. It reduces flowability of powders, increases its cohesiveness many times making it hydrophobic due to air entrapment.

5.2 THEORY OF SIZE REDUCTION

Size reduction involves transferring a particle from the inside of the solid to the surface by application of energy. This energy is transferred into potential energy of the particle surface i.e. surface free energy.

In general, to break a solid is to change its shape beyond certain limits. The ratio of the change in a given dimension to the original value is called the strain of the dimension. The force per unit area applied to carry out this change in dimension is called the stress. Solids can exhibit a very wide range of behaviour when under stress. This behaviour may alter not only according to the chemical and physical constitution of the body but also with the degree and rate of application of the applied force. Stress-strain relationships of different solids will find applications in size reduction.

Fig. 5.1, illustrates the change in strain over a range of stresses.

Fig. 5.1 : Stress-strain relationship for solids

In the region AB, strain is directly proportional to the stress in which reduction in stress would result in corresponding decrease in strain, thus it is an 'elastic region'. Point B is called elastic limit. Slope of the straight line AB is called Young's modulus. Young's modulus is the theoretical stress at which the strain would be unity within the elastic limit. If a stress within the elastic limit is imposed, the material will be deformed, but it will not break. Furthermore, it will return to its original shape when the stress is removed.

In the region BC, rate of change of strain with respect to stress is no longer constant but increasing. The point C is called the 'yield point'. Beyond the yield point, 'plastic deformation' occurs. By release of stress at point D; all strain is not recoverable. In this region, sliding along natural cleavage planes occur. Plastic deformation is terminated by failure or fracture.

In the region DE, the solid changes shape with no change in stress to break at E. Stress corresponding to the point E is called the 'Ultimate stress' ; which is a measure of the strength of the material. The area under the curve at any point represents the strain energy per unit volume absorbed by the material upto that strain. The limiting strain energy per unit volume is the energy absorbed upto the point of failure.

Thus, unless the material has undergone the whole series of changes from its original state to that in which it is at an ultimate stress, it will not break irrespective of the method of application of stress.

The larger the stress at the elastic limit, the stronger the material. The less the difference between the strain at the elastic limit and that at the yield point the more brittle is the material. Generally a brittle body is defined as one which shows very little ductility, thus a body can be both brittle and strong (Fig. 5.2). The ductility of the material is indicated by region CE in which flow occurs with little or no increase in the stress.

Fig. 5.2 : Properties of solid

If a gradually increasing breaking force is applied to a body, it is expected to break first at points of weakness or flaws. These flaws may be cracks and weak joints of agglomeration. This is because stresses concentrate in regions where there are changes of area. Thus maximum concentration of stresses occurs in areas where there are maximum curvatures. The cracks are expected to be elliptical in shape. Fig. 5.3.

Fig. 5.3 : Stress concentration at crack

Griffith postulated that most bodies are mass of cracks, which vary in size from visible ones to those of the order of atomic dimensions and breaking occurs by the way of these cracks through the stress concentration effect. Crack can be initiated on the solid surface when the strain energy to be released in the vicinity of the potential crack atleast equals the surface energy which would be created if the crack were formed. Cracks once formed can be self propagating provided there is enough strain energy in the material. But during comminution processes, cracks are rarely initiated on the surface. Comminution usually occurs through the propagation of existing cracks.

The critical tensile stress (P), required to supply the strain energy for propagation of cracks, breakage and production of new surface is approximately given by :

$$P = \sqrt{\frac{E\gamma}{C}} \qquad \ldots (1)$$

where,
E = Young's modulus,
γ = Density of flaws,
C = Critical crack depth for fracture.

The cracks propagate at an enormous speed and can approach the speed of sound in the material. The propagation of cracks definitely depends on the ability of the material to propagate the strain. Amorphous materials obstruct the propagation of cracks than the crystalline materials. Thus amorphous material tend to break locally at tips, whereas breaking in crystalline material is more diffuse. Product obtained from size reduction, of amorphous material will be a mixture of coarse and fine particles, whereas it will be in a narrower size range in case of crystalline materials.

When the crack propagates, there is penetration of other flaws which may in turn produce secondary cracks. The strength of the material therefore depends on the random distribution of flaws. The probability of containing flaw decreases as the particle size decreases, hence material becomes progressively difficult to grind. There is a minimum length of crack, of about 1 µm, below which van der Waal's forces act. Hence, grinding would proceed down to this size more easily than below it.

If we consider a true single crystal consisting entirely of a precise regular array of ions or atoms, then in such case, there are no cracks. In absence of cracks, breaking can only take place between atoms. But in practice such crystal is not possible.

5.3 ENERGY REQUIREMENT OF SIZE REDUCTION

Though we say that energy given during size reduction is stored as surface free energy of solids ; actual energy requirements are 100 to 1000 times more than predicted values based on surface energy consideration. The bulk of the energy supplied is wasted in :

(a) Particle – particle and particle – machine friction.
(b) Wasteful movement of particles within the mill.
(c) Elastic and plastic deformation of solids.
(d) Production of heat, noise and vibrations.
(e) Losses due to inefficient power transmission.

Thus grinding is a very inefficient process and it is important to use energy as efficiently as possible. The actual energy requirement for particle size reduction is a function of input and output particle sizes, hardness, strength and other mechanical properties of solids, capacity and feeding efficiency.

Various laws to determine energy requirement include :
1. Rittinger's law
2. Kick's law
3. Bonds law
4. Holmes law and
5. Harris law.

1. Rittinger's law : Rittinger proposed that the energy consumed in size reduction of solids is proportional to the new surface produced.

i.e. Energy α New surface

$\therefore$ Energy = K (New surface) = K (Final Surface Area – Initial Surface Area)

= K (Final number of particles ∞ Surface area per final particle –

Initial number of particles ∞ Surface area per initial particle)

$$= K \left(\frac{1}{D_2^3} \infty D_2^2 - \frac{1}{D_1^3} D_1^3 \right)$$

$$= K \left(\frac{1}{D_2} - \frac{1}{D_1} \right) \qquad \ldots (2)$$

where D_1 and D_2 are feed and product particle size respectively and

$$K = K_R \cdot f_c$$

where, K_R is Rittinger's constant and f_c is crushing strength of the material.

2. Kick's law : Kick postulated that deformation energy, the energy required by the material just before rupture called as strain energy, is proportional to volume. Thus unit volume of particles just at the stage of rupture contains same deformation energy independent of particle size. Therefore, in the size reduction process at each stage of grinding, same amount of energy is present.

$\therefore$ Deformation Energy = $K_1 \infty$ Number of stages of size reduction $\ldots (3)$

If D_1 is feed size and D_n is product size after n stages of size reduction with reduction ratio r at each stage, then

$$r^n = \left(\frac{D_1}{D_n} \right)^3$$

$$\therefore \quad n = \frac{3 (\log D_1 - \log D_n)}{\log r} = K_2 \log \left(\frac{D_1}{D_n} \right)$$

Substituting value of n in equation (2),

$$\therefore \quad \text{Total deformation energy} = K_1 K_2 \log \left(\frac{D_1}{D_n} \right)$$

$$= K \log \left(\frac{D_1}{D_n} \right) \qquad \ldots (4)$$

where, $K = K_K f_c$. K_K is Kick's constant.

From above discussion, Kick's law considers the deformation energy requirement, required upto just before rupture whereas, Rittinger's law considers energy required for actual fracture of the particle, once particle has reached the state of deformation. If α represent the energy for preparation of fracture as per Kick and β as the actual energy of fracture, then

$$x = \frac{\alpha}{\beta} \qquad \ldots (5)$$

where x is the particle size. Therefore, when x is large, Kick's law dominates and Rittinger's law dominates for small particles. Rittinger's law is applicable for perfectly brittle materials whereas Kick's law is applicable for elastic materials. It is observed that for practical purposes the energy requirement is in between that predicted by Kick's law and Rittinger's law.

3. **Bond's law :** Bond considered comminution as an intermediate stage in the breakdown of a particle of an infinite size to infinite number of particles of zero size and the energy possessed by the particles is proportional to $\frac{1}{\sqrt{Z}}$. Z is the screen size through which 80% of the particles pass. Therefore work (W) required to be done during breaking of a group particles with Z_1 to group of particles with Z_2 will be proportional to the difference in reciprocals of their roots.

$$W = K\left(\frac{1}{\sqrt{Z_2}} - \frac{1}{\sqrt{Z_1}}\right) \quad \ldots (6)$$

where, K is a constant for the material. Bond suggested $K = 10\, W_i$, where W_i is work index.

$$\therefore \quad W = 10\, W_i \left(\frac{1}{\sqrt{Z_2}} - \frac{1}{\sqrt{Z_1}}\right) \quad \ldots (7)$$

Bond explained selection of factor $\frac{1}{\sqrt{Z}}$ as follows :

If Z is the size of the particle, then surface area per unit volume is proportional to $\frac{1}{Z}$ and the crack length in volume is proportional to one side of that area and therefore $\frac{1}{\sqrt{Z}}$.

Work index W_i is the comminution parameter which expresses the resistance of the material to crushing. It is the kilowatt hours per short ton required to reduce the material from theoretically infinite feed size to 80% passing 100 µm.

4. **Holmes law :** It is the Bond's energy equation as,

$$W = 10\, W_i \left(\frac{1}{Z_2^r} - \frac{1}{Z_1^r}\right) \quad \ldots (8)$$

Holmes reported values of r between 0.25 to 0.73.

5. **Harris law :** This law considers that the rate of change of energy causing fracture diminishes as energy input increases. Resistance of particles to fracture increases as particle decreases and surface area reaches an upper asymptote as energy input increases.

A single equation was developed to combine Rittinger, Kick and Bond equation

$$\frac{dW}{dd} = -C\, d^n \quad \ldots (9)$$

n value is -2 for Rittinger law, -1 as per Kick's law and -1.5 for Bonds law.

The energy requirements for size reduction of some pharmaceutical substances is shown in Fig. 5.4.

Fig. 5.4 : Effect of nature of feed and particle size of energy requirement

Sugar is a brittle or friable, bark is a fibrous and gelatin is ductile and viscid substance. It shows that :

(a) Energy requirement increases as the substance is ground finely.

(b) Energy requirement for grinding of brittle or friable substance is much lower than the ductile substances.

(c) The lower limit of size reduction for friable substance is 3 – 4 µm, it is 40 – 50 µm for fibrous substance and 80 – 100 µm for gelatin.

5.4 EQUIPMENTS FOR SIZE REDUCTION

Mills are equipments designed to impart energy to the material and cause its size reduction. The energy is supplied by different mechanisms such as :

(i) Compression or nipping : It involves gripping the material between two surfaces and force is imposed on it by one or both the surfaces.

(ii) Impact : It involves contact of material with a fast moving part which imparts some of its kinetic energy to the material. This causes creation of internal stresses in the particle, breaking it.

(iii) Cutting : It involves application of force over a very narrow area of material using a sharp edge of a cutter.

(iv) Attrition : It involves collision between the two particles having high kinetic energy or a high velocity particle with a stationary surface.

The mills carry out size reduction by one or combination of the above mentioned mechanisms. Various mills and their mechanisms are given in Table 5.1.

Table 5.1 : Mechanisms of Size Reduction

Mill	Mechanism

1.	Hammer	1.	Impact
2.	Tumbling (Ball)	2.	Impact + Attrition
3.	Fluid energy	3.	Impact + Attrition
4.	Roller, Edge Runner	4.	Nipping
5.	Cutter	5.	Cutting
6.	Colloid	6.	Attrition

5.4.1 Hammer mill :

The hammer mill is an impact mill. It consists of high speed rotor mounted with hammer encased in a casing which has a mesh at the bottom (Fig. 5.5). The hammer may be fixed or pivoted. But generally pivoted hammers are used. The rotor moves at high speeds such that peripheral speed of about 300 – 500 m/s is achieved. The material remains in the casing until it is reduced to desired size. As soon as it is reduced to desired size, it is thrown out from the screen at the bottom. The material in the mill has velocities very close to the velocity of a rotor and fracture takes place due to severity of the blow received or subsequent impact with the casing.

Fig. 5.5 : Hammer mill

The hammers may be of different shapes, a blunt hammer is used for brittle materials and the cutting edge hammer for fibrous materials. The spacing of hammers on rotor is such that it balances the rotor and correspond with the rotor speed so that each piece of feed is likely to be hit by a hammer as soon as it enter the chamber.

Speed of hammers and screen thickness are two important variables affecting the size reduction process in hammer mill.

Speed of hammers : At low hammer speeds, as the kinetic energy of hammer is low, the amount of energy imparted to the material is also very low. The low quantum of energy imparted cannot generate stresses in material to cause fracture. Large amount of kinetic energy is utilised to transport the material from one point to another in the casing. Movement of particles over one another causes abrasion. This causes generation of smooth surface particles. Thus energy is utilised for mass transport than size reduction and no significant size reduction occur.

At very high speed, the contact between the hammers and particles is very low for a short period. Though the hammer has very high kinetic energy it cannot be imparted to the material in the short period of contact. Thus for effective size reduction the hammer should have high kinetic energy and sufficient time of contact to impart it to the material so as to fracture it. Hence no significant size reduction occurs at very high speeds.

Fig. 5.6 : Effect of hammer speed

The high speed of hammers also affects the quality of product obtained by changing the angle at which it is thrown out. So as to understand this effect let us discuss how the fine product comes out. Suppose we have placed 75 μm mesh at the bottom. The particle of 75 μm will pass through it, if it is passing along the vertical axis. In hammer mill, the particle approaches the mesh at certain angle and cannot align itself as it is having high kinetic energy. Therefore, those particles will only pass which can escape without any hindrance across the mesh wall. Thus, the cut-off size of the mesh depends on the angle at which the particle is thrown, when the particle cannot align itself due to high velocity. When hammer speed is high the particles are thrown towards periphery and has very high kinetic energy, therefore, the product coming out is very fine (Fig. 5.6). As hammer speed increases, the velocity of particle increases and its angle of throw decreases and product fineness increases.

Screen thickness : The unhindered escape of the particle largely depends on thickness of mesh. As screen thickness increases, the cut–off size decreases as shown in Fig. 5.7.

Fig. 5.7 : Effect of screen thickness

The energy requirement of mill is comparatively low if operated at proper rates. The space requirement is less and capacity is high. Particle size down upto 40 µm may be obtained. The mill is versatile in application, it is used for fibrous substances such as glycerrhiza, asbestos, crystalline drugs such as caffeine, ascorbic acid, acetanilide and gelatin, waxes, stearates etc. It is also used for wet grinding.

Severe impact in the machine causes wear of hammer due to which sometimes metal particles may contaminate the product.

5.4.2 Tumbling Mills :

Tumbling mills consist of a rotating cylindrical shell containing loose units occupying more than half of its volume. The units may be balls, rods, pebbles, etc. and accordingly mill becomes ball mill, rod mill, pebbles mill, etc. Ball mill is commonly used. The balls due to friction of the shell get lifted to a certain height (Fig. 5.8), and then cascade and cataract down the free surface of other balls in course of being lifted up. Size reduction takes place between the balls when they are rolling over one another prior to lifting i.e. attrition and impact is given by ball when it falls down. Thus comminution mechanism is combination of impact and attrition.

Fig. 5.8 : Ball mill

In the upward movement of the side of the shell, the balls are interlocked and relatively stationary. At the top of their lift, at about the quadrant, the balls cascade down the free surface or cataract in free fall and hit the bottom where material is present. This lifting, sliding and impacting of balls mainly in the downward direction causes comminution.

If the length of shell is very high (approximately five times) as compared to diameter then it is called as tube mill. It may have compartments for different stages of grinding. The product is taken out after sufficient time for batch operation. For continuous operation, overflow is taken out.

Ball mill processing involves many variables of which important are speed of rotation, ball size, ball load, charge load.

Speed of rotation : If ball mills are rotated at very high speed then due to high centrifugal force, balls remain attached to the shell and does not cascade or cataract. (Fig. 5.9). Thus no size reduction occurs. At very low speed, the centrifugal force acting on the ball is very low to lift it and they only roll over one another causing attrition but no impact. Thus significant size reduction does not occur. Therefore, it is necessary to operate the mill so that ball will be lifted and fall from certain height.

Fig. 5.9 : Effect of speed of ball mill

Therefore, the critical speed has to be calculated. The critical speed is the minimum speed at which the media are held against the shell by centrifugal force i.e. the speed at which the centrifugal force is just balanced by the weight of the ball.

Consider a ball with radius 'r' and mass 'M' rotates in the shell of radius 'R' having rotational speed 'N'. If 'V' is velocity of the ball then centrifugal force is given by,

$$\text{Centrifugal force} = \frac{MV^2}{R}$$

At critical speed ($N = N_c$), the weight of ball is exactly balanced by centrifugal force.

$$\therefore \quad Mg = \frac{MV^2}{R}$$

$$\therefore \quad V^2 = gR$$

But $V = 2\pi R \propto N$

$$\therefore \quad (2\pi R)^2 N_c^2 = gR$$

$$\therefore \quad N_c = \frac{\sqrt{g}}{2\pi \sqrt{R}} \qquad \ldots (10)$$

By solving equation (10) we get,

$$N_c = \frac{300}{\sqrt{R}} \text{ revolutions per min.} \qquad \ldots (11)$$

A further modification is suggested taking into consideration centre of gravity of the ball.

$$N_c = \frac{300}{\sqrt{R-r}} \qquad \ldots (12)$$

Dry grinding should be carried out at 65 – 70% of N_C and wet grinding at 70 –75% of N_C.

Ball size : It is observed that larger balls give coarse product as compared to small balls. It is due to the larger voids present as ball size increases and attrition which generates fine product becomes less effective. Therefore, large balls are necessary for coarse grinding and small balls for fine grinding. Generally combination of large and fine balls are used.

A relationship was observed between ball size and feed size.

$$d = K\sqrt{\text{Feed size}}$$

where, d is ball diameter and K is grindability constant having values between 25 to 55 depending on the nature of material. Harder the material, larger is the K value.

Ball load : Maximum size reduction was observed when balls occupy 50% of the internal volume of mill. When the ball load was reduced to 40%, the size reduction decreased by 25%.

Charge load : The material charged in the mill should be optimum generally upto 50 – 60%. Large charge loads may cause 'cushioning effect' and effect of impact will be reduced.

Fig. 5.10 : Energy input versus charge volume

Time of milling : Time of milling is most important in fine grinding. If fine particles are ground for longer period rebonding between particles occur leading to agglomeration.

The ball mill finds wide applications in pharmacy. It can be used for grinding of material of any hardness. It gives very fine product upto 200 mesh. Urea, antibiotics, vitamins, nail lacquers, alum, colours are processed in ball mill. It can be used for dry as well as wet grinding. It can be sterilized, therefore, suitable for sterile processing.

But ball mill is not suitable for sticky substances powders containing more than 1 – 2% moisture. As it involves impact, chances of contamination by impacting ball particles cannot be neglected.

5.4.3 Fluid Energy Mill :

Initial models of fluid energy mill consisted of two jets of material fluidized by air or steam, fed diametrically opposite so that particle collide. Subsequently, fluid energy mill was designed as a cylindrical type (micronizer) and elliptical tube type.

Fig. 5.11 : Fluid energy mill

As shown in Fig. 5.11 it consists of an elliptical tube with diameter upto 20 cm. The material is forced into the grinding chamber through the venturi feed placed near the bottom. The fluid compressed at 100 – 150 psi enters the chamber through the nozzles. In the tube, a fluid vortex is formed which provide the particles with differential speeds and collide with each other as well some impacts with the casing. The particle in the tube is subjected to three forces simultaneously :

(i) forces set up by grinding jets,
(ii) tangential forces due to cyclone, and
(iii) rotational forces.

These forces cause attrition and size reduction to micron size. At the top of the elliptical shape change in direction and tangential forces result in classifying action. Three separate streams are formed, a stream of greatest radius, where most of the collisions occur causing size reduction, the intermediate radius stream where classification of heavier and lighter particles occurs. The heavier particles under centrifugal force again thrown to periphery and small particles pass to the slow moving inner stream and taken out as product. Thus fluid energy mill causes size reduction as well as particle classification.

The ratio of mass of fluid to that of material is generally kept 1 : 1. The fluid may be air, nitrogen or steam. Steam has advantage that at the outlet it condenses and the entrained solids may be removed. This is of particular value when material is toxic. Superheated steam under pressure is cheaper than compressed air.

The feed size is maintained less than 150 μm. Size greater than this makes operation uneconomical, therefore, product may be subjected to pre-milling.

Fluid energy mill offers many advantages for processing of pharmaceuticals such as :

(i) As the fluid under pressure enters the mill, its sudden expansion causes decrease in its temperature. This cooling does not allow the temperature to rise during comminution. Thus, it is a suitable method for thermolabile materials.

(ii) As it does not have any moving part, very little wear of the equipment occurs. Therefore, product is also free from contamination.

(iii) The mill can be sterilized and aseptic milling is possible.

But the mill is not suitable for fibrous and waxy material. It is used for vitamins, antibiotics, iodine, calcium stearate etc. As it involves attrition between fine particles under high velocity it may cause disturbance of electronic configuration at the particle surface causing static charge problems. Therefore, earthing should be provided.

5.4.4 Roller Mill :

It is based on the principle of compression or nipping. It consists of two, three, four or six cylinders, which are usually horizontal and revolve towards each other. It may also consist of a single roll and a stationary plate called as breaker plate. The distance between the rolls is usually adjustable. The multi-roll machine uses rolls in pairs so that the material can be successively passed between pairs. In case of triple roller mill, the rolls are arranged so that their centres form a triangle with one roll at the top ; the material is then fed under the top roll and over the other ones. The shear forces imparted by roller may be intensified by the differing peripheral velocity of the rolls.

Fig. 5.12 : Forces on a particle in crushing rolls

For nipping action between the rolls, it is necessary that the particle must be gripped between the rolls. It depends on the distance between the rolls and size of material to be gripped. This distance can be adjusted using angle of nip. Consider a circular particle with radius r held between two circular rolls with radius R and distance between two rolls be 2a as shown in Fig. 5.12 . The angle between the tangents at the two points of contact between the particle and surfaces is called as angle of nip (θ). There is maximum angle beyond which the surfaces fail to nip the particle, which would slip when pressure was applied to it by the surfaces. The particle is subjected to two types of forces; the compressive force C acting normal to tangent and frictional force µC acting in the direction of tangent. A vertical component of compressive force is $C \sin \frac{\theta}{2}$ acts in upward direction and vertical component of friction force, $\mu C \cos \frac{\theta}{2}$, acts in the downward direction. When downward force equals the upward force then product will be just gripped. Therefore, the condition is

$$\mu C \cos \frac{\theta}{2} = C \sin \frac{\theta}{2} \quad \text{or} \quad \mu = \tan \frac{\theta}{2} \quad \ldots\ldots\ldots$$

where µ is coefficient of static friction.

From Fig. 5.12,

$$\cos \frac{\theta}{2} = \frac{R + a}{R + r} \quad \ldots (14)$$

Using this equation (14), we can determine the maximum size of the particle gripped in the rollers and if reduction ratio of $\left(\frac{r}{a}\right)$ is desired. For most of the practical purposes, the angle of nip is between $10 - 25°$.

Fig. 5.13 : Triple roller mill

Roller mill (Fig.5.13) is most suitable for pastes, ointments and other plastic flowing substance. It is also used for grinding substances such as ascorbic acid, alum, caffeine etc. It is used for dispersion of pigments in lipsticks.

5.4.5 Edge and Runner Mill :

It is also called as pan mill, chasers or mullers. It has rollers or mullers which turn on a horizontal axis and rests under gravity on a bed of material in a pan (Fig. 5.14). A mill using more than two rollers in Chilean mill. The edger runner mills with perforated bottoms are known as grate mills. It may be used for dry or wet grinding. The scrappers are used for directing the material back to the centre of the pan. The rollers are equidistant from the centre of the pan and revolve on solid plates which form a circle in the centre of the pan. The discharge can be rim discharge or bottom discharge.

Fig. 5.14 : Edge runner mill

The size reduction in the mill partly takes by rolling i.e. compression and partly by sliding. The areas in which these actions take place are related to the distance of the rollers from the centre of the pan (R) and the width of the rolls (B), as

$$\frac{\text{Area of rolling action}}{\text{Area of sliding action}} = \frac{4R}{B}$$

Thus to maximise sliding, R is made as small as possible and B as large as possible.

The fineness of the product depends on depth of the bed and roller weight. The basic advantage of the edge runner mill, that it produces a mixture of sizes which jointly constitute a material with very low porosity i.e. high bulk density (Fig. 5.15). This is due to sliding and compressive action of the rollers, which induces the particles to marry in with one another thus minimizing voids. Another explanation given is the particles are made spherical.

Fig. 5.15 : Particle rounding during milling in edge runner mill

Thus in edge runner milling there is increase in the number of different particle sizes, selective crushing of softer material and making of particles more spherical, which yields product with high bulk density. The high bulk density material is less prone to segregation during transport and storage.

End runner mill (Fig. 5.16) is another mill working on the same principle. It consists of a mortar made of porcelain or other suitable material. A heavy pestle is mounted vertically within the mortar in an off-centre position. Size reduction occurs due to compression due to weight of pestle and the shear developed by relative movement of the pestle and mortar. The shear varies with the face of the pestle. The pestle is friction driven by the mortar through the ground material. A scraper is used to redirect the material to the milling zone.

Fig. 5.16 : End runner mill

5.4.6 Cutter Mill :

In the process of cutting, the finest edge of a cutter penetrates the material causing its plastic deformation. First the material is displaced and a furrow is formed. If the cutting knife has a saw-like edge it causes abrasion also. The different cutting tools such as knives, shears, saws, spikes, may be used. Knives and shears are useful for plastically deformable materials, saws are applied for brittle substances and spikes for all kinds of substances. Kaiser reported two types of shears which are commonly used. The first one which requires continuous sheet of material to be fed to it, so that it is cut with precision into regular rectangular pieces (Fig. 5.17). The second one which is commonly used in pharmaceuticals cuts pieces of assorted sizes into random shapes and sizes. Saws are not used now-a-days. Spikes are used on the surface of roll crushers.

Feed Casing   Stationary blade Rotating blade   Rotor   Sieve   Blade holder Ground product

Fig. 5.17 : Section through a horizontal cutting mill

Cutting mill find application in size reduction of plastic, elastic and fibrous materials which are otherwise difficult to reduce. But major limitations are that its rate is slow and very fine product is not obtained. These mills also create safety problems.

5.4.7 Special Grinding Technique :

1. Freeze Grinding : Many substances when cooled to extremely low temperatures of – 80 to – 196 °C become brittle, e.g. waxes with low melting point. The cooling agents employed may be liquid nitrogen (– 195.8°C), solid carbon dioxide (– 78.5 °C).

The mill contains fixed or loose hammer mounted on a rotor moving at the speed of around 4000 r.p.m. fitted in a casing like a hammer mill. The material to be ground passes through a heat exchanger. Suitable arrangement is done for air because air present in the feed contracts on cooling. Drying tower is also present.

This technique offers advantages such as increased production rates, prevents product degradation, fine product size, reduces explosion hazards etc. It is suitable for substances which are heat - sensitive, oxygen sensitive and volatile materials. Almonds, apricot kernels, ginger, clove, cinnamon and nutmegs which contain oils and form paste when ground at room temperature may be satisfactorily subjected to freeze grinding. Heat and oxygen sensitive drugs like adrenaline, antibiotics, vitamins may be processed by this technique. Polymers such as polyvinyl chloride, polyvinyl alcohol may be made brittle and ground by this technique.

2. Dry and Wet Grinding : Wet grinding may be defined as grinding of materials containing about 50% of water by volume in the uncombined state. If wetting of materials acceptable before, after and during grinding, then it offers many advantages. Generally, water is used as a wetting liquid.

The proportion of wetting liquid required depends on the properties of liquid such as its density, viscosity, surface tension and particle size of the feed and product. The slurry for grinding should not be excessively thinned because it reduces capacity and causes wear of grinding medium and lining. The quantity of liquid during grinding should be sufficient to fill the total void spaces. Many times the material to be ground may be hydrophobic and create problems. In such cases, surface active agents may be added to aid grinding.

Advantages of Wet grinding :

1. Power consumption is low. Bond index is about 75% as compared to dry grinding.
2. Dust problems are reduced.
3. Milling capacity increases by 10 – 65%.
4. Tumbling mills can be rotated at higher speeds.

5. Static charges problem is avoided.
6. As wet screening is efficient than dry screening, better particle size control can be obtained.

Disadvantages :
1. Wear of the grinding media and liners is more.
2. Flocculation problem may occur.
3. Drying step is required in many cases after milling and it becomes costly.

Size Control During Milling :

Ideally material should cease to be comminuted as soon as it reached the desired size. For this purpose, open or closed circuit is utilized.

Open Circuit Milling :

In open circuit, the material is fed into the mill at a calculated rate so that correct product is produced in one pass [Fig. 5.18 (a)]. In this, the feed is screened prior to entering the mill so as to remove material already sufficiently small. In open circuit the controls which are relied on are feed rate, retention time and internal size classification.

(a) Open circuit milling   (b) Closed circuit milling
Fig. 5.18 : Size control during milling

As the material remains for predetermined time in the mill, a fraction of feed which gets reduced to desired size at early stages of cycle is unnecessarily ground for remaining part of the cycle. This increases power consumption, some fraction is ground far below the desired size and capacity of milling also decreases. Fine particles may cause cushioning effect and may also reach the agglomerative stage.

Closed Circuit Milling :

In closed circuit milling [Fig. 5.18 (b)], the material of desired size is removed by a classifier and oversize is returned to the mill. In closed circuit, it is not necessary that size reduction should take place in a single pass. But precaution is taken that material is removed as soon as it reaches the desired size. The material returned to the mill by the classifier is known as the circulating load, and its weight is expressed as a percentage of the weight of new feed. Closed circuit reduces over–grinding of feed, increases energy available for useful grinding, most of the product is very close to the desired size. Capacity of milling increases by about 35% as compared to open–circuit milling. It is commonly used in ball milling. But it increases a size separation step which increases cost of setup. But adoption of closed circuit milling is only possible on a relatively large scale.

***

MANUAL CORRECTIONS
CH. 5

as possible. The actual energy requirement for particle size reduction is a function of input

... (2)

Substituting value of n in equation (2),

$$\therefore \text{Total deformation energy} = K_1 K_2 \log\left(\frac{D_1}{D_n}\right)$$

$$= K \log\left(\frac{D_1}{D_n}\right) \quad ...(4)$$

where, $K = K_K \, f_c$. K_K is Kick's constant.

At very high speed, the contact between the hammers and particles is very low for a short friction of the shell get lifted to a certain height (Fig. 5.8), and then cascade and cataract down

$$\therefore (2\pi R)^2 \, N_C^2 = gR$$

$$\therefore N_C = \frac{\sqrt{g}}{2\pi \sqrt{R}} \quad ...(10)$$

By solving equation (10) we get,

$$N_C = \frac{300}{\sqrt{R}} \text{ revolutions per min.} \quad ...(11)$$

A further modification is suggested taking into consideration centre of gravity of the ball.

$$N_C = \frac{300}{\sqrt{R-r}} \quad ...(12)$$

Dry grinding should be carried out at 65 – 70% of N_C and wet grinding at 70 – 75% of N_C.

... (13)

compressive action of the rollers, which induces the particles to marry in with one another thus

Before milling   **After milling**

Scraper

(a) **Open circuit milling**   (b) **Closed circuit milling**

Fig. 5.18 : Size control during milling

SIZE SEPARATION

6.1 INTRODUCTION

Size separation or classification is an operation in which particles of desired size are separated from other fractions. Particle size separation plays an important role in pharmaceutical processing, as particle size affects properties of the formulation as well as it's processing. Narrow particle size distribution is necessary in suspensions to avoid Ostwald ripening causing coarseness to the formulation. Particle size distribution control is most important in the processing of granules to form tablets.

Techniques based on different principles are utilised for mechanical size separation. Sieving, sedimentation and centrifugation are widely used techniques.

6.2 SIEVING

A sieve or a screen is a surface having number of apertures of given dimensions. The material of mixed size is passed on the screen surface and agitated. The particles will either pass through or be retained on the screen depending on their size. This operation may be repeated successively with smaller sieves and particles are classified into different size fractions. Thus sieving is a technique which classifies the particles solely on the basis of size, independently of other properties such as density, surface area etc. Sieving can be carried out for dry as well as wet powders.

The sieves are often referred to by their mesh size or sieve number. Sieve number indicates number of wires or apertures per linear inch. There are different standards set for the sieves such as German Standard DIN 4188, American Society for Testing Materials (ASTM) Standard E 11, the American Tyler series, the French series. AFNOR and the British Standard, BSS 410. These standard specify the gauge of the wire and permitted tolerances. The successive meshes as per BSS 410, show mesh space alteration by a factor of $\sqrt[4]{2}$. Therefore, if alternate screens in the series are if selected for sieving then mesh spacing will decrease by $\sqrt{2}$ and the area of the aperture will be halved. The ASTM standard E 11 is shown in Table 6.1. Same mesh number on the various standard corresponds to different aperture size depending on the thickness of the wire used in the woven wire cloth.

Table 6.1 : BSS 410 Wire-Mesh Sieves

Mesh number	Nominal aperture size (µm)	Mesh number	Nominal aperture size (µm)
3	5600	36	425
3.5	4750	44	355
4	4000	52	300
5	3350	60	250
6	2800	72	212
7	2360	85	180
8	2000	100	150
10	1700	120	125
12	1400	150	106
14	1180	170	90
16	1000	200	75
18	850	240	63
22	710	300	53
25	600	350	45
30	500	400	38

(a) Woven-wire sieves

(b) Perforated plate sieves

(c) Wedge - wire sieves

Fig. 6.1 : Screening surfaces

The types of screening surfaces used depend on the aperture required and the nature of the work. Woven wire clothes employing bronze, stainless steel, steel, brass and copper, are widely used screen surfaces. Non–metallics used for screen surface include materials like nylon, silk and polyurethane. These materials have high resistance to abrasion or impact. The aperture shape also differs e.g. square mesh is used for coarse screening and rectangular for fine screening. The rectangular screens have more open area than the square screens of the same wire diameter

(Fig. 6.1). Diameter of wire used for screens depends on nature of work and capacity. Thin wire is used for fine screens which increases open area but screen becomes fragile. Punched plates with square or circular holes are also used for heavy duty operations. Other shapes such as slots may be used for sieving fibres.

Wedge wire screens (Fig. 6.1) are used for fine screening machines such as sieve bends. Such screens are strong and have relatively large open areas. The wedge profiles minimizes particle binding.

Coarse powders are screened in dry condition. Wet screening of dilute slurries is suggested for powders which aggregate strongly, clog the mesh or get electrostatically charged on vibrating screens.

Screening equipments may use stationary or vibrating screens. But in pharmaceutical processing generally vibrating screen is used. A stationary screen like sieve bend finds application in wet screening of pharmaceuticals especially of mineral origin and closed circuit wet grinding.

6.2.1 Sieve Bend :

The sieve bend has a curved screen made up of wedge bars (Fig. 6.2). The feed slurry enters tangentially at the top of the screen surface. As the slurry steam passes each opening a thin layer is peeled off and directed to the underside of screen. The sieve bend may separate particles upto 50 μm and capacities upto 180 m^3 h^{-1} per square meter of screen area may be obtained. But when separation occurs, a thin layer of pulp remain adhered to the convex side or back of the screen due to wall effect. Therefore, periodic removal of adhered particles is necessary.

Fig. 6.2 : Sieve Bend

6.2.2 Moving screens :

The screens may have revolving, reciprocating, gyratory or vibrating action. In pharmaceutical operation later two are commonly used.

On small scale the nest of sieves with rim diameters in the range of 8 – 18 inches are mounted on a sieve shaker (Fig. 6.3) and agitated for predetermined time. The agitation time is selected such that the underflow rate becomes negligible.

For large scale processing the screen with gyratory movement i.e. a sifter is used especially for wet and dry screening down upto 40 μm. It consists of nest of circular screens mounted on a table which is mounted on springs on a base. (Fig. 6.4). A table has a motor below it. The motor drives eccentric weights and produces horizontal gyratory motion. The screens may have diameter upto 5 ft. It sieves the powder into different fractions in short period of time.

Fig. 6.3 : Vibrating sieve shaker

Fig. 6.4 : Gyratory shaker

The vibrating machines may also have rectangular screens and may be slightly inclined. The inclination is between $5 - 30°$.

Fig. 6.5 : Alpine air-jet sifter

Alpine air jet sifter (Fig. 6.5) is a method for sieving fine materials. Air is drawn upwards through a sieve, from a rotating slit which is positioned below the gauze and scans its whole area. The jet aims upwards, keeping the screen aperture clear, and maintaining the charge of material in a fluidized state. Negative pressure is simultaneously applied to the bottom of the sieve which removes fine particles to a collecting device. The oversize particles are retained on the screen. This is known as reverse flow scavenging which effectively reduces screen blinding. This technique can be used for sieving down to 10 μm.

Effectiveness of Screens :

Fig. 6.6 : Screening mass balance

Effectiveness or efficiency of screen is its ability to separate the oversize and undersize particles. A screen will have 100% efficiency if it passes all undersize particles through it retaining only oversize particles in the overflow.

The equation for efficiency of screen may be obtained by using material balance across the screen. Let us consider F, H and U denote flow rates in kg/hr for feed, overflow and underflow respectively across the screen. f, h and u are fraction of oversize particles in the feed, overflow and underflow respectively (Fig. 6.6).

Overall Material Balance across the screen is

$$\text{Feed} = \text{Overflow} + \text{Underflow}$$

i.e. $\quad F = H + U \quad$ ... (1)

Material Balance of oversize material will be :

$$Ff = Hh + Uu \quad \text{... (2)}$$

Material Balance of undersize particles is

$$F(1-f) = H(1-h) + U(1-u) \quad \text{... (3)}$$

Solving equation (1), (2) and (3), we get,

$$\frac{H}{F} = \frac{f-u}{h-u} \quad \text{... (4)}$$

and $\quad \dfrac{U}{F} = \dfrac{h-f}{h-u} \quad$ ... (5)

Recovery of oversize material in overflow will be

$$\frac{Hh}{Ff} = \frac{h(f-u)}{f(h-u)} \qquad \ldots (6)$$

and recovery of undersize particles in underflow is

$$\frac{U(1-u)}{F(1-f)} = \frac{(h-f)(1-u)}{(h-u)(1-f)} \qquad \ldots (7)$$

Equations (6) and (7) gives effectiveness of the screen in separating the coarse material from underflow and fine material from overflow. Overall effectiveness E of the screen is obtained by multiplying the two equations

$$E = \frac{h(f-u)(1-u)(h-f)}{f(h-u)^2(1-f)} \qquad \ldots (8)$$

If no aperture is broken or deformed, the amount of oversize particles in the underflow is negligible. Thus considering $u = 0$, the equation becomes :

$$E = \frac{(h-f)}{h(1-f)} \qquad \ldots (9)$$

Equation (9) can be used to find out overall efficiency of the screen.

Factors affecting screening :

1. **Feed Rate :** Low feed rates and longer sieving time, ensure complete separation of particles and increase effectiveness of the screen. But this reduces capacity of the operation. High feed rates reduces residence time of the particles and increases thickness of bed on the screen. Thus fine particles have to travel larger distance to reach the screen surface. This reduces efficiency of screen.

2. **Nature of feed material :** The probability of the material passing through the aperture is proportional to the percentage of 'open area' in the screen. 'Open area' is defined as the net area of the apertures to the whole area of the screening surface.

Feed particles near the aperture size tend to block the aperture, this is called as 'blinding'. Blinding of screen reduces the open area available for screening. Thus, particles having size near the aperture size will be reported in the overflow, reducing efficiency. This is shown in Fig. 6.7 by a efficiency curve ; which is a plot of percentage feed of each fraction reporting in overflow, against the geometric mean diameter on logarithmic scale. Similarly, capacity of screen also gets reduced due to blinding. Thus screens with slightly greater aperture size than the desired size should be used for screening.

Fig. 6.7 : Efficiency curve

The shape of feed particles also affects screen efficiency. Non-spherical particles will have small cross-section in one orientation while large in the other. Screens will have low efficiency for flat, plate-like and needle shaped crystals. During dry screening, higher moisture content of the feed tend to 'agglomerate on screen and causes blinding of screen. Therefore, moisture content should be maintained low.

3. Screen vibration : Screens are vibrated so as to increase their efficiency by reducing blinding and causing material segregation. At very high vibration rates, particles bounce and thrown far away. This reduces it's strikes with screen and in turn screen efficiency. Very low vibration rates may form a bed with cushioning effect, inhibit bouncing of particle and reduces efficiency.

Mogensen sizer :

In conventional sieving the principle of separation is that the sieves retain the particles larger than the aperture and allow passage of the smaller ones. But we have seen that sieve efficiency is low for particles with borderline sizes.

Mogensen developed a sifting device (Fig. 6.8) which operates on the principle that there is a definite and quantifiable probability that a particle will pass through an aperture larger than the maximum diameter of that particle. The separation limit amount to only a fraction of the clear mesh width. The resultant poorer selectivity is improved by passing the material repeatedly through several sieves placed one below the other. As this process does not classify particles strictly according to mesh width, it is also known as sieve like process.

Fig. 6.8

The material is classified by several sieves placed one above the other and having increasing inclination and decreasing mesh width from top to bottom in the sieve stack. But the mesh width used in large in comparison with the separation limit. In other words, separation is carried out in the region of high probability of passage. Due to this input of large quantities of materials is possible. The individual screen shows poor sieving effect but it is compensated by repeating the separation process through further sieves. The separation is further sharpened by increasing angle of inclination and decreasing mesh width of the sieves from top to bottom of the sieve stack. A vibrator is provided to produce the necessary sieving movement. Mogensen sizer is used in preparing pharmaceutical industry to obtain infusions. The capacity of Mogensen sizer is such that a particular screening duty can be met with a machine occupying a fraction of the floor space required by a conventional screen and blinding and wear is greatly reduced.

6.3 SEDIMENTATION

Classification of solids on the basis of their velocity in a fluid medium is carried out in sedimentation and hydraulic separation methods.

6.3.1 Theory :

Suppose if a solid particle falls in a vacuum, it is subjected to constant acceleration and its velocity increases indefinitely, which is independent of size or density of the particle. In other words, a lump of lead and feather will fall at the same rate.

But when solid moves in a fluid medium such as air or water, resistance is given to this movement and it increases with velocity. When equilibrium is achieved between the gravitational forces and the opposing forces of fluid, the body falls at a uniform rate, velocity which is attained is called as terminal velocity. In Chapter 'Fluid Flow', we have seen viscous drag acting on sphere in contact with fluid is given by Stoke's law as :

$$\text{Drag} = 3\pi d u \eta \qquad \ldots (10)$$

Consider, a spherical particle with diameter d, and density ρ_s is falling under gravity in a viscous fluid with viscosity η, density ρ_f under free settling conditions. Then the sphere will be acted upon by three forces : a gravitational force acting downwards, an upward buoyant force due to displaced liquid, and a drag force D acting upwards. Then equation for motion of the sphere is given as :

(Gravitational force) – (Buoyant + drag) force = Force deciding velocity

$$mg - m'g - D = m\frac{dx}{dt} \qquad \ldots (11)$$

where m is mass of sphere, m' is mass of displaced liquid, x is the particle velocity and g is the acceleration due to gravity.

At terminal velocity, change in velocity is zero i.e. $\frac{dx}{dt} = 0$.

$$\therefore \quad D = (m - m')g \qquad \ldots (12)$$

But mass is a product of volume and density. Substituting it in equation (12), we get

$$D = \frac{\pi}{6} d^3 g (\rho_s - \rho_f) \qquad \ldots (13)$$

where $(\rho_s - \rho_f)$ is known as effective density.

Substituting this value of D from equation (10), we get

$$\frac{\pi}{6} d^3 g (\rho_s - \rho_f) = 3 \pi d u \eta$$

$$\therefore \quad u = \frac{gd^2 (\rho_s - \rho_f)}{18 \eta} \quad \ldots (14)$$

This is Stoke's law for settling solid.

The Stoke's law assumes the particle to be a smooth sphere and fluid has low Reynolds number and particle is settling freely without any hindrance ; which occurs when solid content is less than 15 percent by weight.

Newton calculated the drag acting on a sphere due to turbulent flow as :

$$D_t = 0.055 \pi d^2 u^2 \rho_f \quad \ldots (15)$$

Substituting this value in equation (13), we get

$$u = \sqrt{\frac{3 gd (\rho_s - \rho_f)}{\rho_f}} \quad \ldots (16)$$

Thus Stoke's law gives terminal velocity under laminar and Newton's law for turbulent resistance. Stoke's law is valid for particles less than 50 μm in diameter, whereas Newton's law for larger particles upto 500 μm. Both laws show that terminal velocity of solids in a particular fluid is a function of particle size and density.

As the proportion of solids in the slurry increases, the effect of crowding of particles becomes more apparent. The system now behaves like a viscous liquid with density of slurry is very high than the fluid, settling of solid under such condition is hindered settling. Hindered settling reduces the effect of size, and density of particle becomes important factor in sedimentation of solid.

Example 6.1 : Calculate the settling velocity and Reynolds number of a dust particle of 60 μm diameter in air at 21 °C and 100 kPa pressure. Assume that particles are spherical and density is 1280 kg m^{-3}. Viscosity of air = 1.8×10^{-5} Ns m^{-2} and density of air = 1.2 kg m^{-3}.

Solution : Stoke's equation : $u = \dfrac{d^2 g (\rho_s - \rho_f)}{18 \eta}$

For 30 μm particles $\quad u = \dfrac{(60 \times 10^{-6})^2 \times 9.81 \times (1280 - 1.2)}{18 \times 1.8 \times 10^{-5}}$

$$= 1.4 \text{ ms}^{-1}$$

Reynolds Number $\quad Re = \dfrac{D u \rho}{\eta}$

$$= \dfrac{(60 \times 10^{-6} \times 0.14 \times 1.2)}{1.8 \times 10^{-5}} = 0.56$$

∴ Settling velocity of particle = 1.4 ms^{-1}

Reynolds number of particle = 0.56

6.4 EQUIPMENTS

Various equipments used for size separation of solids employing sedimentation and related processes such as elutriation and centrifugal sedimentation can be considered as follows :

1. Sedimentation Tanks
2. Elutriator and zigzag sifter
3. Mechanical classifiers
4. Cyclone separators.

6.4.1 Sedimentation Tank :

If a uniform suspension of solids is placed in a cylinder then as settling proceeds, three zones are observed. A clear liquid zone at the top, layer of particles with terminal velocity
i.e. a constant composition zone and a sediment. A constant composition zone is not seen in case of thick slurries with wide particle size distribution. The sediment is separated. Thus sedimentation may be used to separate a concentrated sediment and a dilute overflow.

Thickners are the tanks employing gravitational sedimentation principle for obtaining concentrated slurries. These may be batch or continuous units. Clarifiers are also designed on the same basis but handle relatively dilute slurries.

A continuous thickner (Fig. 6.9) consists of a cylindrical tank with diameter ranging from 2 to 50 m and depth 1 to 7 m. The slurry is fed into the centre through a feed-well which is placed well below the surface, so as to cause minimum disturbance. The clarified liquid overflows through the launders at the top. At the centre of the tank there is a shaft with side arms having blades to rake the settled solids towards the central outlet. Thus, solids in the thickner move continuously downwards and then inwards towards the underflow outlet ; while liquid moves upwards and radially outwards.

Fig. 6.9 : Thickner

6.4.2 Elutriator and Zig-Zag Sifter :

Elutriation is a process of grading the particles using an upward current of fluid, usually air or water. The process is reverse of gravity sedimentation and hence Stoke's law applies.

An elutriator consists of one or more sorting columns (Fig. 6.10) in which the fluid is rising at a constant velocity. The dilute slurry of solid is introduced at the bottom of the first column. Those particles having a terminal velocity less than that of the velocity of fluid will pass into the overflow, while those having greater terminal velocity than the fluid velocity will pass to the underflow. The overflow of preceeding column acts as a feed for the next. The different relative velocities exist in the sorting columns. The different relative velocities are obtained by using columns of different diameters. The velocity of the stream in the first column is highest and in last column it is lowest. Thus, the coarser and denser solids are separated at the first column and the fine product is obtained at the last. Use of water in the elutriator many times causes flocculation problem, therefore, air elutriation may be used in such cases. Air elutriation gives more rapid separation and the separation tends to be sharper than in the liquids owing to the lower resistance of air to particle fall.

Fig. 6.10 : Elutriator

Fig. 6.11 : Hydraulic separator

A hydraulic separator using the same principle is shown in Fig. 6.11, but the sorting columns have same diameter and separate water streams at different velocities are entered at the bottom of each column. The size of each vessel is increased, partly because the amount of liquid to be handled increases and partly to reduce, in stages, the surface velocity of fluid flowing from one vessel to the next.

Zig-Zag Sifter :

It is a gravity cross-flow classifier. It consists of a vertical tube of rectangular cross-section and number of sharp bends through which a stream of air flows upwards from the bottom and is turned at each bend (Fig. 6.12). The material to be classified is fed at one of the bends. The coarse material slides down to the lower side, crossing the airstream at the next bend. This causes intensive whirling. The fine material is transported upwards by the air to the upper side of the sifter. Separation takes place in the region of the bend, where the stream of coarse and fine particles cross the high speed air-stream. Separation efficiency at each individual stage is small. But repeatation of the separation at each bend sharpens separation. The separation range for zig-zag sifter lies between 100 μm to 100 mm. The capacity can be increased by using number of sifter tubes in parallel (Fig. 6.12).

Fig. 6.12 : Zig-zag sifter

6.4.3 Mechanical Classifiers :

In mechanical classifiers, the material is separated using horizontal current of fluid. These are used for free settling solids in contrast to elutriators which may be used for both free as well as hindered settling. The material with lower settling velocity is carried away in a liquid overflow, and the material of higher settling velocity is deposited at the bottom of the equipment and is dragged upwards against the fluid flow by some mechanical means.

The slurry is fed to inclined trough (Fig. 6.13) where it forms a settling pool. Particles having high falling velocity quickly fall to the bottom of the trough. The settled material is conveyed up the inclined trough by mechanical rakes or a helical screw. The conveying mechanism also serves to keep the fine particles in suspension in the pool by agitation. When the coarse particles leave the pool, they are slowly turned over by the raking action and separation efficiency is increased.

Fig. 6.13 : Principle of mechanical classifier

In rake classifier, (Fig. 6.14) the rakes have eccentric motion, which dips them into the settled material and move it up the inclined plane for a short distance. The rakes are then withdrawn and return to the starting point and the cycle is repeated. The material is slowly moved up the incline to the discharge. The spiral classifier using a revolving spiral can be operated at steeper slopes than the rake classifier.

Fig. 6.14

The feed to the mechanical classifier should not be introduced directly into the pool as it may cause agitation in the pool and disturb settling process. If the feed rate is increased, the horizontal carrying velocity increases and the size of particles leaving in the overflow also increases.

The speed of rakes or spirals should be kept high for coarse separations, while for finer separation, less agitation and lower rake speeds are used. The mechanical classifiers are useful for slurries containing less than 50% solids. The mechanical classifiers are not suitable for very fine separations.

6.4.4 Cyclone Separator :

Very low rates of separation are obtained for separation under gravitational force, especially at low velocities and low particle size. Thus, the separation may be aided by application of centrifugal force. The equipment designed on the basis of centrifugal force for size separation is cyclone separator. It may be used for dry as well as for wet separation. Hydrocyclone is used for wet separation. A typical hydrocyclone (Fig. 6.15) consists of a cono-cylindrical vessel, open at its apex or underflow. The cylindrical portion of the vessel has a tangential feed inlet. An overflow pipe is present at the top of cylinder and it extends into the body of cylinder with a removable section known as a vortex finder. A vortex finder prevents short-circuiting of feed directly into the overflow. The tangential inlet of the feed under pressure causes swirling motion to the stream. This generates a vortex in the cyclone, with a low pressure zone along the vertical axis.

Fig. 6.15 : Cyclone Separator

A particle in the cyclone is subjected to two opposing forces. The centrifugal force which acts to move the particle to the cyclone wall and the drag force of the fluid acts to carry the particle into the centre. The centrifugal force is given as :

$$\text{Centrifugal force} = \frac{m\, u_t^2}{r} \qquad \ldots (17)$$

where, m is mass of particle, u_t is tangential air velocity and r is radial distance from cyclone axis.

Thus, the particles just outside the central core of the cyclone are subjected to the maximum centrifugal force due to highest velocity and low radial distance. The faster settling particles move to the wall of the cyclone, where the velocity is lowest and migrate to underflow. The slower moving particles move towards the zone of low pressure along the axis and carried upward through the vortex finder to the overflow. Alongwith the outer region of downward flow and an inner region of upward flow, there exists a position at which there is zero vertical velocity. This envelope of zero vertical velocity exists throughout the cyclone. Particles are thrown outside this zero velocity envelope by greater centrifugal force, while particles are swept to the centre by greater drag force. The particles in the zero velocity envelope are acted upon by equal centrifugal and drag force and have an equal probability of passing into the overflow or underflow.

A performance or partition curve for cyclone is plot of percentage of each particle size in the feed which reports in the underflow to the particle size (Fig. 6.16). The cut-off point or separation size, of the cyclone is defined as the point on partition curve for which 50% of particles in the feed of that size report in the underflow, i.e. particles of this size have equal chance of reporting in overflow or underflow. It is generally referred as d_{50} size. The efficiency of cyclone (I) is given by :

$$I = \frac{d_{75} - d_{25}}{2\, d_{50}} \qquad \ldots (18)$$

where d_{75} and d_{25} are points at which 75% and 25% of feed particles report to the underflow.

Fig. 6.16 : Partition curve for hydrocyclone

As feed rate to the cyclone increases, there is improvement in efficiency by improving centrifugal force acting on the particles. Increase in feed rate or pressure drop, increases centrifugal force on the particle and finer particles are carried to underflow i.e. d_{50} is decreased and efficiency increases. Increase in density and viscosity of the slurry, hinders settling and sharpness of separation decreases. Flat coarse particles also report in the overflow, thus shape of particle is also important.

As the vortex finder diameter increases, the cut-off point becomes coarser and capacity increases. Cyclones with larger diameters are suitable for large size separation and high capacity. As size of cyclone reduces, the cut–off point and capacity both decreases.

6.5 CENTRIFUGATION

Centrifugal separation is an extension of gravitational sedimentation, where the settling rates are increased by application of centrifugal force. In centrifugal separation, two or more phases are separated due to difference in the density of two phases. The centrifugation technique is used for separation of liquid-liquid as well as for solid-liquid mixtures. If there is gradient in the size of dispersed phase then complete classification can also be done.

6.5.1 Theory :

The centrifugal force (F_c) acting on the particle moving in a circular path is given as :

$$F_c = m r \omega^2 \quad \ldots (19)$$

where, m is mass of particle, r is radius of path and ω is angular velocity, which is equal to v^2/r. Substituting value of ω in equation (19) we get,

$$F_c = \frac{mv^2}{r} \quad \ldots (20)$$

The rotational speed is generally expressed as revolutions per minute (r.p.m.). Then substituting $\omega = \frac{2\pi N}{60}$ in equation (19) we get,

$$F_c = \frac{mr(2\pi N)^2}{(60)^2} = 0.011 \, mr \, N^2 \quad \ldots (21)$$

where N denotes revolutions per minute.

In sedimentation, the gravitational force acting on the particle F_g is mg. Therefore, centrifugal acceleration is $0.011 \, rN^2$. The centrifugal force is generally expressed in comparison with 'g'.

The centrifugal force depends on radius, speed of rotation and mass of the particle. Thus, if radius and speed of rotation are fixed then centrifugal force will differ on the basis of weight of the particle. Similarly, for two immiscible liquids, the centrifugal force per unit volume will depend on their density. Thus, the solids will be separated as per their weight and liquids as per their densities. A heavier liquid will be at the periphery of the rotating bowl and lighter liquid to the interior.

Consider that the particles are moving in laminar flow under the accelerating force (a). Then their velocity will be given by Stoke's law,

$$u = \frac{d^2 a (\rho_s - \rho_f)}{18 \eta} \quad \ldots (22)$$

When the force is centrifugal force, it will be given by equation (21) as,

$$F_c = ma = mr \left(\frac{2\pi N}{60}\right)^2$$

$$\therefore \quad a = r \left(\frac{2\pi N}{60}\right)^2$$

Substituting this value of a in equation (22), we get,

$$u = \frac{d^2 r \left(\frac{2\pi N}{60}\right)^2 (\rho_s - \rho_f)}{18 \eta}$$

$$\therefore \quad u = \frac{d^2 N^2 r (\rho_s - \rho_f)}{1640 \eta} \quad \ldots (23)$$

Example 6.2 : How many "g" can be obtained in a centrifuge which is rotating the liquid at 2000 r.p.m. at maximum radius of 5 cm ?

Solution :

$$F_c = 0.011\, m\, r\, N^2$$

and

$$F_g = mg$$

$$\therefore \quad \frac{F_c}{F_g} = \frac{0.011\, r\, N^2}{g}$$

$$= \frac{0.011 \times 0.05 \times (2000)^2}{9.81} = 225$$

Thus, centrifugal acceleration will be 225 times the gravitational acceleration.

Example 6.3 : An o/w emulsion was subjected to centrifugation at 1500 r.p.m., radius of separation is 3.8 cm. Calculate the velocity of oil through water in both gravitational and centrifugal separations.

Solution :

Data : Globule diameter = 5.1×10^{-5} m
Density of oil = 894 kg/m³
Density of water = 1000 kg/m³
Viscosity of water = 7×10^{-4} Ns/m²

Gravitational separation :

$$u = d^2 g (\rho_s - \rho_f) / 18 \eta$$

$$= \frac{(5.1 \times 10^{-5})^2 \times 981 \times (1000 - 894)}{18 \times 7 \times 10^{-5}} = 2.15 \times 10^{-4}\ m/s$$

Centrifugal separation :

$$u = \frac{d^2\, N^2\, r\, (\rho_s - \rho_f)}{1640 \eta}$$

$$= \frac{(5.1 \times 10^{-5})^2 \times 1500^2 \times 0.038 \times (1000 - 894)}{1640 \times 7 \times 10^{-5}}$$

$$= 2 \times 10^{-2} \text{ m/s}$$

As we have applied Stoke's law, it should be confirmed that flow is laminar by Re calculation.

$$\therefore \quad Re = \frac{D u \rho}{\eta}$$

$$= 5.1 \times 10^{-5} \times 0.02 \times 1000 / (7 \times 10^{-5}) = 1.5$$

∴ It is correct to apply Stoke's law in both cases.

6.5.2 Pressure Differential in Centrifugation :

During liquid – liquid separation, the pressure differential is created across the radius of the centrifuge. It can be obtained as follows :

Consider a differential cylinder with thickness 'dr' and height 'b' placed at radius 'r' from the axis (Fig. 6.17). The differential centrifugal force will be given as :

$$dF_c = (dm) \, r \, \omega^2$$

where, dF_c and dm are differential force, and differential mass of cylinder respectively and ω is angular velocity of the cylinder with radius 'r'.

Fig. 6.17

But, $\quad dm = $ differential volume × density

$$= 2\pi (r \cdot dr) \, b \times \rho$$

Area over which dF_c acts is $2\pi r b$. Force per unit area is pressure, therefore, differential pressure (dP) acting on cylinder is

$$dP = \frac{dF_c}{2\pi r b} = \frac{dm \, r \, \omega^2}{2\pi r b}$$

$$= \frac{2\pi (r \cdot dr) \rho \, b \, \omega^2 \, r}{2\pi r b}$$

$$dP = \rho \, \omega^2 \, r \cdot dr \qquad \ldots (24)$$

Integrating equation (24) over r_1 to r_2 and P_1 to P_2 respective pressure, we get,

$$(P_2 - P_1) = \frac{\rho \omega^2 (r_2^2 - r_1^2)}{2} \qquad \ldots (25)$$

Equation (25) gives radial variation in pressure across the centrifuge.

6.4.3 Centrifuges :

The equipments for centrifugal separation are broadly considered under category bowl or basket centrifuges and tube centrifuges.

(A) Basket or bowl centrifuges : The bowl centrifuges basically consist of a drum or a basket revolving at high rotational speed in which feed is entered at the centre. Separated fractions are collected by suitable arrangement.

(i) Perforated or sieve basket centrifuge : It consists of a vertical or horizontal sieve drum. These centrifuges are used for separation of crystals or granular material from the liquid. It can be considered as a centrifugal filtration unit (Fig. 6.18). The basket has perforations of size 3 mm. A suitable filter cloth may be mounted on the perforated surface for separation of finer particles. The basket is rotated at speeds of about 1000 r.p.m. The material of construction of the basket should have enough strength to withstand high strain developed due to centrifugal forces in the process. It provides 'g' value upto 300 – 1500.

Fig. 6.18 : Simple perforated basket centrifuge

These centrifuges may be operated as batch or continuous. The conical sieve centrifuge (Fig. 6.19) makes it possible for the centrifugal solids to slide to the larger diameter as a result of the components of centrifugal force directed parallel to sieve insert. This continuous centrifuge is also known as sliding centrifuge. Oscillating sieve centrifuge (Fig. 6.20) can also be used for continuous separation.

Fig. 6.19 : Conical sieve centrifuge

Fig. 6.20 : Oscillating sieve centrifuge

A peeler centrifuge (Fig. 6.21) is a horizontal drum continuous centrifuge. It has a peeler knife, which scraps off the cake deposited on the sieve and sends it out through a chute. The separated liquid flows down to the bottom.

Fig. 6.21 : Peeler centrifuge

A pusher or telescoping bowl centrifuge (Fig. 6.22) is a horizontal single or multistage centrifuge. The slurry is fed to the innermost stage and then centrifuged. The cake formed on the sieve wall is pushed forward from time to time by pusher plates and thus passes into the next centrifugation stage. The circular collar of the drum is used as the pusher plate for the next drum towards the outside. These centrifuges have high capacity for solid handling and used for separation of drug plant residues after extraction process.

Fig. 6.22 : Three-stage pusher centrifuge

The perforated basket centrifuges are used in the chemical and pharmaceutical industries and in the preparation of fruit juices. It is used for separation of aspirin crystals from mother liquor. It is suitable for separation of particles in the range of 10 μm to 10 mm and solid content upto 10 to 60%. The residual moisture content of solids is as low as 3%. Enclosure of centrifuge makes handling of toxic and volatile materials easy.

(ii) Non-perforated basket centrifuge : A solid basket centrifuge is a batch operation equipment (Fig. 6.23). The basket rotates at high speeds of 13,000 to 50,000 r.p.m. The slurry is continuously fed at the centre and the fractionation occurs at the periphery. The solids at the wall, above which is a heavier liquid and lighter liquid at the surface. The liquids are separated by skimmers or weirs. The solids may be separated manually at the end of process.

Fig. 6.23 : Non-perforated basket

A horizontal bowl centrifuge with scroll or screw discharge (Fig. 6.24) is used for continuous discharge of solids. A horizontal screw rotates inside the conical ended bowl of the machine and conveys solids with it, while the liquid discharges over an overflow towards the centre of the machine and at the opposite end to the solid discharge. The speed of the screw, relative to the bowl, must not be great. For example, if the bowl speed is 2000 r.p.m. a suitable speed of the screw might be 25 r.p.m. relative to the bowl i.e. the screw speed is 2025 or 1975 r.p.m.

This equipment is suitable for solid content upto 30%.

Fig. 6.24 :

(iii) Plate or disc centrifuge :

(a) (b) Fluid flow between two plates
Fig. 6.25 : Plate separator

In plate centrifuge or plate separator the clarifying area is enlarged by incorporation of large number of conical plates (Fig. 6.25). The plates are 0.5 to 0.75 mm thick placed 0.3 – 2 mm apart. The plates have angle of inclination of about 30 – 40°. The plates split the stream of liquid into many thin layers. The separation spaces are connected in parallel and they produce very short deposition paths. The solid particles get separated from the liquid when it has reached the upper conical surface of the individual separation space. The deposited solid particles slide down continuously forming a coherent layer on the plate surface. The solids are collected into the solid-space of the drum. The liquid flows inwards and leaves the plate at its inner edge. The rate of output per unit time (Q) is given as follows :

$$Q = \frac{d^2 \Delta \rho g}{18 \eta} \infty \frac{2\pi}{3g} \omega^2 (\tan \phi) z \left(r_a^3 - r_l^3\right)$$

where,
- Q = throughput rate (kg/hr.)
- d = particle size of solid
- $\Delta \rho$ = effective density i.e. $\left(\rho_s - \rho_l\right)$
- ϕ = angle of inclination
- ω = angular velocity
- r_a = outer radius of separator
- r_l = inner radius of separator
- z = number of individual separation spaces.

Plate separator offers advantages, such as good clarifying effect, automatic cleaning of plates can be done by correct setting of the angle and distances between the plates.

The plate separator may be modified for the continuous discharge of solids by using nozzle (Fig. 6.26).

Fig. 6.26 : Plate separator with nozzles

(B) Tube centrifuge : These are high speed centrifuges with a tubular bowl having length-diameter ratio of from 4 to 8 (Fig. 6.27). It is a batch type centrifuge used for particle size below 300 µm. It is used for solid concentrations below 1 – 2%. The tubes of smaller diameter are used because they have to withstand high force generated during centrifugation. Liquid enters the tube at the bottom. The central cylindrical layer of liquid flows upwards from the bottom. It provide the acceleration of about 13000 – 17000 r.p.m.

Fig. 6.27 : Operation of a tube centrifuge

***

MANUAL CORRECTIONS

(a) Plain weave   (b) Twilled weave

Fig. 6.1 : Screening surfaces

Wedge wire screens (Fig. 6.1) are used for fine screening machines such as sieve bends. Such screens are strong and have relatively large open areas. The wedge profiles minimizes particle blinding.

upwards through a sieve, from a rotating slit which is positioned below the gauze and scans its whole area. The jet aims upwards, keeping the screen aperture clear, and maintaining the charge of material in a fluidized state. Negative pressure is simultaneously applied to the

Fig. 6.6 : Screening mass balance

Mogensen sizer :

Mogensen developed a sifting device (Fig. 6.8) which operates on the principle that there

is

movement. Mogensen sizer is used in preparing pharmaceutical industry to obtain infusions. The capacity of Mogensen sizer is such that a particular screening duty can be met with a machine occupying a fraction of the floor space required by a conventional screen and blinding and wear is greatly reduced.

words, a lump of lead and feather will fall at the same rate.

which is attained is called as terminal velocity. In Chapter 'Fluid Flow', we have seen viscous

Zig-Zag Sifter :

It is a gravity cross-flow classifier. It consists of a vertical tube of rectangular cross-section and number of sharp bends through which a stream of air flows upwards from the bottom and is turned at each bend (Fig. 6.12). The material to be classified is fed at one of the bends. The coarse material slides down to the lower side, crossing the airstream at the next bend. This causes intensive whirling. The fine material is transported upwards by the air to the upper side of the sifter. Separation takes place in the region of the bend, where the stream of coarse and fine particles cross the high speed air-stream. Separation efficiency at each individual stage is small. But repetition of the separation at each bend sharpens separation. The separation range for zig-zag sifter lies between 100 µm to 100 mm. The capacity can be increased by using number of sifter tubes in parallel (Fig. 6.12).

settling and sharpness of separation decreases. Flat coarse particles also report in the

v^2/r. Substituting value of ω in equation (19) we get,

6.5.3   Casing   Sieve drum   **Fig. 6.24**

$z\left(r_a^3 - r_l^3\right)$

FILTRATION

7.1 INTRODUCTION

Filtration is an important separation process. In pharmaceutical industry it is frequently used in manufacture of liquid dosage forms. It is a method of choice for sterilization of some heat sensitive liquids. Air filtration is commonly used technique for environment control in pharmaceutical manufacturing units and especially sterile manufacture.

Filtration is a process in which solid is separated from a fluid with use of a septum. The septum is called a filter medium, the solid free fluid is obtained as filtrate and a deposit of solids formed on the septum as cake. If the amount of solids to be separated from liquid is less than 1% then the process is termed as 'clarification' and in this case filtrate is the primary product.

7.2 MECHANISM OF FILTRATION

The fluid and slurry pass over a filter medium, where the solids are retained and fluid is allowed to pass. The filter medium is made up of different materials but mainly fibres or membranes are used. The particles are retained by the filter medium by different mechanisms as mentioned below :

Fig. 7.1 : Particle retention mechanisms

1. **Direct interception :** It occurs when a particle or a droplet collides on one of the fibres.

2. **Inertial impaction :** It results when the particle or droplet in the airstream cannot overcome the pressure drop during flow through the tortuous path in the filter bed. It collides and adheres to a fibre.
3. **Diffusion :** When extremely small aerosols and particles wander in, 'Brownian motion' within the flow pattern of the airstream. This enhances their chances of colliding with each other and filter medium fibres.
4. **Electrostatics :** Gas flowing through the filter medium causes a triboelectric effect causing generation of charges on the filter surface. The particle containing charge gets attracted to the surface.

7.3 TYPES OF FILTRATION

The filtration process may be of two types viz. surface filtration and depth filtration. (See Fig. 7.2)

Surface Filtration : It is also called as surface straining. Particles having size more than the pore size of the medium are retained on the surface of the filter. Adsorptive forces are also involved but their magnitude is very low. It is largely due to direct interception.

During surface filtration two effects take place.

1. The pores get partially blocked by the particles and slowly the effective pore size goes on reducing. This may be caused by (a) by retention of extremely fine particles within the pores by adsorptive forces. (b) due to partial intrusion of soft, deformable, particles into the pores, due to forces generated by fluid flow. Deformable particles may block the pore to greater extent.
2. A cake develops on the surface of the filter medium. The cake itself may act as a filter medium.

Depth Filtration : In depth filtration, the separation process occurs within the medium only, as the particles are often much smaller than the pores of the medium. Direct interception is the mechanism for particle retention. Brownian movement also plays a role in retention of very small particles of about 1 μm.

Fig. 7.2 : Surface and Depth filtration

7.4 FILTER MEDIUM

An ideal filter medium should have following properties :
(i) It should have ability to retain wide range of particles from the suspension.
(ii) It should offer minimum resistance to the flow of filtrate.
(iii) It should allow easy discharge of cake.
(iv) It should not swell when it is in contact with filtrate and washing liquid.
(v) It should have sufficient strength to withstand pressure drop and mechanical stress during filtration.
(vi) It should have high chemical resistance.

7.4.1 Surface Filtration Media :

There are three types of surface filter media.

(a) Screen type filters : These are two dimensional structures having uniform pore size. Woven fibres are most commonly used screen filters. These may be made up of natural or synthetic non-metallic fibres or metallic wires. Cotton cloth is most widely used. It has a limited tendency to swell in liquids and can be used upto 100 °C. It is easily damaged by acids and alkalies. Generally, a cotton cloth with very thin duck weave i.e. muslin cloth is used as a filter medium. A duck weave has threads of equal thickness and texture running over one and under one of the wrap. A duck weaved cloth has higher porosity, hard surface and can withstand higher pressure. It also allows easy discharge of cake. Cloth is subjected to preshrinking before use to ensure its fitting on filters such as drum filter. Nitrated cotton cloth provides much harder surface. Glass cloth which has glass yarns offers high thermal and corrosion resistance, high tensile strength and easy to handle. But it lacks flexibility.

Synthetic clothes, such as nylon, acrilan etc. are superior to natural clothes. They do not swell, have high acid and alkali resistance. These clothes are resistant to fungal and bacterial growth. Synthetic fibres resist relatively high temperature and have a smooth surface for easy cleaning and discharge of cake.

Metallic screens or fabrics made up of steel, copper, bronze, nickel etc. are used. These are suitable for handling corrosive liquors and high temperature filtration. The metallic clothes may have more than 50,000 holes/cm^2 and the hole sizes down upto 20 μm.

Perforated sheets and screens are used for coarse separation. The polymeric cast membranes with suitable pore sizes can also be used. e.g. membrane filters.

(b) Edge type filters : Edge type filters involve the use of cartridge type element (Fig. 7.3) with flow directed outside inwards. The element is composed of a stack of discs or washers of paper, plastic or metal clamped together by compression. Flow takes place from the edge inwards between the discs which may be in intimate contact in the case of non-rigid disc materials or through the controlled clearance space between individual discs provided by spacing washers. In stacked paper discs filter, the cut-off point of 1 μm may be obtained. It can trap and retain finely dispersed water in oils or similar fluids. It does not get affected by sudden pressure changes.

Fig. 7.3 : Edge type filter

(c) Stacked disc filters : It employs individual discs which are stacked over a perforated inner tube (Fig. 7.4), with intermediate spacing washers. Flow is between, and subsequently through, the filter discs into the inner tube.

Fig. 7.4 : Stacked disc filter

7.4.2 Depth Filtration Medium :

An ideal depth filter medium has increasingly dense layers from outside to inside, which increases chance of finer particles being trapped on their passage through the filter. There are three classes of depth filter medium.

(a) Fibrous medium : It is a layer or mat containing numerous fine fibres having diameter in the range of 0.5 to 30 μm. These fibres are randomly oriented and intermixed with one another so that they form numerous tortuous passages in which the particles are trapped. The fibres are of cotton, cellulose, rayon, polypropylene, micro glass-fibre. The efficiency of the filter media is dependent of fibre diameter. The lower the diameter of the fibre, the closer it gets compacted and smaller is the diameter of the flow path. The layers of fibre are bound together using resins, so that its structure is maintained throughout the process. It is used for collection of particles in the sub-micron range. Filter media made up of a permanently charged dielectric polymer called electret have an open structure and has high collection efficiency and low pressure drop. These filter media are suitable for clean air systems in hospitals and pharmaceutical units to reduce significantly the microbial counts. Binder free media made of borosilicate microfibres are made by welding together the fibres by temperature and pressure. These fibres are chemically, biochemically and biologically inactive and neutral.

(b) Porous media : It is made up of polymeric materials or sintered ceramics or metals. These materials form a capillary type passage.

(c) Cake type media : These comprise of a layer or bed of loose, separate, discrete particles formed into a cake on a supporting screen usually by the action of fluid flow. The materials are diatomaceous earth, clays, cotton fibres, wood fibres, clays etc. These are not suitable where stability, compactness are desired.

7.5 THEORY OF FILTRATION

In the process of filtration the fluid passes through the filter medium, which offers resistance to its passage. Pressure differential across the filter is the driving force for the operation. The rate of filtration is given by :

$$\text{Rate of filtration} = \frac{\text{Driving Force}}{\text{Resistance}} \quad \ldots (1)$$

In the filtration process, the solution passes through the bed of solids, and Poiseulli's and Kozeny's concept can be applied in the modified form as follows :

$$\frac{dV}{d\theta} = \frac{A \, \Delta P}{R} \quad \ldots (2)$$

where, $\frac{dV}{d\theta}$ = Volumetric flow rate

A = Area of filtration

R = Resistance to flow through the filter.

Resistance for filtration is offered by the filter medium, pre-coat if any and the filter cake. Resistance of filter cake is nothing but specific resistance of the cake i.e. resistance per unit cake thickness multiplied by thickness of cake. The resistance is also proportional to viscosity of the fluid.

$$\therefore \quad R = \eta \, r \, (L + L_c) \quad \ldots (3)$$

where, r = Specific resistance of cake

η = Viscosity of fluid

L_c = Thickness of cake

L = Equivalent length of filter medium and precoat (a fictitious thickness).

If V is the volume of fluid filtered containing w fraction of solid content per unit volume. A is the area on which cake is formed, then thickness of filter cake L_c is given as :

$$L_c = wV/A \quad \ldots (4)$$

Substituting the value of cake thickness in equation (3), we get

$$R = \eta \, r \left(L + \frac{wV}{A} \right)$$

$$\therefore \quad \frac{dV}{d\theta} = \frac{A \, \Delta P}{\eta \, r \left(L + \frac{wV}{A} \right)} \quad \ldots (5)$$

As this equation is developed on the basis of Poiseulli's equation, the basic assumption is that the fluid flow is laminar and the solid is non-compressible i.e. specific resistance does not change with pressure difference.

Using above equation, the *factors affecting filtration* can be said to be as follows :

1. Rate of filtration can be increased by increase in surface area.

2. Volumetric flow rate is inversely proportional to viscosity. Therefore, higher filtration rates can be obtained by filtration of high temperature liquids when viscosity is low.

3. Filtration rate increases as pressure differential across filter increases but the cake should be non-compressible. But some cakes are compressible as the cakes of soft and flocculant materials. For such cases the compressibility is considered while calculating specific resistance of the cake. In such cases,

$$r = r' \Delta P^s \quad \ldots (6)$$

where, r is the specific resistance of the cake under pressure P, ΔP is the pressure drop across the filter, r' is the specific resistance of the cake under a pressure drop of 1 atm and s is a constant for the material called its compressibility. Thus values of r' and s are determined from experimental runs under various pressures.

4. As we have discussed in Kozeny's equation (eq. 2) for flow of fluid through the bed of solids, the resistance is highly dependent on particle size and shape. As the particle size of cake particles decreases, filtration rate decreases.

5. In the above discussion we have considered specific resistance of the cake; which considers that the cake has uniform porosity throughout the thickness. But the cake is subjected to two forces, the hydrostatic force due to the slurry present above it and the compressive stress due to viscous drag when fluid flows through the cake. The hydrostatic pressure is highest at the upper surface of the cake and lowest near the filter medium. But the compressive stress increases from top to bottom of the cake. If these two forces are balanced then resistance will remain same throughout the cake, but the compressive stress generally shows higher effect. Thus cakes of most of the materials show higher compression near the filter medium. This effect is more pronounced at higher pressure differentials. This effect is not seen in highly rigid cakes.

7.6 FILTER AIDS

Filtration rates are very low for highly compressible materials due to very high specific resistance. Filter aids are the substances incorporated in the concentrations upto 5% to the high resistance cakes to decrease their resistance and increase filtration rates. Filter aids are the special type of filter medium i.e. cake type depth filtration medium. Filter aids impart rigidness and porosity to the cake due to their peculiar irregular shape, low surface area and narrow particle size distribution. This rigid structure provides support for the compressible particles in the slurry.

An ideal filter aid should have following properties :

1. It should be chemically inert and stable under various conditions.
2. It should be non-compressible and insoluble in the fluid used.
3. It should be useful over wide range of pressure drops. It should be inexpensive.
4. There should be easy and economic method for it's separation from the cake after use.
5. It should not add fibres or particles to filtrate.

6. It should be non-toxic.

Various agents used as filter aids are purified talc, kieselghur or diatomaceous earth, charcoal, kaolin, asbestos, cellulose and volcano glass called perlite. Diatomaceous earth is processed from fossilized diatoms, it is almost pure silica (SiO_2). It is inert and insoluble.

Pearlite is aluminium silicate, which is around 20–30% less dense than diatomaceous cake. It shows some compressibility but is less costly. Cellulose is highly compressible and expensive also, therefore, it is used only when the slurry is incompatible with cellulose. Seitz or asbestos i.e. alumino silicate is also used as filter aid, but it may cause contamination of filtrate with the fibres. The choice of filter aid is governed by the output given and filter cake thickness. Some properties of Seitz and Pearlites are given in table 7.1.

Table 7.1 : Filter aids

	Seitz			Pearlite	
	Coarse	Medium	Fine	Coarse	Fine
Specific filter cake density (g/l)	258	212	196	163	148
Specific filter cake thickness (mm/m^2/kg)	3.9	4.7	5.1	6.1	6.8
Specific filter capacity at 10 mm cake thickness (l/m^2/h)	7,900	65,000	2,300	52,000	24,000

The filter aid should be used in optimum concentration. It is as shown in Fig. 7.5, the rate of filtration increases with increase in concentration of filter aid and then decreases. It can be explained on the basis of Kozeny's equation. As the filter aid concentration increases, the porosity and thickness of cake increases simultaneously. The former enhances rate of filtration whereas the later decreases it. Upto critical optimum concentration the rate of increase in filtration rate due to increase in porosity is very high as compared to decrease due to increase in cake thickness. At optimum filter aid concentration, the porosity has reached very close to maximum porosity and any further addition of filter aid contributes mainly to increase in thickness, hence rate of filtration decreases.

Fig. 7.5 : Effect of Filter aid concentration

The filter aid is used by three methods :

1. Body mix method : The filter aid in the concentration of 0.01–4% is mixed with the slurry to be filtered. The slurry containing filter aid is then filtered.

2. Precoat method : While working high pressure drop, this method is preferred. The cake of filter aid with suitable thickness is first formed by filtration of filter aid and then slurry is filtered. Precoating is done to prevent clogging of filter medium or to prevent passage of fines through the filter medium and mainly to give mechanical strength during filtration.

3. Special precoat method : It is adopted for rotary drum filter. The filter aid slurry is first filtered and deposition of cake is allowed by removing cake loosening and removal technique. Once the filter aid cake (precoat) of desired thickness is obtained the slurry is filtered. The cake removing knife scraps the cake along with a small thickness of the precoat everytime.

Separation of filter aid from the cake is difficult, therefore, it is not advisable to use filter aid when desired product is cake.

7.7 FILTRATION EQUIPMENTS

Various filtration equipments for liquid-solid separation are as follows :

7.7.1 Filter Press :

(a) Plate and Frame Filter Press : It consists of plates and frames arranged alternately. A plate is a square shaped solid structures with raised edges and corrugated surface. Frame is a hollow structure with thickness between 20 – 150 mm. These are made up of stainless steel, cast iron or wood. The size of the plate is between 4 in ∞ 4 in to 4 ft. ∞ 4 ft. i.e. the area varies between 100 mm^2 to 1.2 m^2. A filter cloth is placed on the surface of a plate. Plates and frames are hung alternately on tensioned rods, and compressed by a hydraulic device.

The plates and frames are designed in two types non-washing type and washing type.

In *Non-washing type* filter press, the plates and frames have one hole at one of the top corners. (Fig. 7.6). The holes on plates and frames align to form a channel. The holes on the frame open inside the frame, but the hole on plate is not connected to inside. Thus when feed slurry is forced through the channel, it can pass only inside the frame i.e. the space between two plates formed by the frame. As slurry is pumped the pressure develops inside the chamber, is maintained at around 100 lb/in^2. Slurry under pressure gets filtered through the filter cloth on the plate surface. The filtrate passes over plate and gets collected at the bottom. There are two types of filtrate collection systems commonly used : open and closed collection system.

(a) Filter plate   **(b) Frame**

(c) Washing plate

Fig. 7.6 : Filter press : Plates and frames

In open collection system, the filtrate collection hole of each plate opens separately to the outside by stopcocks. The filtrate from each plate gets poured into a semicylindrical trough. In closed collection system, the holes at the bottom of the plate coincide with the corresponding holes on the frame and form a channel. The filtrate flows through this closed channel and is taken out at one end.

In open collection system the filtrate is exposed to atmosphere, therefore, chances of contamination and volatilization of filtrate are high as compared to closed channel system. But open channel has an advantage that if the filter cloth on any of the plate is broken, it can be easily identified and that plate can be removed from the operation just by closing the filtrate outlet stopcock. Whereas in closed channel system, identification of a problem giving plate is difficult, it can be identified and removed only after complete dissembling of the equipment. Washing type plate and frame filter press is required when washing of cake is desired.

Fig. 7.7

In Washing type plate and frame filter press, there are two different types of plates (Fig. 7.7). The plates and frames are provided with different number of buttons on their outer surface which serves as identification mark. The plates may have 1 or 3 buttons and frames has 2 buttons i.e. there are 1 – button and 3 button plates and 2 button frames. The plates and frames have two holes at the top and two holes at the bottom. The corresponding holes coincide with one another and form two channels of which one is the channel for feed slurry during filtration cycle and another is used for washing solvent in washing cycle. The plates and frames are arranged so that on one side of the frame is one button plate and on other side a three button plate (i.e. $\overset{P}{1} - \overset{F}{2} - \overset{P}{3} - \overset{F}{2} - \overset{P}{1}$ button). The one and three button plates differ with respect to wash inlet hole. The wash inlet hole can bring the washing liquid on the surface of a three button plate but not on one button plate. Working of washing type press has two cycles a filtration cycle and washing cycle. The filtration cycle is same as for the non-washing type. Once the cake of sufficient thickness (i.e. to fill up the frame) has developed washing cycle starts. The washing liquid is passed through wash inlet, it passes over the 3 – button plate beneath the filter cloth. The outlet hole of 3-button plate is closed. The pressure develops and under pressure it passes through the cakes and filter cloth on 1 - button plate, over the surface of 1 - button plate. The washing is taken out by 1 – button plate. The washings may be collected by any of the collection methods as described filtrate collection.

Advantages :
1. Larger filter area is provided in smaller floor space.
2. Operates under high pressure, therefore, rate of filtration is high.
3. Washing of cake can be done easily.
4. Easy maintenance.

Disadvantages :
1. Batch operation involves significant non-productive time between two batches.
2. High labour cost, high non-productive time makes the operation expensive. Therefore, so as to prolong the production time, it is generally recommended for slurries containing less than 5% solids.

(b) Chamber Press : It is similar to plate and frame filter press except that the filter elements consist only of the corrugated filter plates. The filter chamber is formed between two successive plates. All the chambers are connected by means of a comparatively large hole in the centre of each plate (Fig. 7.8). The filter cloth with a central hole covers the plate and the slurry is passed through the inlet channel. The clear filtrate is taken out through the outlet. It can be used for higher solid contents, as labour cost is low as compared to plate and frame press.

Fig. 7.8 : Filtration process in a chamber filter press

7.7.2 Nutsch filters :

Nutsch filters consist of a flat filtering plate in a false bottomed tank. Sand and other loose inert materials were initially used as a filtering medium. It can be used for vacuum filtration. The tank construction for vacuum application requires materials for greater strength so as to withstand high pressure differentials. In Nutsch filter a single chamber is divided into two chambers by a perforated section. The upper chamber operates under atmospheric pressure and retains the unfiltered slurry. The perforated false bottom supports the filter medium. The lower chamber is designed for negative pressure, and to hold the filtrate. Nutsch filters are useful for providing frequent and uniform washings.

A rotating tray horizontal filter (Fig. 7.9) is a continuous filter which consists of a series of Nutsch filters. It consists of a circular horizontal table that rotates about a centre axis. The table is comprised of a number of hollow pie-shaped segments with perforated or woven metal tops. Each section is covered with a suitable filter medium. Each segment receives the slurry in succession, where it is dewatered. Wash liquor is sprayed onto each section in two applications. The cake is finally dewatered by passing dry air through it. Finally the cake is removed from the surface by a discharge scroll. Belt filters consist of series of Nutsch filters moving along a closed path. Nutsch filters have a supporting perforated plate covered with a filter cloth. The washed cake is removed either by turning the unit over or by a shaker mechanism. Whereas, in belt filter there is an endless supporting perforated rubber belt covered with the filtering cloth. The cake thickness is between 1 – 25 mm. It is simple with facility of automatic washing and removal of cake. But it requires larger area and washing is poor at the belt edges.

Fig. 7.9 : Cross section of a rotary horizontal vacuum filter showing filtrate removal system, filter cloth and discharge scroll

7.7.3   Edge Filters :

The edge filters consists of pack of filter medium and filtration occurs on the edges of this medium. Metafilter and streamline filter are examples of edge filters.

Fig. 7.10 : Edge filters

Metafilter : It consists of large number of metal rings packed on a fluted rod (Fig. 7.10). The grooves on the surface of rod provides a channel for discharge of the filtrate. The metallic ring has number of semicircular projections on one surface to provide spacings between the rings. The rings when packed on the rod form a tapering channel. The slurry to be filtered pumped under pressure; vacuum may also be used. Filter aid coat may be given prior to filtration. Large number of such units may be used in one chamber in large scale production. The cake deposited may be removed by back-flushing of water.

Fig. 7.11 : Metafilter

Due to its robust design it can withstand high pressure. It can be designed with high corrosion resistance, recurring cost is low as no filter medium is required. It is useful for coarse straining as well as for removal of the fine particles. It is suitable for filtration of viscous liquids also e.g. syrups. But it is used for slurries with very low solid content.

Streamline filter : It consists of paper discs compressed to form a filter pack. The filtrate passes through the fine interstices between the discs and a cake is formed on the edges.

7.7.4 Leaf Filter :

A filter leaf consists of metal framework or a grooved plate over which the filter cloth is fixed.

(a) Cross-section of typical filter leaf   (b) Typical leaf filter circuit

Fig. 7.12 : Leaf filter

Number of such filter leaves are connected and first immersed in the slurry in the feed tank (Fig. 7.13). The cake is picked up under positive or negative pressure. The leaves are then transferred to the wash tank followed by a cake-removal tank. In cake removal stage, cake is removed by blowing air under pressure. Leaf filters are horizontal or vertical.

Fig. 7.13 : Filter leaf in tanks

It requires large floor space. The portion of cake may get separated during transfer from one tank to other. It is used only for clarification.

7.7.5 Rotary Drum Filter :

(a) Rotary-drum filter with discharge

It is a continuous filter generally operated under vacuum. It consists of a hollow metal cylinder on which a mesh is mounted as a support for filter cloth (Fig. 7.14). The cylinder is divided into three sections, pick up or cake building section, dewatering section and cake removal section. The drain pipes starting from these sections open on a seat valve on one side of a rotating cylinder. The seat (rotary) valve connects the first two sections to vacuum and the third zone to the air under pressure. A cylinder is submerged in the feed trough and rotates at a very low speed of around 0.1 to 3 r.p.m.

(b) Belt discharge filter with cloth washing

Fig. 7.14 : Rotary drum filter

The drum will pick-up the slurry as soon as it comes in contact with the slurry in trough. The drain pipe connects pick-up zone to the vacuum alignment of it's opening on seat valve with a vacuum zone of the stationary plate. In the pick up zone the slurry gets filtered under vacuum and cake builds up on the filter cloth. In initial zone of dewatering section the cake is dewatered. This dewatered cake is subjected to the washing, water is sprayed on the cake and simultaneous dewatering takes place. The washing may be collected separately or may be mixed with the filtrate. The cake at the end of dewatering section is compact and tightly bound to the filter cloth. In the cake removal section two processes take place :

(a) Loosening of cake and

(b) Discharge of cake.

The cake is loosened by blowing air under high pressure beneath the cake. The hole of drain pipe of this zone on seat valve gets aligned with the blowing section of the stationary plate. The cake gets loosened due to this blowing treatment. Cake discharge may be done by different techniques such as scraper method, string discharge and belt discharge (Fig. 7.15). In scraper method a knife or a scraper is set at a small distance from the drum surface and scraps away the filter cake from the filter cloth. In pre-coat method a self adjusting knife is used which scraps a small thickness of the precoat alongwith the cake. In string discharge number of endless strings are placed at about 1/2 inch pitch over the width of the drum. The run of these strings is extended to form an open conveyor system passing over a discharge and return roller. As compared to scraper, the wear of filter cloth is minimized by string discharge.

Fig. 7.15 : Cake discharge methods

Belt discharge system makes the filter cloth to pass on the rollers and material is discharged on first roll and before its passage to the feed trough it is subjected to washing. Therefore, higher filtration rates may be achieved using belt discharge.

Rotory drum filter is used for separation of calcium carbonate, starch, magnesium carbonate, mycelia from fermentation liquor.

Advantages :

1. Continuous filter with low labour cost and high capacity.
2. Versatility in application suitable for thick slurries containing 15–30% of solids.

Disadvantages :

1. Equipment is complex and application of vacuum makes it expensive.
2. Due to application of vacuum, the cake may crack and washing and drying stage may not be carried out efficiently.
3. As vacuum is applied, it is unsuitable for liquids near boiling point.
4. The gelatinous or slimy precipitates forming impermeable cake may cause filtration problems.

7.7.6 Membrane Filtration :

Membrane filters are microporous surface filters with pore size in the range of 0.005 μm to 12 μm. The membranes with the pore size 0.2 μ to 0.45 μ are used for sterilization. The membrane filters are also used for microfiltration, reverse osmosis and ultra-filtration (which are discussed separately).

The ideal characteristics of membrane filter are as follows :

1. It should have good flexibility to allow easy handling.
2. The extractable content should be low.
3. It should have narrow pore size distribution.
4. It should be autoclavable and should withstand repeated autoclaving without shrinkage.
5. It should be inert and compatible with aqueous as well as organic solvents and extreme solution pH.

The membrane filters are made up of polymers such as cellulose acetate, cellulose nitrates, polytetrafluoro ethylene (PTFE), polyvinyl chloride, nylon etc. Cellulose acetate filters are commonly used for sterility testing especially when alcohol is present in the sample, but it dissolves in ketone. PTFE filters are hydrophobic and suitable for filtration of gas and non-aqueous filtration. These are stable upto 260°C. PVC filters are suitable for extreme pH solutions.

The membrane filters are available as discs and cartridges. The pores occupy around 60 - 85% of the total volume of the filter, hence due to high porosity filtration rates are maintained high e.g. water flows at the rate of 38.5 ml per cm^2 through 0.45 μm filter. The membranes have thickness of about 150 μm.

Filter life is limited due to clogging. It is significantly low for thick solutions of large or fibrous molecules like blood, gelatin, colloids, slimy plant extracts etc. The filter life can be increased by prefiltration, dilution, serial filtration, mechanical agitation or using filter aids. Prefilter is generally used. The prefilter having disc diameter less than the final filter used. The selection of prefilter pore size is a critical factor governing life of membrane. If the prefilter with very large pore size is used then the large fraction of dirt gives load on the final filter. In such cases, the final filter gets exhausted (i.e. pressure drop across it is too high) too early when the resistance of cake on prefilter is negligible. If the prefilter is too small it gets exhausted too early, when final filter is unexhausted. Thus a prefilter should be selected such that the resistance across the prefilter and final filter increases at the same rate and exhausting them at the same time at the end of filtration cycle.

Integrity Testing of Membrane Filter :

Integrity tests are carried out to predict the performance of a filter. Various integrity tests commonly used are as follows :

(a) Bubble point test
(b) Diffusion test
(c) Forward flow test
(d) Bacterial challenge test.

(a) Bubble Point Test : It is the most commonly used method for determination of the pore size and pore size distribution of the membrane filter.

The method is based on capillarity theory. According to this theory, the height of liquid column in a capillary is inversely proportional to the capillary diameter. As the capillary diameter is reduced the height of liquid column in the capillary increases. The water which has risen in the capillary can be pushed back by a pressure which has equivalent height that of the liquid column. The minimum pressure necessary to force the liquid out of the capillary is called as 'bubble point pressure'. By knowing bubble point pressure, the maximum pore size on the membrane can be calculated by using equation derived below.

Consider a cylindrical pore in the filter medium. The liquid in this capillary is acted upon by two forces :

(i) Surface tension forces of the liquid, which oppose the flow of the liquid. This force is proportional to the circumference of the pore.

(ii) Hydrostatic force, which promotes flow of liquid, and is proportional to the surface area of the pore.

$$\text{Surface tension forces} = \text{Circumference} \propto \gamma \cos \theta$$
$$= \pi D \gamma \cos \theta$$
$$\text{Hydrostatic forces} = \text{Area of pore} \propto \text{Pressure}$$
$$= \frac{\pi}{4} D^2 P$$

where, γ = Surface tension of liquid (for water 72 dynes/cm)
θ = Solid liquid contact angle

D is diameter of pore and P is pressure.

At bubble point pressure (P_b), the two forces are at equilibrium :

$$\therefore \quad \pi D \gamma \cos \theta = \frac{\pi}{4} D^2 P$$

Error! or Error!

Thus, by knowing bubble point pressure, pore diameter can be calculated.

To determine the bubble point pressure the membrane filter is saturated with water and liquid level is maintained above the membrane. Air is below the membrane, the pressure of air is slowly increased and minimum pressure at which bubbles start continuously appearing in the liquid above membrane is taken as bubble point pressure.

Wetting of the filter medium is most important, if medium is hydrophobic it may not get wetted by water. Wetting agents may be used in such cases. It was observed that bubbling occurs below the anticipated bubble point pressure. It occurs because the gas dissolves in the liquid in the capillaries and diffuses through it and forms bubbles when it comes out in liquid at low pressure. Bubble point test may also be used to check efficiency of membrane filter, apart from its integrity. A bubble point for 0.22 μm filter is 55 psi and 32 psi for 0.45 μm (with water).

(b) Diffusion Test : This test is generally applied for filters in the form of cartridges or multistack discs, where large volume of liquid has to be displaced before the bubbles can be detected. This test is based on Fick's law of diffusion. If the pressure differential across the wetted membrane is maintained below bubble point pressure, then air will flow through the liquid filled pores by diffusion process. The pressure applied is about 80% of the bubble point pressure. The wetted membrane is maintained at this pressure for two minutes and amount of air diffused is measured, which indicates the pore size of the membrane.

(c) Forward Flow Test : It also measures rate of diffusion of air through the wetted filter, but at pressures well below the bubble point pressure.

(d) Bacterial Challenge Test : In this integrity test, the culture of an organism of defined size is filtered through the membrane. The filtrate is checked for sterility or absence of the particular organism. The micro-organisms used to test different filters are given below :

Pore size (μm)	Test Organism
0.2	*Pseudomonas diminuta*
0.3	*Pseudomonas aeroginosa*
0.45	*Serratia marcescens*
0.65	*Saccharomyces cerevisiae*

Thus, the filter is challenged with a micro-organism of defined size. But the limitation of this test is that, it is not an in use test.

7.7.7 Ultrafiltration :

Ultrafiltration is a technique used for the concentration and purification of macro-molecular and colloidal substances in solution. It is suitable for concentration of thermolabile substances. It is pressure activated filtration of colloidal solutions through membranes which are capable of retaining the solute molecules (Fig. 7.6). The solute molecules to be separated have size between $20 - 1000$ A°. The solute may be lyophilic or lyophobic in nature, with molecular weight in the range of $1000 - 10,000$. The membranes used for ultrafiltration are made up of cellulose nitrate, polysulfone, polyvinylidene fluoride etc.

In ultrafiltration, the solute that does not pass through the membrane, accumulates near the membrane causing higher solute concentrations than bulk. This is known as *concentration polarization*. Concentration polarization reduces the rate of filtration. The retained solute should be transported back to the bulk of the solution by moving the suspension.

Advantages : It is a non-thermal process and removes around 90% of the water at any temperature between 4°C to 100°C, avoiding thermal or oxidative degradation of the product. The capital cost is low. It does not affect physical stability of formulations such as emulsions during concentration.

But the pumping power required is significantly high.

Applications :

1. It is an ideal method for fractionation and purification of blood fractions. It is widely used in purification and concentration of albumin and hormones without denaturation of end product.

2. Diafiltration, a process where purified reconstituting fluid is continuously added as ultrafiltration proceeds so that ultrafiltration is carried out at constant solute concentration. This process is used in preparation of diagnostics.

3. Ultrafiltration is used for the purification of iron-dextran complex used in parenteral treatment of iron deficiency anaemia. The complex is obtained as

    Dextrin $\xrightarrow{\text{Hydrolysis}}$ Dextran + Iron $\xrightarrow{\text{Complexation}}$ Iron–Dextran Complex

    The product obtained by this process contains 6% dextran, 2% glycerol, 6% ferric hydroxide, 8% sodium chloride and 1.5% citric acid. The dextran, glycerol and ferric hydroxide formed iron–dextran complex colloidal suspension with molecular weight 50,000 – 2,00,000. Excess glycerol, citric acid and sodium chloride are removed by ultrafiltration.

4. It may be used for removal of pyrogens, sterilization of IV solutions, concentration of viruses, enzymes, hormones, separation of plasma from blood components.

7.7.8 Reverse Osmosis :

Osmosis is a process which involves movement of solvent (water) from the region of higher concentration to lower concentration across a semipermeable membrane. Reverse osmosis is an exactly opposite process where solvent moves from lower concentration to higher concentration. In reverse osmosis the osmotic pressure across the membrane is exceeded by the hydrostatic pressure (Fig. 7.16). It is a pressure driven diffusion process for separation of dissolved solutes. It is generally used to separate the small solute molecules. The membrane used should be semipermeable with respect to the solute which is to be removed.

Fig. 7.16

Though principle is similar for ultrafiltration and reverse osmosis, there are many differences in the two processes. (See Table 7.2).

Table 7.2 : Differences between Reverse Osmosis, Ultrafiltration and Microfiltration

Sr. No.	Parameter	Reverse Osmosis	Ultrafiltration	Microfiltration
1.	Solute Mol. Wt. separated	Low (100 – 1000)	High (1000 – 10,000)	–
2.	Pressure differential across membrane	High (500 – 2000 psi)	Low (50 – 200 psi)	Low (15 – 50 psi)
3.	Water flux	Low (2 – 50 gal/ft^2/day)	High (10 – 100 gal/ft^2/day)	High 0 – 200 gal/ft^2/day
4.	Desired product	Solvent (water) separated from dissolved solute (i.e filtrate)	The concentrated solution of macro-molecules (i.e. retainate)	Retainate, emulsified oils, fine suspended solids.

Different types of membranes used in reverse osmosis are anisotropic cellulose acetate membranes, ion exchange or polyelectrolyte membrane and anisotropic aromatic polyamide hollow fibres. These membranes are used in the form of hollow fibre module, spiral wound or plate and frame type.

Reverse osmosis is often used in place of distillation, because its energy requirement is only 25% of the distillation process. But as it involves high labour cost for continuous monitoring of quality, it is not commonly used for production of water for injection.

7.7.9 Microfiltration :

It is a technique to separate relatively large size particles as compared to reverse osmosis and ultrafiltration. It is also a pressure activated filtration for retention of suspended solids and micro-emulsions ; but allows passages of molecules and dissolved species. The transmembrane pressure differential is low and permeate flux rate is high. The membrane materials are cellulose acetate, polytetrafluoroethylene (PTFE), nylon as well as ceramics such as α–alumina, zirconia and silica. It may be a membrane type with pore size less than the suspended solids or depth type (e.g. cartridge filters) with pore size larger than particle size.

This technique is popular due to high flux rates. It can be used for separation of hydroxide precipitates having densities very close to water due to which conventional separation techniques such as centrifugation is less efficient. It is also used in pharmaceutical industry for pollution treatment.

7.8 AIR FILTRATION

Separation of fine solids and aerosol droplets from air is an important step in environment and pollution control in pharmaceutical industry. The filtration equipments handling air are categorised as primary, secondary and final stage filters. The difference is given in table 7.3 :

Table 7.3 : Difference in categories of filters

	Primary filter	Secondary filter	Final stage filter
Air velocity	High > 0.5 ft./sec.	Low ; 0.1 – 0.5 ft/sec.	Very low ; < 0.1 ft/sec.
Cut-off particle size	> 5 μm	0.5 – 5.0 μm	< 0.5 μm
Filtration efficiency	Low ; 85 – 90%	Medium ; 90 – 95%	High ; > 95

Filtration efficiency is the percentage of particles retained by the filter and cut-off size is the lowest particle size below which retention is not possible.

Some important equipments used for handling air are as follows :

7.8.1 Bag Filters :

Fig. 7.17 : Bag filters

It consists of the filter medium in the form of cylinder or bags (Fig. 7.17) Number of such bags are fitted in one holder, in such a way that bags remain open and receive same quantity of air. This arrangement is called as 'bag house'. The bags are made up of cotton cloth, polyester, porous metals, glass fibre, etc.

The bags may be cleaned intermittently. The cleaning may be manual or may be achieved using air jets with high pressure. Many times disposable bags are also used.

The bags can show very high collection efficiency for dust particles, if they are maintained open, rigid and inflated. These may be used as primary as well as secondary filters. Air velocities through the bags should be maintained low, not more than 1 ft/sec. Bag filters are used for dust separation from exhausted air from fluidized bed dryer, spray dryer, cutter mill etc. But maintenance cost and pressure drop across the bags is high, therefore, should be used when high efficiency is required.

7.8.2 Electrostatic Precipitators :

It is a method based on development of charge on the fine solid particles and separate them by application of electric field. The air containing powder passes through the ionizer screen, where the electrons collide with air molecules and generate positive ions. These positive ions get adhered to the fine dust particle, imparting positive charge to it. The air containing charged dust particles flows slowly between the closely spaced metal plates alternately charged positive and negative, the voltage is around 6000 volts. The positively charged particles repel the positively charged plate and get attracted towards negative plate and become neutral; where they are collected (Fig. 7.18). Positive ionization is generally preferred because it avoids overproduction of ozone in the air filtration systems. The larger particles in the air are removed prior to it's entry in the ionization section. The solids retained on the plates may be removed by washing. It can be used for separation of particles from 10 μm down to 0.001 μm.

Fig. 7.18 : Two stage electrostatic filter

Resistivity of the particle is an important factor affecting separation process. The resistivity of the particles should be between 10^2 to 10^8 Ωm. It's major advantage is low pressure drop but equipment cost is very high. It is used for separation of mist, cleaning of volatilized fumes, etc.

7.8.3 Wet Scrubbers :

It is a wet separation process used for separation of dust particles from gases with use of liquid. The liquid is generally water. The particles are made to come in contact with the liquid surface and collected by it. The particles collected are washed off and the slurry is removed from the scrubber.

Fig. 7.19 : Wet Scrubber

A venturi scrubber which is commonly used, consists of a venturi section where water is sprayed. The spraying of water creates suction, and the fumes are drawn into the scrubber. In the scrubber the particles are removed in the scrubbing water and clean air with entrained droplets leaves the chamber. The slurry is taken out at the bottom as a drain. The efficiency of separation depends on the energy of the sprayed fluid. The other designs of scrubbers are spray chamber as in humidifier, packed towers etc.

7.8.4 Louvres :

Louvres are the air cleaning devices based on the aerodynamic principle. These consist of V shaped pocket comprising of the louvre slits on the either side and solid at the end (Fig. 7.20). The air containing dust particle passes through the louvre slits and during change of direction the particles are separated. The separated particles are collected by the dust chute.

Fig. 7.20 : Louvers

7.8.5 High Efficiency Particulate Air (HEPA) Filters :

The HEPA filter contains glass fibres as a depth filtration medium. This medium is supported by corrugated metal dividers or the medium is molded to have pleats or dimples for separation (Fig. 7.21). The later design without metal divider accommodates more medium in smaller space. The air having velocity between 5 – 12 ft/min enters the filter medium and particles are separated from air by impaction, diffusion and interception mechanism. The larger particles are separated by interception and impaction and finer particles by diffusion.

Fig. 7.21

The pleats on the filter medium are uniform and deep around 120 to 200 pleats are present in 2 ft ∞ 4 ft ∞ 6 in. HEPA filter. The pleats align the flow path of the air molecules flowing through the filter. Similarly, as the resistance of filter medium is approximately uniform throughout, equal volume of gas moves simultaneously through each pleat of the filter. This uniform velocity of gas in combination with alignment gas molecules by the pleats, results in flow of air in laminar fashion for some distance. Thus laminar flow is maintained in the HEPA filters. The air passing to the HEPA filter should be first subjected to prefilters and secondary stage filters. The maintenance of laminar flow depends on air flow rate, placement of equipment and obstructions in the flow. The higher the flow rate, higher is the separation by interception and impaction and lower is the efficiency due to diffusion. At low flow rate it is exactly opposite condition. The HEPA filter has an average minimum efficiency of 99.97% for 0.3 µm aerosol.

Integrity and Efficiency Testing of HEPA Filter :

Di-octylphthalates (DOP) test is commonly used to test HEPA filters. DOP is a group of oily, high boiling point liquids. In this test a monodisperse aerosol of DOP having size 0.3 µm and concentration 66.6 ppm by weight is passed through the filter at controlled flow rate. The air entering and leaving the filter is sampled and analysed for aerosol concentration by light scattering technique. The percentage of aerosol passing the filter is then determined as follows :

$$\% \text{ Aerosol passing (P)} = \frac{\text{Aerosol concentration after leaving the filter}}{\text{Aerosol concentration before entering the filter}} \infty\ 100$$

and   Filtration efficiency (E) = 100 – P

Efficiency should not be less than 99.97%.

For testing of integrity of HEPA filter or presence of pinholes, the aerosol having dispersed size is passed through the filter. The percentage 0.3 µm particles is around 20 – 30% and others are larger and smaller than this size.

***

MANUAL CORRECTIONS

CH. 7

(i)   It should have ability to retain wide range of particles from the suspension.

(iii) It should allow easy discharge of cake.

Pharmaceutical Engineering   27 Flow of Fluids

contamination and volatilization of filtrate are high as compared to closed channel system.

button plate but not on one button plate. Working of washing type press has two cycles a

strength so as to withstand high pressure differentials. In Nutsch filter a single chamber is

Nutsch filters. It consists of a circular horizontal table that rotates about a centre axis. The

moving along a closed path. Nutsch filters have a supporting perforated plate covered with a

7.11).

Scraper discharge   **String discharge**   **Belt discharge**

multistack discs, where large volume of liquid has to be displaced before the bubbles can be

  (d) Bacterial Challenge Test : In this integrity test, the culture of an organism of

have size between 20 – 1000 A°. The solute may be lyophilic or lyophobic in nature, with molecular weight in the range of 1000 – 10,000. The membranes used for ultrafiltration are made up of cellulose nitrate, polysulfone, polyvinylidene fluoride etc.

differences in the two processes. (See Table 7.2).

Table 7.2 : Differences between Reverse Osmosis, Ultrafiltration and Microfiltration

given in table 7.3 :

Table 7.3 : Difference in categories of filters

NEW MANUAL CORRECTIONS

(a) Reverse osmosis   **(b) Ultrafiltration**

Particle board frame   Corrugated aluminium separators   Filter media   Airflow

Neoprene gasket   HEPA Filter media   Cross section of filter media

Fig. 9.19 : Concentration – Time Curve

139	140	141	142	143	144	
145	146	147	148	149	150	
151	152	153	154	155	156	
157	158	159	160	161	162	
163	164	165	166	167	168	
169	170	171	172	173	174	
175	176	177	178	179	180	

MANUAL CORRECTIONS

CH. 2

Fig. 2.6 : Pressure energy

Fig. 2.8 : Pressure differential

CH. 6

Fig. 6.8 : Magensen sizer

CH. 7

(a) Non-washing type   **(b) Washing type**

Fig. 7.13 : Filter leaf in tanks

Fig. 7.20 : Louvers

(a) Corrugated plate type (b) 'Dimple pleat' type

Fig. HEPA filter

CH. 9

Fig. 9.2 : Crystal forms

Spiral   Spiral   Thick liquor   Thick liquor

CHAPTER 8

MIXING

8.1 INRODUCTION

Mixing is the most widely encountered unit operation. It is defined as complete intermingling of two or more dissimilar portions of material, so that the final product attains desired level of uniformity. In a completely mixed system, each particle of any one ingredient is close as possible to the particle of each of the other ingredient.

Mixing is considered as a contacting mechanism, by which the materials are brought together, to achieve process objectives such as :

(i) to obtain a uniform mixture.

(ii) to cause mass transfer to occur.

(iii) to effect chemical reaction.

(iv) to obtain emulsion or suspension.

Mixing may be carried out to supply oxygen to the micro-organisms in the fermentor etc. Danckwert has coined the terms positive, negative and neutral mixing. *Positive mixing* is a condition where the components of the system get spontaneously and completely mixed if sufficient time is provided e.g. two miscible liquids or two gases. *Negative mixing* requires continuous input of energy so as to keep the two phases of the system in a mixed state. e.g. suspension or immiscible liquids. *Neutral mixing* is a condition where neither mixing nor demixing occurs unless the system is acted upon by some forces, e.g. mixing of solids.

8.2 LIQUID MIXING

In this section we are dealing the liquid-liquid mixing and mixing of liquids with small proportions of solids.

8.2.1 Mixing mechanisms

The important mechanisms for liquid mixing are :

1. Bulk transport : It involves movement of large portion of material from one location to another in the system. It causes rearrangement of various portions in the system. Bulk transport can not be considered as a very effective mixing mechanism.

2. Laminar Mixing : It is associated with the high viscosity liquids. Under laminar flow conditions, in the vicinity of the agitator blade large velocity gradient exists. In these regions deformation and stretching of the fluid element occurs. It may be visualised that due to shear given to the highly viscous liquid under laminar flow, the laminas or streamlines get converged. The convergence of streamline occurs but volume is same therefore there is decrease in thickness and increase in area of fluid element occurs. This is stretching of fluid. [Fig. 8.1 (a)].

The stretched fluid element is subjected to :

(i) shear mixing e.g. in cylinder geometry folding continues till layer is few molecules thick and

(ii) distributive mixing, where the fluid element is cut and redistributed throughout the system [Fig. 8.1 (b)]. Thus in laminar mixing, stretching and folding or cutting of the liquid layer occurs. The process of stretching and folding progresses in exponential manner.

(a) Stretching and elongation

(b) Cutting and Folding

Fig. 8.1 : Laminar mixing

3. Turbulent Mixing : It is the mechanism which plays an important role in mixing of low viscosity fluids. (generally less than 10 poise).

The agitator imparts inertial energy to the fluid due to which the fluid circulates in the system and reaches back to the agitator. During circulation in the system, eddy diffusion occurs which causes mixing. The rate of mixing due to eddy diffusion is much higher than the laminar mixing.

Kolmogoroff proposed the theory to explain turbulence. According to this theory, the turbulence is analysed on the basis of velocity fluctuations at a point with respect to direction and magnitude and dissipation of energy through eddies. Consider a point in the fluid flow, the velocity at this point is sum of vectors in x, y and z directions. In turbulent flow this sum fluctuates continuously. Similarly, fluctuation is also with respect to direction depending on the component which dominates. This causes turbulence in the fluid.

Kolmogoroff states that a turbulent flow has large number of different size eddies. There are large primary eddies, which have size close to the size of agitator diameter. These eddies show high velocity fluctuations of low frequency and contain maximum kinetic energy. These large eddies interact with slow moving streams and produce small eddies of high frequency which further disintegrates and finally its energy is dissipated into heat. The properties of the large eddies are dependent on the agitator, whereas the properties of smaller eddies are independent on the agitator size but is dependent on viscosity of the fluid. Thus turbulent mixing involves large number of eddies having different life spans and properties causing mixing to occur.

The liquid in turbulent state may be expressed in terms of scale and intensity of turbulence. Scale of turbulence refers to the size distribution of eddies in the turbulent region. Higher the proportion of smaller eddies, lower is the scale of turbulence. Intensity of turbulence is related to velocity at which eddies move.

4. Molecular Diffusion : Laminar and turbulent mixing cause increase in contact areas between the components. But for complete intermingling of the components into each other, molecular diffusion is the mechanism responsible. Molecular diffusion is discussed in details in Chapter 4. Rate of mixing by diffusion is dependent on the concentration gradient which is related by Fick's Law.

$$N_A = -D A \Delta C \qquad \ldots (1)$$

where N_A is rate of diffusion, D is diffusivity of the molecule, A is area across which diffusion occurs and ΔC is concentration gradient. The diffusivity of molecules is dependent on fluid velocity and molecule size.

8.2.2 Mixing Equipments

Equipments for fluid mixing are classified as follows :

A. Batch Mixing Equipments
    1. Mechanically Agitated vessel.
    2. Jet mixers.
    3. High shear mixing equipments :
        (a) Homogenizer
        (b) Colloid mills
        (c) Ultrasonic homogenizers.
B. In-line Static Mixers (Pipe mixers)

A. Batch Mixing Equipments :

1. Mechanically Agitated Vessel :

The mechanically agitated vessel for mixing has three components. viz. a vessel, an impeller for agitation and baffle if required to prevent swirling.

The vessels are generally cylindrical tanks of varying sizes. The base of the tank may be flat, conical or contoured. If deep cones are used, proper care should be taken so that complete mixing occurs, especially near the surface. Contoured base is preferred for handling of suspensions.

Fig. 8.2 : Mechanically agitated vessel

Impellers : Impellers are the devices which supply energy for the fluid mixing. The energy imparted gives fluid velocity with three components radial, axial and tangential. The flow pattern of fluid depends on balance between these components. The radial component of the flow acts in a direction perpendicular to the impeller shaft. An axial component is acting parallel to the impeller shaft and tangential component is acting in a tangential direction to the circle of rotation around the impeller shaft. Accordingly, the flow patterns may be axial, radial or tangential. In axial flow the fluid flows along the axis of the impeller to the bottom of the mixing tank. The impeller blades displace the fluid in an axial direction which is then brought upto the top of the tank and drawn down along the axis of the impeller shaft. The radial flow promotes lateral and vertical flow currents. The impellers are categorized depending on the flow pattern they produce. (Fig. 8.3).

(a)

(b)

(c)

Fig. 8.3 : Flow patterns induced by impellers

The three main categories of impellers are viz. propeller, turbine and paddles.

(a) Propellers : Propellers are high speed, compact agitators suitable for low viscosity liquids upto 5000 cp. Propellers produce flow having combination of axial and tangential patterns. Axial flow dominates. Propellers are generally three bladed marine type (See Fig. 8.4). The propeller draws the liquid from the top of it, which leaves the propeller in the form of a cylindrical spiral comprised of three helics of different velocity. The propellers are used in the speed range of 400 rpm to 1750 rpm. Lower speeds are recommended for high viscosities (greater than 200 cp), and lower volumes. Higher speeds are suitable for low viscosities and larger volumes. For large volumes, or high depth stirring, it is better to use two or more propeller blades on single shaft. The impeller diameter to tank diameter ratio is low in case of propellers.

Fig. 8.4 : Propeller type agitator

Volume of fluid displaced by the propeller per revolution is known as volumetric displacement (V) ; which is proportional to the propeller diameter and pitch.

$$V = \pi D^2 \frac{P}{4} \qquad \ldots (2)$$

where, D and P are propeller diameter and pitch respectively. Therefore, pumping rate or volume of liquid displaced by the propeller (Q), is given by

$$Q = VN = \pi D^2 P \frac{N}{4} \qquad \ldots (3)$$

where, N is rotational speed of the propeller.

Power consumed by the propeller is highly affected by viscosity of the fluid. It is discussed in details later in this chapter.

The propeller should be properly positioned in the tank, so that complete mixing from top to the bottom occurs. Side entering, off centre or bottom entering arrangement of propellers is also used for efficient mixing of liquids. (Fig. 8.4).

(b) Turbines : Turbine is an impeller with a number of blades, which may be straight or curved (Fig. 8.5). The impeller diameter to tank diameter ratio is less. A flat blade turbine produces radial and tangential flow, but as speed increases, radial component dominates the flow pattern. A pitched blade turbines produce axial flow. The turbines are generally operated in the speed range of 50 – 200 r.p.m. (See Fig. 8.5)

Fig. 8.5 : Turbine type impellers

A flat blade turbine can be operated in either a clockwise or anti-clockwise direction. These are suitable for dispersion applications. Curved blade turbine, provide greater blade area and shear at the tip is lower, due to this, it is suitable for handling of abrasive materials and to preserve structure of fibrous or crystalline suspensions. The use of curved blades reduces the number of blades required and hence the power consumption.

In pitched blade turbine the blades are set at some angle to the horizontal centreline of the impeller. Generally, the angle is 45°. These produce axial flow ; and are suitable for suspension of solids. Pitched blade turbine reduces power requirements. The power consumption of a 45° pitched turbine is half that of flat blade turbine.

The turbines may be open turbine and centre disc turbine and shrouded turbine. The centre disc turbine is useful for mixing the fluids with viscosities below 20,000 cp. Shrouded turbine reduce the tangential component of the flow, swirling is reduced ; but are not suitable for suspensions as cleaning becomes difficult.

Turbines are used for mixing low viscosity liquids, but as compared to propellers they can be used over a wide viscosity range upto 1,00,000 cp. These are used in mixing, dissolution and dispersion operations, but as the axial flow is less these are less suitable for suspending heavy solids as compared to propellers. The shear produced by turbines is more than the propellers but pumping rate is lower than propellers. Therefore, turbines are suitable for high shear low pumping rate operations such as emulsification. The shear imparted by turbines can be further increased by use of diffuser rings. A diffuser ring is a stationary perforated or slotted ring which surrounds the impeller. The liquid discharged passes through the diffuser ring reducing the swirling and increases the shear forces. The swirling or vortexing occurs with turbines except shrouded turbine, therefore the tanks should be baffled.

Number of turbines required on one shaft is dependent on tank diameter, volume and specific gravity of the liquid to be handled. This is given by,

$$\text{Number of turbines} = \frac{\text{WELH}}{\text{Tank diameter in inches}} \quad \ldots (4)$$

where, WELH is water equivalent liquid height. It is defined as the maximum liquid height in inches to be placed into the tank multiplied by the specific gravity of the mixture.

The power requirements of turbines is given by equation,

$$\text{HP} = \rho \text{HP}_{600} \left(\frac{T}{600}\right)^{2.74} \cdot f \quad \ldots (5)$$

where, HP = Power requirement of turbine (horse power)

HP_{600} = Horse power requirement by a standard turbine of the same diameter at tip speed of **600** ft/min. (Standard table is available)

T = Actual tip speed in ft/min.

ρ = Specific gravity of the fluid

f = Correction factor.

(c) Paddles :

Fig. 8.6 : Paddle type impellers

Paddles are the low speed agitators having large mixing element mounted on shaft (Fig. 8.6). A simple paddle consists of one or more horizontal arms mounted on a shaft. The arms may be vertical or pitched at an angle of 45°. The paddle speed is in the range of 10 – 100 r.p.m. The ratio of paddle diameter to tank diameter is about 0.9. The paddles produce mainly the tangential flow. The pitched paddles produce some axial flow, therefore unless the paddle is pitched, baffles are required for mixing. Due to low axial flow, paddles are not suitable for mixing of suspensions or fluids where separation can occur. Paddles are suitable for mixing of liquids and low gravity solids or for slow agitation of viscous materials. Apart from simple paddle, other examples of this class include gate mixer, anchor blade mixer and mixer with stationary blade intermeshing with moving element.

A gate agitator has an element with vertical and horizontal plates. These plates give strength to the agitator. It is used for mixing of emulsions which will become viscous during cooling. It is a low shear agitator suitable for viscous liquids and creams. But a modification of gate mixer has an high shear attachment. The high shear attachment which has separate motor attached, is activated initially to emulsify the liquids, so the complete reduction and dispersion of internal phase occurs in hot condition. Once emulsification has been completed, the low shear agitator provides agitation to the cream during its cooling when viscosity builds up. The scrapers may be attached to the gate mixer so as to scrap the cream from the vessel wall and cause uniform and fast heat transfer.

The anchor type agitator is useful in heat transfer equipments due to very low clearance between the blades and vessel wall. Clearance between anchor blade and vessel wall is around 0.25 to 0.75 inches and rotates at the speed of about 15 to 60 r.p.m. It is a low shear agitator suitable for high viscosity liquids or creams. Stationary paddles intermeshing with the moving element suppresses the swirling motion in the mixer.

In the mechanically agitated vessel, the swirling or vortexing is a common problem when working with high shear agitators such as propellers and turbines. Axial and radial flows are not induced in the liquids. This may cause problems such as entrapment of air, settling of separated phase, foam formation etc. These problems can be tackled by use of suitable baffle system in the tank.

Baffles :

Baffles are the obstructions purposefully placed in the mixing tank to redirect the flow. Baffles used are of different sizes and shapes (Fig. 8.7). Wall baffles are most common, but bottom baffles and partition baffles may also be used. The number of baffles used in the vessel varies from two to eight. In a standard tank, generally four long vertical plates or wall baffles are placed symmetrically around the perimeter of the tank. The baffle width is about one tenth the tank diameter. The baffle height is higher than the liquid height.

Wall baffles hinder the tangential flow of the fluid and impart radial and axial flow. Baffles increase relative velocity of the impeller and the fluid. Introduction of baffles exert an extra fluid resistance and extra shear thereby improving blending performance. But addition of baffles also results in higher power consumption in the process. Baffles are not recommended for laminar region mixing. Bottom baffles increase the suspension of solids but may also trap the solids. Surface baffles are useful in preventing or limiting the surface entrainment of gas.

Fig. 8.7 : Different types of baffles

In some turbulent applications, wall baffles are not recommended. For example, many times in solid-liquid mixing, solids build up on the baffles and cause quality control problems. Baffles are very difficult to clean and cause the cleaning operation to be much longer than that for unbaffled tanks.

2. Jet Mixer :

Jets are high velocity fluid streams entering the low velocity liquids. The entering fluid stream may be or air of liquid. In a jet mixer, a high velocity jet of liquid emerges from a submerged nozzle into a low viscosity liquid in a mixing vessel. The momentum is transferred from a high velocity jet to the liquid in the vessel which causes mixing action and circulation within the tank. The jet expands in the vessel and entrains the surrounding fluids. If the mixing tank is larger in size, then several nozzles may be used. A pump is used to withdraw part of the liquid from the vessel and recycle it through the nozzle.

Fig. 8.8 : Jet mixing

In the jet, the entraining liquid enters the jet cone normal to the jet centreline. The jet cone angle determines the mixing efficiency of the jet. The jet in a tank is so positioned that jet centreline is at $\frac{1}{3}^{rd}$ the tank diameter from the opposite side.

Air jets use air or an inert gas as the jet fluid e.g. vapour jets are observed in perforated plate columns for distillation or extraction. If liquid circulation is desired then jet diameter is confined, using draf tube so that more buoyant force will be present in the air which will entrain the liquid. The confined turbulence causes efficient mixing and circulation of fluid.

Jet mixing is not effective in laminar mixing regime. In such cases, the jet often becomes a layer in the flow. Jet mixing is also not suitable for viscous liquids.

3. High Shear Mixing Equipments :

In pharmaceutical field, high shear equipments are frequently required where low particle size and dispersions are required e.g. emulsions, micro-emulsions, microspheres, etc.

(a) Homogenizer : Homogenizers are of two types homogenizer mixers which can be considered as modified turbines and pressure homogenizer.

Fig. 8.9 : Homogenizer - mixer

The homogenizer mixers have a turbine and a stator with a fixed clearance between them (Fig. 8.9). The turbine rotates at a very high speed, due to which pressure differential is created. Material below the homogenizer is drawn to the turbine due to the pressure differential. The material is forced to pass through the small openings on the stator. This causes high hydraulic and mechanical forces and the material is mixed. The stator has different types of openings e.g. very fine openings for emulsification, slots for breaking pellets etc. The ultra-turrax type homogenizer (Fig. 8.10) is used for fine grinding and dispersion of solids or emulsification where low globule size is desired.

Fig. 8.10 : Ultra - Turrax type homogenizer

Fig. 8.11 : Pressure homogenizer

A pressure homogenizer consists of a heavy duty plunger pump at the outlet of which a stainless steel fluid end is connected. The fluid end has a valve seat and a valve with a surrounding ring having a very close clearance (Fig. 8.11). A plunger pump forces the liquid under high pressure and low velocity to the valve seat. The liquid enerts the close clearance between valve and valve seat, where its velocity increases rapidly to around 700 ft/s. This sudden increase in velocity causes cavitation. The cavitation bubbles collapse at the valve, causing it to vibrate. The liquid coming out 'collides with an impact ring. This is the mechanism of homogenization. The output from the homogenizer is at the flow rates of 15 – 14000 gal/h and pressure 1500 to 10,000 psi. It is useful in the viscosity range of 1 to 2000 cps. The product size of 0.5 to 20 μm is obtained. The capacity of homogenizer and quality of dispersed product can be improved by premixing the fluids and final mixing only be carried out in the homogenizer. Homogenizers are not suitable mixing solids in the liquids because it may cause wear of the fluid end. It is more suitable for low viscosity liquids than high viscosity.

(b) Colloid mill : Colloid mill is a continuous mill based on the principle of attrition between a stator and a rotor (Fig. 8.12). It is used for preparation of emulsions, suspensions and ointments. It is observed that it causes disruption of aggregates than size reduction, thus it is basically suitable for homogenization.

Fig. 8.12 : Colloid mill

The feed flows by gravity or is pumped through the inlet, where it comes in contact with the rotor surface. The rotor is revolving at 3000 – 15000 r.p.m. and has peripheral speed of about 10 to 50 m/s. The feed is forced by the rotor through the gap between rotor and stator. The feed then reverses the direction of flow and moves towards the centre of the rotor on the other surface. This flow is counter current to the centrifugal force. The material is discharged through the outlet. The rotor and stator are made up of stainless steel or carborundum. The surface of rotor may be smooth or it may be serrated.

The clearance between rotor and stator is adjustable. It may be as low as 25 μm and upto 750 μm. The rotor speed is an important factor in controlling size of the product. For a feed of 200 μm, it was observed that size reduced to 1 μm at peripheral speed of 10 m/s and 0.001 μm at 40 m/s. The peripheral speed of the rotor be kept low for high viscosity fluids. Colloid mill is suitable for feed viscosity range of 1 to 30,000 cp. The capacity is in the range of 2 lit./min. to 400 lit./min. depending on the mill size and rotor speed. Surface active agent may be used so as to prevent reaggregation of the fine particles. Large amount of heat is generated in colloid mills, therefore, unless suitable cooling system is attached, it cannot be used for thermolabile materials and emulsions.

(c) Ultrasonic homogenizer : Ultrasonic homogenizer is based on the utilization of cavitational energy of the ultrasonic waves (frequencies above 20,000 Hz). The ultrasonic waves if passed through the medium, then areas of compression and rarefaction are formed. Cavities are found in the areas of rarefaction, which collapse as soon as the area changes to compression. During collapse, the walls of the bubbles are compressed. Such compressed bubbles just prior to collapse have tremendous pressure generated inside them. The collapse generates powerful shock waves which produces shear effect responsible for size reduction and homogenization. This method is primarily used for emulsification. The equipments for emulsification are based on generation of intense vibrations by liquid whistle (Fig. 8.13). The homogenizer consists of a powerful positive displacement pump, which forces the material in a flat jet over a blade which is forced to vibrate. The mixture of frequencies generated by the material passing over a blade, induces cavitational forces, which can be of the order of 60 tonnes/sq. in. A high proportion of this energy is utilised for dispersion. Critical factors affecting the homogenization in ultrasonicator are velocity of flow, size, shape of orifice and distance between orifice and blade edge.

Fig. 8.13 : Ultrasonic homogenizer

There are several advantages of ultrasonic homogenization. It is extremely efficient, e.g. its output is 20 – 500 lit/min. requiring only 2 – 4 horse power motor. The cavitation is caused by gases in solution itself, no additional aeration of product is required. There is no rise in temperature during processing, therefore, method is suitable for thermolabile and volatile materials. The emulgent concentrations required reduces drastically, in some cases, it has reduced to one tenth of the conventional concentrations. It is versatile and can be used for emulsions, mixing and solid dispersions.

3. In – line Static Mixers (Pipe Mixers) :

A pipe mixer utilizes the energy of the flowing fluid to cause mixing. The stationary baffles introduced in the pipe leads to mixing of the fluids flowing through it.

A static mixer by Kenics Corp. consists of stationary units housed in a pipe. The pipe diameter is about 1 cm to 0.5 m or more. The stationary units are number of elements on right and left hand helices (Fig. 8.14). These elements are alternated and oriented so that each leading edge is at $90°$ to the trailing edge of the one ahead. The length of individual element is 1.5 diameters. The viscous liquid in laminar flow is mixed by stretching, slicing and folding mechanism. As the liquid proceeds in the pipe, the product mixedness improves.

At the leading edge of each stationary element the flow divides and follows a semi-circular channel created by the element shape (Fig. 8.14 [b]). At each succeeding element the two flows are further divided, resulting in an exponential progression of flow division. The progression is described by following formula :

$$S = 2^n \qquad \ldots (6)$$

where S is the number of striations produced and n is the number of elements. After the flow has passed through 20 elements, over a million striations exist [Fig. 8.14 (c)]. The thickness of striations, d is defined as :

$$d = \frac{D}{2^n} \qquad \ldots (7)$$

where D is the inside diameter of the pipe.

(a) In-line mixer

(b) Mixing elements

(c) Laminar mixing

Fig. 8.14 : Pipe mixer

The above discussed mechanism is only for laminar mixing. But in case of liquid-liquid or liquid-gas, mixing occurs in the turbulent region, due to break-up of gas bubbles or liquid droplets takes place. Due to pressure drop, the droplets are formed exposing high interfacial area across which mass transfer occurs causing mixing. The flow rate of the liquid if increased, the droplet size decreases. It gives continuous output and its working volume is low.

In static mixers, it is important to control the flow rates of the two components because there is no back mixing of fluids and composition of fluid is different throughout the pipe. If it is not possible to control flow rates of the material it may be mixed in a mixing chamber (Fig. 8.15) . In the mixing chamber, the material remains for sufficient time. The composition of the material in the chamber is same throughout the chamber.

Fig. 8.15 : Continuous tank mixer

8.2.3   Power requirement in liquid mixing :

Power required for mixing of fluid is dependent on large number of parameters. It is dependent on the variables related to the fluid and those related to the agitator.

For a Newtonian liquid which is under agitation in a vessel, the power requirement will be dependent on following variables :

Liquid related variables : Density (ρ) and viscosity (η) of liquid.

Vessel related variables : Vessel diameter (T) ; liquid height in vessel (H).

Impeller related variables : Rotational speed of impeller (N), diameter of impeller (D) and its width (W).

Thus we can say,

$$P = f(\rho, \eta, g, N, D, T, W, H, \text{other dimensions}) \qquad \ldots (6)$$

where, P is power requirement. This gives actual energy received by the liquid. Total energy will be P plus energy losses of motor, gear box etc.

As large variables affect the power requirement, dimensional analysis is a method which will simplify the relationship. After dimensional analysis following equation will be generated.

$$\frac{P}{\rho N^3 D^5} = f\left\{\frac{\rho N D^2}{\eta}, \frac{N^2 D}{g}, \frac{T}{D}, \frac{W}{D}, \frac{H}{D} \text{ etc.}\right\} \qquad \ldots (7)$$

where, $\dfrac{P}{\rho N^3 D^5}$ = Power Number (Po)

$\dfrac{\rho N D^2}{\eta}$ = Reynolds Number (Re)

$\dfrac{N^2 D}{g}$ = Froude Number (Fr)

Thus power requirement relationship has been converted in terms of dimensionless numbers and some ratios of geometry which are constant. The general relationship can be written as :

$$Po = K\,(Re)^n\,(Fr)^m \qquad \ldots (8)$$

Froude number is the ratio of inertial forces to gravitational forces and it becomes significant when the liquid surface is disturbed by the impeller and vortex appears. Below Reynolds number of about 300, the Froude number has little or no effect. Therefore, under such circumstances equation (8) becomes,

$$Po = K (Re)^n \qquad \ldots (9)$$

If Reynolds number is high, then effects of Froude number are eliminated by use of baffles or off–center stirring.

For a given system, if power number is measured with variations in impeller speed, fluid density and viscosity and plotted against Reynolds number on log-log paper, a 'Power Curve' is obtained. A typical power curve is shown in Fig. 8.16.

Fig. 8.16 : A Typical Power Curve

A power curve shows, in laminar region at Re less than 10, the curve is linear with slope – 1. The equation becomes

$$Po = \frac{K}{Re} \qquad \ldots (10)$$

At high Reynolds numbers, greater than about 10^4, the flow is turbulent and in this region power number is constant.

$$Po = B \qquad \ldots (11)$$

In between laminar region and turbulent zone ($10 < Re < 10^4$), a transition region exists where no simple mathematical relationship exists between Po and Re.

Power curves for various geometries and fluid conditions are available in literature. Using these curves, the power requirement for mixing can be easily obtained if impeller speed, geometry and fluid properties are known. The relationship becomes complicated for Non-Newtonian fluids and are not discussed here.

Some approximate values for power consumption in a typical stirred tanks under different conditions are given by Table 8.1.

Table 8.1 : Power consumption for different operations

No.	Operation	Approximate power consumption in kW/m³
1.	Suspending light solids, blending low viscosity liquids.	0.2
2.	Dispersion of gas, liquid-liquid contacting, suspending moderate density solids.	0.6
3.	Emulsification, suspending heavy solids.	2
4.	Blending pastes, doughs.	4

8.3 MIXING OF SOLIDS WITH LIQUIDS :

The mixing of solids with liquids shows variations in the mechanisms involved and in turn equipments required depending on the ratios of two phases. Rheology of the blend changes as the proportions of two phases change.

At low solid concentrations, the flow is generally Newtonian and impellers are suitable. So as to keep the solids in suspended form the size of impeller blade is increased and speed is reduced. At high concentrations of solids, the pastes and doughs which are formed are too highly viscous to be mixed and blended in conventional mechanically agitated vessels. The high viscosity of such mixture leads to laminar flow conditions. The mixing mechanism which prevails in the equipments is laminar and distributive mixing. The streamlines of the fluid in laminar flow show relative motion during flow leading to increased interfacial areas and stretching or elongation of the regions which are folded over each other. Molecular diffusion may occur when the lamina reduces to few molecule thickness. The distributive mixing involves slicing and replacing of portions of mass under mixing process.

8.3.1 Equipments

Equipments used for mixing of high proportions of solids with liquids are as follows :

1. Z-blade Mixer : It is also known as a kneader, sigma blade or double arm mixer. It consists of a twin trough and two z-shaped blades (Fig. 8.17). The blades revolve towards each other and can be designed to overlap or to rotate tangentially with a speed ratio of about 2 : 1. The blades are so shaped and mounted that the material turned up by one blade is immediately turned under by an adjacent one. A kneading and rolling action is imparted to the mass being mixed by the action of the two blades which are turning at different speeds. The shearing action is also given due to close clearance between the blades and the inner wall of the mixer. It is suitable for mixing the materials having viscosity in the range of **100,000 to 500,000 cp.** The sigma blender may be closed to prevent losses of volatile ingredients or it may be jacketed for heating or cooling. These mixers can be emptied easily just by tilting them. But the power requirement of mixer is high. It is also used for mixing dry powders.

Fig. 8.17 : Z-blade mixer

2. Planetary Mixer : It consists of mixing element mounted on a moving shaft (Fig. 8.18). To impart the planetary mixing action, the mixing element rotates about it's own axis as it moves in a circle and the pan remains stationary. The mixing element is mounted off centre on a rotating arm. During the travel of the blade around the circumference of the mixing vessel, it gives shearing action.

Fig. 8.18 : Planetary mixer

3. **Screw Mixers :** There are vertical helical screw (Fig. 8.19) and conical orbital screw (Nauta mixer) (Fig. 8.20 [a]) mixers. The helical screw mixer causes the axial flow of the viscous material.

Fig. 8.19 : Vertical helical mixer

A Nauta Mixer is a conical orbital screw mixer. A mixing screw rotates on its own axis and simultaneously moves in the orbit at the periphery of the conical container. It produces three mixing currents (Fig. 8.20 [b]). The mixer screw rotates to lift the material to the top of the cone. This imparts upward spiral motion. The rotating arm guides the whole screw in a circular path along the wall of the conical container, so that the material is also conveyed in a horizontal direction (Fig. 8.20 [c]). The material drops off the screw to the opposite side of the cone, and is lifted up repeatedly (Fig. 8.20 [d]). The resultant action is to impart a mixing effect in three dimensions (Fig. 8.20 [e]). In mixing the pastes, the operation can be made
effective by pouring about half of the liquid ingredients from the top of the tank, then with the screw agitator running downward the dry ingredients are added. The dispersion of solids in liquid occurs by hydraulic shear. Once the satisfactory dispersion is achieved, remaining liquid is added to achieve proper consistency.

(a) (b)

(c) (d)

(e)

Fig. 8.20 : Conical orbital mixer (Nautamix)

A Nauta mixer can be jacketed as well as subjected to vacuum. Cleaning of the mixer is difficult. Nauta mixer is used in wet granulation. It is used for efficient kinetic maceration of crude drugs and is suitable for drug plants containing mucilage and swelling substances also.

4. High Speed Mixers : The mixers containing high speed impellers are used. The impellers may move at the speeds of **1000 to 3000 rpm**. In this mixer, the mechanism does not involve that clumps of related particles are pushed, folded and relocated as in case of z-blade or planetary mixer. With high impeller speed the individual particles or lumps are impacted by impeller to give rapid bulk circulation of material. Common mixers of this category are Lodige mixer, Diasona mixer and Gral mixer. These mixers have an arrangement of blades and choppers causing high impaction. The mixing time is significantly reduced.

Diasona mixer (Fig. 8.21), consists of a vertical bowl in which a high speed mixer blade is revolving at the bottom. A chopper blade present above the mixer blade, causes breaking of lumps and agglomerates. It is highly efficient in powder mixing, which occurs in only two minutes or less . The lid is provided with the spray nozzle through which the binder solution is sprayed for wet granulation. Granulation takes around 8 min. The discharge of mass is easy. It may be pneumatic discharge.

Fig. 8.21 : Diasona mixer

An 'intensifier' (Fig. 8.22) is an modification of Diasona, where instead of single rotating blade, more compact multiple blades and choppers are used. This increases chances of all the mixture passing through the zone of high impaction. Mixture is more uniform and obtained in short time.

Fig. 8.22 : Intensifier

Lodige mixer (Fig. 8.23), consists of a cylindrical vessel in which the plough shaped blades are mounted on a central high speed rotating shaft. At the rear end, the chopper blades are provided. The spray nozzles are present above the chopper, for spraying the binder solution. The choppers are in operation during dry mixing of the powders and break the aggregates efficiently. The plough shaped blades transfers the material back and forth across the blender. The blades are revolved at variable speeds so as to maintain the contents in fluidized condition. The granulation time is reduced to as low as 30 to 60 sec. The powder requirement increases as wetting of powder occurs.

Fig. 8.23 : Lodige mixer

Gral mixer (Fig. 8.24) is a modification of planetary mixer. It has two mixing elements. The large planetary mixing element provides large scale mixing motion. An additional small chopper blade which is placed off centre and above the large blade. It breaks the agglomerates. The shaft or blades are not fixed in the container and can be cleaned easily.

Fig. 8.24 : Gral mixer

The high speed mixers are also used for dry mixing of cohesive powders. But the high energy input in the mixer causes rise in temperature of the mixture.

8.4 MIXING OF SOLIDS

Mixing of solids differs from the liquid mixing process in following respects :

1. The solid particles do not have ability to move without external energy supply. There is no mechanism like molecular diffusion. Rate of randomization of particles is dependent on the flow characteristics which are imposed.
2. Solid particles show property of segregation depending on size, shape, density, etc.
3. In liquid mixing, the ultimate element is at molecular level, whereas in solid mixing, the ultimate element is several times larger than molecules.

8.4.1 Mechanisms of mixing and segregation

Mixing of solids occur by following mechanisms, alone or in combination :

(a) Convective mixing : It involves transfer of group of particles from one location to another in the system. It is observed in mixers having a stationary container and a moving mixing element, e.g. ribbon mixer.

(b) Shear mixing : In a powder mass shear and other forces acting between the particles. This induces formation of a slip plane causing mixing across two different regions. e.g. stirred vertical cylinder.

(c) Diffusive mixing : Mixing due to diffusion occurs when particles roll over a sloping powder surface. The random movement of particles on the surface results in redistribution of the particles. When particles in the mixture have identical properties diffusion can act as a true randomizing mechanism e.g. double cone mixer.

These mechanisms are also responsible for causing segregation in the particulate system. If the particles in the system have identical properties then only it is possible that only mixing will occur. If three mechanisms are compared, in convection mixing the particles do not have the same individual freedom of movement associated with shear and diffusional mixing and the resultant mixture is generally less prone to segregation.

Segregation in powder system occurs due to difference in particle size, shape, density etc. Particle size plays an important role in segregation. It is a general observation that particles with a size greater than 75 µm segregate easily and tendency reduces with particle size upto 10 µm. Below 10 µm, no appreciable segregation occurs. Shear segregation may occur when a powder flows in such a way that a velocity gradient is set up, any one layer of particles will have a velocity relative to a neighbouring layer and in such cases, particles can percolate or roll into a new particle layer. Smaller particles have greater mobility as compared to larger ones and segregation may occur. This will occur in a drum mixer, if two different size particles are rotated. Powders are generally subjected to vibrations during storage, transportation and processing. The vibrations of powder mass creates voids into which the fine particles can drop more readily than coarse particles causing segregation.

8.4.2 Degree of Mixing :

The mixedness or goodness of mixing of the powder system is important to be analysed especially in pharmaceuticals. Because the pharmaceutical systems involve mixing of particles with different properties and in different ratios. A powder mixture can be visualised as shown in Fig. 8.25. A 'perfect mixture' of two powder in equal proportions, where each particle has a neighbouring particle of other component. Such an arrangement is practically impossible to occur in any mixer. A 'random mixture' is the one in which probability of finding the particle of one component at any point is equal to the proportion of that component in the mixture.

(a) Segregated particles   **(b) Perfect mixture**   **(c) Random mixture**

Fig. 8.25 : Powder mixture

The quality of mixture has been expressed in qualitative and quantitative terms. Following qualitative terms are defined by Danckwerts :

(a) Scale of scrutiny : It is that maximum size of the regions of segregation in the mixture which would cause it to be regarded as imperfectly mixed. Scale of scrutiny is to be taken into consideration while determining sample size for mixedness analysis. For example, suppose a tablet contains, 200 mg of drug A and 50 mg of excipient then to analyse distribution of drug and excipient sample size should be 250 mg. If this sample shows A and B in the desired ratio then only we can say randomization has occurred.

(b) Scale of segregation : It is a measure of the size of regions of segregation within the mixture. The smaller the scale of segregation, the better the mixture. For example, a pigment is dispersed in lipstick mass, then scale of segregation in this case will be the area of the mass where pigment has not reached in desired concentration. As mixing progresses, scale of segregation reduces.

(c) Intensity of segregation : It is the measure of divergence. It can be regarded as the amount of dilution that has occurred in the segregated areas. Lower the intensity of segregation, the better the mixture. We can consider that it is related to distribution of segregated regions. In the above example of pigment dispersion, if the pigment is distributed uniformly as lump or segregated region, the size of the region is scale of segregation and as it is uniformly distributed, intensity of segregation is low.

Fig. 8.26 : Scale and Intensity of segregation

A mixer reduces both the scale and intensity of segregation within the mixture. High intensity of segregation may be tolerated so long as the scale of segregation. Similarly, a larger scale of segregation may be tolerated if the intensity of segregation is reduced.

'Quantitative terms' such as mixing indices are used to describe goodness of mixing in a powder mixture. It compares the maximum to minimum variance in a powder mixture.

Consider that the mixture of two components is completely segregated, then in such mixture,

$$S_0^2 = pq \qquad \ldots (11)$$

where S_0^2 is variance of completely segregated mixture and p & q are proportions of two components estimated from the mixture. This is the maximum variance.

For a completely randomized state of the same powder mixture, containing N number of particles, variance will be given as :

$$S_R^2 = \frac{pq}{N} = \frac{S_0^2}{N} \qquad \ldots (12)$$

where, S_R^2 is variance of randomized powder mixture. It is the minimum variance which can be obtained for a given powder mixture.

Once the two limiting variances S_0^2 and S_R^2 are calculated, Lacey 'Mixing Index' (M_l) which is defined as the ratio of how much mixing has occurred to how much could have occurred can be obtained

$$\text{Mixing Index } M_l = \frac{S_0^2 - S_d^2}{S_0^2 - S_R^2} \qquad \ldots (13)$$

where S^2 is the variance in the sample powder mixture.

But Lacey index is little insensitive to mixture quality as for bad mixtures also the index value is high. It ranges from 0.75 to 1.

Pool, Taylor and Wall have proposed alternative formula for Mixing Index where variance of segregated mixture is omitted. It is calculated as

$$M' = \frac{S_d^2}{S_R^2}$$

This mixing index (M') is greater than unity for a non-random mixture and approaches unity as system moves towards state of randomization.

8.4.3 Rate of Mixing :

Once suitable mixing index is calculated for the powder mixture, then rate of mixing can be obtained as follows :

$$\frac{dM}{dt} = K(1-M) \qquad \ldots (14)$$

where, M is mixing index and K is mixing rate constant.

Integrating equation 14, we get,

$$M = 1 - e^{-Kt} \qquad \ldots (15)$$

Mixing rate constant K, depends on the physical nature of the materials being mixed and on the geometry and operation of the mixer.

8.4.4 Powder Mixers

The powders to be mixed may be free flowing or cohesive. A cohesive powder is one where the bulk of powder has developed macro-structure which inhibits flow, and when flow occurs it will be erratic or stick-slip type. For free flowing powders, the mixers which are used include tumbler mixers and ribbon blender.

Tumbler mixers : These are mixers which cause mixing by diffusive mechanism. It consists of an enclosed vessel, which rotates about an axis causing the particles in the mixer to tumble over each other on the mixing surface. As only diffusive mechanism is used, it is suitable for free flowing and granular materials only. The various geometries of the mixing vessel include horizontal and inclined cylinders, cube, double-cone, V and Y - mixers. The vessel is attached to a shaft and rotates at low speeds of around 15 to 60 rpm. The capacity of the vessel is about 50 m^3. The mixer is operated at half the total capacity. The speed of the mixer should be kept half the critical speed. Critical speed of a tumbler mixer is that minimum speed at which the centrifugal force acting on the particle is just balanced by the gravitational force. Internal baffles and lifting blades or impellers may also be incorporated. The impeller may break the agglomerates and redistribute the powder.

(a) Twin core   **(b) Cubic**   **(c) Tetrahedral**

Fig. 8.27 : Timber Mixers

As the tumbler mixer is closed, it is easy to clean and suitable for obtaining high purity product. The gentle operation of tumbler mixer avoids any significant comminution of the material, therefore, it is commonly used for lubrication of granules. The mixing performance of tumbling mixer is highly dependent on speed of rotation of the mixer. The equilibrium efficiency of the tumbler mixers is very low. Addition of any ingredient over a period of time is not possible to the tumbler mixer due to its enclosed nature. Though these mixers are simple to construct they are difficult to jacket. Except inclined cylinder, all tumbler mixers are batch type.

Ribbon Blender : It is a widely used convective mixer (Fig. 8.28). It consists of a ribbon like conveying scroll, which rotates in a stationary trough. The two ribbons conveying the material in opposite directions are fitted on the same shaft. The capacity of these blenders is generally 20 m^3.

Fig. 8.28 : Ribbon blender

As it does not rely on natural circulation, it can be used to mix wet powders. The mixer can produce homogeneous mass though there is significant difference in particle size, shape, etc. But dead spaces are observed in the ribbon blender and it is not suitable for cohesive powders.

For cohesive powders, the mixers which are used include Nauta mixer, Lodige mixer, Intensifier and Gral mixer. These mixers having an impaction device, breaks the agglomerates continuously causing efficient mixing.

8.5 DEAERATION AND DEFOAMING OF MIXTURES

Air may enter the mixture through the vortex formed during mixing or air contained in the powders will get entrained in the mixture in which it is dispersed. This entrapped air should be removed because it creates many problems. The problems include :

(i) Oxidation of drugs,

(ii) Rancidity of unsaturated oils in the mixture,

(iii) Product may develop grainy texture,

(iv) May cause problems in filling of the formulation,

(v) May form spongy surface on storage.

Versator (Fig. 8.28) is an equipment which consists of a open bowl containing a rotating shaft on which a disc is mounted. The disc rotates in the range of **900 rpm to 6000 rpm**. The material to be deareated is fed at the centre of the spinning disc by a feed tube. The film is formed at the centre and has thickness of few mm. Under high centrifugal force, the mass moves towards periphery causing decrease in film thickness. The turbulent flow is caused in a thin film during its movement towards periphery. The chamber is subjected to vacuum. The vacuum and internal pressures in the turbulent mass combine to effect removal of gaseous constituents. This product is deaerated, defoamed and degassed when it reaches the periphery, where it is collected.

Fig. 8.29 : Versator

***

MANUAL CORRECTIONS

together, to achieve process objectives such as :

2. Laminar Mixing : It is associated with the high viscosity liquids. Under laminar flow conditions, in the vicinity of the agitator blade large velocity gradient exists. In these regions deformation and stretching of the fluid element occurs. It may be visualised that due to shear given to the highly viscous liquid under laminar flow, the laminas or streamlines get converged. The convergence of streamline occurs but volume is same therefore there is decrease in thickness and increase in area of fluid element occurs. This is stretching of fluid. [Fig. 8.1 (a)].

the velocity at this point is sum of vectors in x, y and z directions. In turbulent flow this sum

mixing occurs, especially near the surface. Contoured base is preferred for handling of suspensions.

Fig. 8.2 : Mechanically agitated vessel

Impellers : Impellers are the devices which supply energy for the fluid mixing. The energy imparted gives fluid velocity with three components radial, axial and tangential. The flow pattern of fluid depends on balance between these components. The radial component of the flow acts in a direction perpendicular to the impeller shaft. An axial component is acting parallel to the impeller shaft and tangential component is acting in a tangential direction to the circle of rotation around the impeller shaft. Accordingly, the flow patterns may be axial, radial or tangential. In axial flow the fluid flows along the axis of the impeller to the bottom of the mixing tank. The impeller blades displace the fluid in an axial direction which is then brought upto the top of the tank and drawn down along the axis of the impeller shaft. The radial flow promotes lateral and vertical flow currents. The impellers are categorized depending on the flow pattern they produce. (Fig. 8.3).

Fig. 8.3 : Flow patterns induced by impellers

    (a)   **Propellers :** Propellers are high speed, compact agitators suitable for low viscosity

Off-centre inclined   **Side-entering**

Fig. 8.4 : Propeller type agitator

Flat Blade Turbine   Pitched Blade Turbine   Disk Style Turbine

increased by use of diffuser rings. A diffuser ring is a stationary perforated or slotted ring which surrounds the impeller. The liquid discharged passes through the diffuser ring reducing the swirling and increases the shear forces. The swirling or vortexing occurs with turbines except shrouded turbine, therefore the tanks should be baffled.

Simple Anchor   Stationary blad intermeshing   Gate   Double action gate

pitched, baffles are required for mixing. Due to low axial flow, paddles are not suitable for

Fig. 8.7 : Different types of baffles

angle determines the mixing efficiency of the jet. The jet in a tank positioned is so that jet centreline is at $\frac{1^{rd}}{3}$ the tank diameter from the opposite side.

Stator heads

Fig. 8.9 : Homogenizer - mixer

The homogenizer mixers have a turbine and a stator with a fixed clearance between them (Fig. 8.9). The turbine rotates at a very high speed, due to which pressure differential is created. Material below the homogenizer is drawn to the turbine due to the pressure differential. The material is forced to pass through the small openings on the stator. This causes high hydraulic and mechanical forces and the material is mixed. The stator has different types of openings e.g. very fine openings for emulsification, slots for breaking pellets etc. The ultra-turrax type homogenizer (Fig. 8.10) is used for fine grinding and dispersion of solids or emulsification where low globule size is desired.

(a) Homogenizer : A pressure homogenizer consists of a heavy duty plunger pump at the outlet of which a stainless steel fluid end is connected. The fluid end has a valve seat and a valve with a surrounding ring having a very close clearance (Fig. 8.11). A plunger pump forces the liquid under high pressure and low velocity to the valve seat. The liquid enerts the close clearance between valve and valve seat, where its velocity increases rapidly to around 700 ft/s. This sudden increase in velocity causes cavitation. The cavitation bubbles collapse at the valve, causing it to vibrate. The liquid coming out 'collides with an impact ring. This is the mechanism of homogenization. The output from the homogenizer is at the flow rates of 15 –

mills, therefore, unless suitable cooling system is attached, it cannot be used for thermolabile

its

possible to control flow rates of the material it may be mixed in a mixing chamber (Fig. 8.15). In the mixing chamber, the material remains for sufficient time. The composition of the

Fig. 8.15 : Continuous tank mixer

density and viscosity and plotted against Reynolds number on log-log paper, a 'Power Curve'

In between laminar region and turbulent zone ($10 < Re < 10^4$), a transition region exists

diffusion may occur when the lamina reduces to few molecule thickness. The distributive

Fig. 8.17 : z-blade mixer

(Nauta mixer) (Fig. 8.20 [a]) mixers. The helical screw mixer causes the axial flow of the

three mixing currents (Fig. 8.20 [b]). The mixer screw rotates to lift the material to the top of the cone. This imparts upward spiral motion. The rotating arm guides the whole screw in a circular path along the wall of the conical container, so that the material is also conveyed in a horizontal direction (Fig. 8.20 [c]). The material drops off the screw to the opposite side of the cone, and is lifted up repeatedly (Fig. 8.20 [d]). The resultant action is to impart a mixing effect in three dimensions (Fig. 8.20 [e]). In mixing the pastes, the operation can be made

Lodige mixer (Fig. 8.23), consists of a cylindrical vessel in which the plough shaped

The quality of mixture has been expressed in qualitative and quantitative terms. Following qualitative terms are defined by Danckwerts :

Once suitable mixing index is calculated for the powder mixture, then rate of mixing can be obtain as follows :

Pharmaceutical Engineering　　　　　　　32Mixing

As the tumbler mixer is closed, it is easy to clean and suitable for obtaining high purity

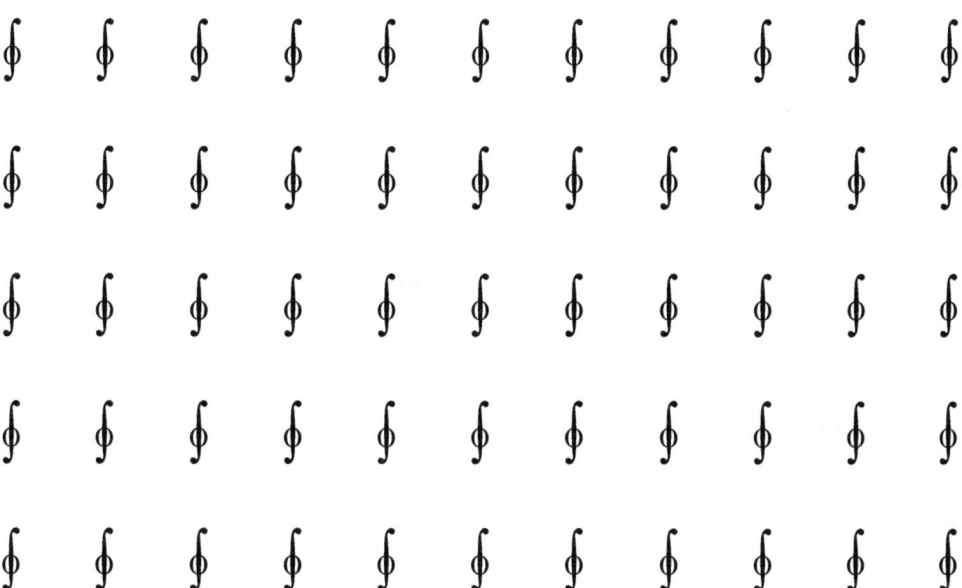

LABELLING

Propeller　　Emulsor head and fine screen　　Slotted head

Right head element　　Left hand element

Mixing arm　　Mixing blade　　Container　　Rotational path of blade edge

Rotational path of blade shaft　　Mixing bowl in lowered position (raised on to mixing arm of massing)

Pivoting arm　　Mixer screw　　Conical mixer vessel　　Discharge pipe

Mixing bowl
(raised position)   Chopper   Three-bladed
mixing shaft

A – Feed Assembly
B – Disc Chamber
C – Scoop Assembly
D – Disc

CH. 8

MANUAL CORRECTIONS

(a) Axial   (b) Radial   (c) Tangential

pitched, baffles are required for mixing. Due to low axial flow, paddles are not suitable for

A pressure homogenizer consists of a heavy duty plunger pump at the outlet of which a stainless steel fluid end is connected. The fluid end has a valve seat and a valve with a surrounding ring having a very close clearance (Fig. 8.11). A plunger pump forces the liquid under high pressure and low velocity to the valve seat. The liquid enerts the close clearance between valve and valve seat, where its velocity increases rapidly to around 700 ft/s. This sudden increase in velocity causes cavitation. The cavitation bubbles collapse at the valve, causing it to vibrate. The liquid coming out 'collides with an impact ring. This is the mechanism of homogenization. The output from the homogenizer is at the flow rates of 15 – 14000 gal/h and pressure 1500 to 10,000 psi. It is useful in the viscosity range of 1 to 2000 cps. The product size of 0.5 to 20 μm is obtained. The capacity of homogenizer and quality of dispersed product can be improved by premixing the fluids and final mixing only be carried out in the homogenizer. Homogenizers are not suitable mixing solids in the liquids because it may cause wear of the fluid end. It is more suitable for low viscosity liquids than high viscosity.

Fig. 8.17 : Z-blade mixer

(a) Homogenizer : Homogenizers are of two types homogenizer mixers which can be considered as modified turbines and pressure homogenizer.

Jet   Cavitation zone   Blade   Flow Flow

Curved vane turbine   Turbine with diffuser ring   Shrouded turbine

Fig. 8.14 : Pipe mixer

EXTRACTION

9.1 INTRODUCTION

Extraction of drugs suggests extraction of active constituent from solid drugs; i.e. solid from solid. This type of extraction is known as 'solid-liquid extraction' or 'leaching'; because solid is extracted with a liquid medium. The 'liquid-liquid extraction' involves the liquid phases, which are completely or partially immiscible. In leaching, the liquid phase used for extraction is termed as 'menstruum or solvent'. The solution containing extracted substance is known as extract or miscella (when oil is extracted). Lixiviation is the term used for solid-liquid extraction where solvent is water. The dissolution of extractive substances out of the disintegrated cells is termed as 'rining'. In 'liquid-liquid extraction' the solute is extracted from the solution. 'Diluent' is a liquid in which solute is present. The liquid used as a extracting agent is known as 'solvent'. In liquid-liquid extraction the phase which remains after separation of extract is known as 'raffinate'. The solid-liquid and liquid-liquid extraction are discussed below :

9.2 SOLID-LIQUID EXTRACTION

In general, the leaching process involves mixing of solid-solvent in a mixer and separation of the two in a suitable separating device such as a separator or thickner. Leaching may be carried out batchwise or continuously.

Different methods by which leaching may be carried out as follows :

(a) Simple Single Contact :

A batch of solid is mixed with sufficient amount of solvent and contacted for sufficient time so as to bring all solute into the solution. The mixture is then allowed to settle and extract is decanted from the residual inert matter.

Certain amount of extract is lost with the residue. 'Factor A' is the ratio of amount of extract decanted to that removed with the inert matter.

$$\text{Factor A} = \frac{\text{Amount of extract decanted}}{\text{Amount of extract lost with inert matter}}$$

Factor A increases as the time of sedimentation is increased. But in practice as the inert material has to be removed in manageable state (where it contains appreciable amount of solution), the factor A is low. Thus single stage contact method suffers from the disadvantage of high losses of solute in residue.

(b) Simple Multiple Contact :

In this method a fresh batch of solvent is contacted with the residue remaining after first extraction. This is repeated several times, each time the concentration of the solution entangled in the residue reduces. Thus solute recovery is improved as compared to simple single contact, but the extract obtained is dilute. Therefore, subsequent recovery of the solute from dilute solution becomes expensive.

(c) Continuous Counter-Current Contact :

Continuous counter current contact is provided in a series of stages (Fig. 9.1). The fresh drug comes in contact with the concentrated solution, whereas almost exhausted drug is contacted with the fresh solvent. Therefore, concentrated extract is removed at one end of the extraction battery, while the exhausted inert material is removed at the other end. The solution entrapped in the inert material is dilute.

Thus, continuous counter current contact overcomes disadvantages of simple single stage and simple multiple contact. The loss of solute in the entrapped solution is less and at the same time extract obtained is concentrated.

Fig. 9.1 : Counters Current Extraction Methods

The counter current contact may be carried out as :
(a) Discontinuous absolute extraction, in which the extraction solvent and drug are moved against each other.
(b) Continuous relative counter current extraction where only on phase, generally the solvent is in motion and the other phase i.e. solid remains stationary.
(c) Absolute counter-current contact involves continual movement of both the extraction solvent and the drug material.

9.2.2 Recovery and Equilibrium Stages Determination :

Triangular diagram is used for determination of recovery of the solute and calculation of number of equilibrium stages required for the given extraction process.

In a triangular diagram Fig. 9.2, there are three components solute, solvent and inert matter.

(a) The apices represent the pure components, (b) mixtures of any two components are represented by point on the sides, (c) mixtures of all the three components are presented by points inside the triangle.

Fig. 9.2 : Triangular Diagram

Each side of a triangle may be scaled in weight % or mole %. Analysis of single contact, simple multiple contact and continuous counter current contact are as follows :

(a) Simple Single Contact : In Fig. 9.3, F represents composition of dry feed and S represents dilute solution or extract. R_1 represents the composition of residue on dry basis and E_1 is the desired concentration of the extract.

Fig. 9.3 : Simple Single Contact

When feed (F) is contacted with solvent (S), the resulting mixture composition will be indicated by point M. Location of point M on the line SF depends on the ratio of feed to solvent.

$$\frac{\text{Weight of extracting solutions S}}{\text{Weight of Feed F}} = \frac{[S]}{[F]} = \frac{MF}{MS}$$

As the mixture finally resolves into extract E_1 and solid residue R_1, point M lies on line E_1R_1 and

$$\frac{[E_1]}{[R_1]} = \frac{MR_1}{ME_1}$$

$$\therefore \quad [E_1] = \frac{MR_1}{E_1 R_1}([F]+[S])$$

But in actual practice the residue is not dry but it is solution entangled in the inert matter represented by point R. Therefore, factor A will be given as follows :

$$\text{Factor A} = \frac{MR}{ME_1}$$

Position of point R depends on the manageability of the underflow :

When residue R is treated further to remove the solvent from it, a dry residue of composition R_2 is obtained. Solute concentration in R_2 is greater than R_1 because there is deposition of solid solute after evaporation of solvent from the entangled solution.

(b) Simple Multiple Contact : Consider that feed having composition F is contacted with solution S_1 and objective is to obtain extract of composition E_3. When the feed is almost exhausted.

Fig. 9.4 : Simple multiple contact

The first stage of contact will be exactly the same as discussed for single stage contact. The residue of first batch R_1 is contacted with fresh solvent S to obtain new extract E_2. (Fig. 9.4.) Similarly, residue R_2 of second stage is subjected to next stage of extraction to obtain extract E_3 and residue R_3. The material balances for these stages will be as follows :

Stage I :

[F] and [S_1] denote feed and solvent quantities respectively.

$$[S_1] = [F] \frac{M_1 F}{M_1 S}$$

$$\text{Wet Residue }[R_1] = \frac{M_1 E_1}{R_1 E_1}([F]+[S_1])$$

$$\text{Extract }[E_1] = \frac{R_1 M_1}{E_1 R_1}([F]+[S_1])$$

Stage II :

$[S_2]$, $[R_2]$ and $[E_2]$ denote quantities of solvent, wet residue and extract respectively.

$$[S_2] = [R_1]\frac{M_2 S}{M_2 R_1}$$

$$[R_2] = \frac{M_2 E_2}{R_2 E_2}([R_1] + [S_2])$$

$$[E_2] = \frac{R_2 M_2}{E_2 R_2}([R_1] + [S_2])$$

Stage III :

$[S_3]$, $[R_3]$ and $[E_3]$ are quantities of solvent, wet residues and extract respectively

$$[S_3] = [R_2]\frac{M_3 S_3}{R_2 M_3}$$

$$[R_3] = \frac{M_3 E_3}{R_3 E_3}([R_2] + [E_3])$$

$$[E_3] = \frac{R_3 M_3}{R_3 E_3}([R_2] + [S_3])$$

Finally after recovery of all the solvent from the wet residue, the dry residue of composition R_3' is obtained.

$$\left[R_3'\right] = [R_3]\frac{SR_3}{R'R_3}$$

Thus from the simple multiple contacts the end product is a dry residue and three extracts of different strengths. This technique is advantageous when several solutions of different strengths are desired.

(c) Continuous Counter Current Contact : In this system residue of the previous stage is contacted with the extract from the next stage.

Fig. 9.5 : Continuous Counter-Current Extracation

As shown in Fig. 9.5, solvent and feed enter at the opposite end. At each stage extract becomes concentrated with respect to solute and comes in contact with the solids containing more amount of solute. The material balance at each stage will be as follows :

Stage I : $\qquad [S] + [R_2] = [R_1] + [E_1]$

Stage II : $\quad [E_1] + [R_3] = [R_2] + [E_2]$

Stage III : $\quad [E_2] + [F] = [R_3] + [E_3]$

If we calculate difference between the entering and leaving stream at any stage and term it as Net Rightward Flow (NRF) then it can be as follows :

Stage I : $\quad [S] - [R_1] = [E_1] - [R_2]$

Stage II : $\quad [E_1] - [R_2] = [E_2] - [R_3]$

Stage III : $\quad [E_2] - [R_3] = [E_3] - [F]$

Thus throughout the extraction battery net rightward flow is constant. NRF is represented by a point which lies in the plane of a triangular diagram. It lies along the straight line through the terminal conditions E_3F and SR_1. Thus, the point obtained by the intersection of E_3F and SR_1 is termed as 'Operating Focus'. (Fig. 9.6).

Fig. 9.6 : Continuous counter-current contact

The material balance shows that E_1 and R_2 lie on the straight line passing through operating focus denoted by 'O'. Similarly, if Factor A mass of solvent per unit residue is same in all the cells in the battery then 'A Line' can be obtained which is parallel to the base line. Points R_1, R_2 and R_3 lie on the A line.

Construct triangular diagram as follows :

1. On a triangle locate points E_1, E_2, E_3, F and R_1.
2. Draw lines SR_1 and E_3F. The lines intersect at operating focus 'O'.
3. Draw line E_1O, which intersects 'A' line at R_2.
4. Draw lines SR_2 and E_1R_1; which intersect each other at point M_1 representing the composition of the mixture in Stage I.
5. Similarly proceed upto E_3.

Solid-Liquid Extraction Equipments :

9.2.3.1 Simple Single Stage Contact

(a) Mixers

(b) Vortical Extractor

(c) Ultrasound Extractor

(d) Electrical Discharge Extractor

9.2.3.2 Counter Current Contact

(A) Continuous Relative Extractors

    (a) Percolation Battery

    (b) Rotocel Extractor

    (c) Basket Extractor

(B) Continuous Absolute Extractors

    (a) Screw Extractor

    (b) Hilderbrandt Extractor

    (c) Pulsation Column Extractor

9.2.3.3 Extraction Centrifuges

9.2.3.1 Simple Single Stage Contact

(a) Mixers : For simple single contact various mixers with or without stirrers are used. The examples of mixers without stirrers include tumbler mixers, cube mixers. The mixers with stirrers are Ploughshare mixer, Planetary mixer, Intensive mixer.

(b) Vortical Extractor : In vortical or turbo extractor the drug to be extracted is stirred in the solvent with a high-speed mixer or homogenizer. The shredding and shearing forces break the material to finer size. In the plant materials the cells disintegrate and the active constituents are washed out from the destroyed cells. Therefore equilibrium is achieved very fast. The energy supplied by the stirrer/homogenizer and size reduction causes increase in temperature during extraction. This may cause decomposition of the thermolabile constituents. Therefore suitable cooling arrangement must be provided. Particle size reduction during extraction make separation of the residue difficult. Separation of the residue is generally carried out by filtration, sedimentation or centrifugation. The yields obtained by turbo extraction are higher than the that obtained by the simple mixers. It has been used for the extraction of valerian roots, cinchona bark and belladonna leaves. Combination of vertical extractors may be used for batch or continuous operations.

(c) Ultrasound Extractor : Ultrasound extraction uses the energy of ultrasound for accelerating the rate of extraction. Ultrasound i.e. frequencies above 20,000 Hz., may be produced with :

    (i) Magnetostrictive ultrasonic transmitters, or

    (ii) Piezoelectric ultrasonic transmitters.

Magnetostrictive ultrasonic transmitters are based on the change in length undergone by the ferromagnetic substances due to magnetization. Generally nickel steel rods are used which begin to vibrate in a magnetic field produced by high frequency alternating current. The amplitude is maximum when frequency of the alternating current is the same as a natural frequency of the vibrating rod.

Piezoelectric ultrasonic transmitters are based on the reciprocal piezoelectric effect produced when a quartz crystal undergoes compression or expansion (change in length) when electric current is applied. The crystal begins to vibrate when placed between the condenser plates and current is applied. The frequency is equal to the frequency of the applied current and amplitude is greatest when frequency of vibration is equal to the natural frequency of the quartz.

Ultrasound causes fast extraction due to :

(a) Increase in the permeability of the cell wall,

(b) Spontaneous formation of bubbles in the liquid below its boiling point i.e. cavitation effect, due to dynamic stressing and

(c) Increase in the mechanical stressing i.e. internal friction of the cells.

Ultrasound shortens the extraction time to 5–15 min. from several hours in conventional simple contact techniques. The extraction efficiency depends on the frequency of ultrasound, capacity of apparatus and length of time.

Application of ultrasound has shown to cause oxidation various drugs. It is due to the formation of hydrogen peroxide produced by radical decomposition of water. Its application on large scale is also limited due to the high cost.

(d) Electrical Discharge Extractor : In this technique cavitation phenomenon is achieved by the electric discharge. The equipment (Fig.9.7) consists of an electric source, capacitor, and a sparkgap and two electrodes in the extraction vessel. The electric source charges the capacitor to the threshold tension where the capacitor discharges through the spark gap and electrodes. The high frequency discharge causes cavitation effect. This has been used for the extraction of Rauwolfia and Belladonna.

Fig. 9.7 : Electrical Discharge Extractor

9.2.3.2 Counter Current Contact

(A) Continuous Relative Extractors

(a) **Percolation Battery :** In this method, the fresh solvent is fed to the tank containing the solid that are nearly exhausted; it flows through several tanks in series and finally strong solution or miscella is withdrawn from the tank that has been freshly charged. The material in any one tank is stationary until it is completely extracted. Such arrangement of series of tanks containing solids at various stages of extraction is termed as extraction battery and process is Shanks process.

The piping connection of the battery may be so arranged that fresh solvent can be fed to any tank and concentrated miscella can be withdrawn from any tank. In the battery it is possible to charge or discharge one tank at a time. The remainder of the battery advances in strict counter-current way. Robert diffusion battery is a percolator battery suitable for extraction of crude vegetable drugs (Fig. 9.8). As the size of the drug particles is considerably large, extraction mainly takes place by diffusion and dissolution of active constituents from the destroyed cells is negligible. In Robert battery, heaters are provided. The two main heaters are required, one handles solvent and the other handles solution. As shown in Fig. 9.8 consider that first cell is nearly exhausted and cell 3 contains fresh feed. Drug in cell 3 contains air space, therefore solution coming to cell 3 is double heated and passes in the upward direction thereby removing entrapped air. The operation is continued till the material in cell 1 is completely exhausted.

Fig. 9.8 : Robert Diffusion Battery

Percolators have many disadvantages especially at industrial scaler. It is uneconomical to soak and well the material before it is put in the percolator. A considerable increase in pressure in the percolator is expected with strongly swelling plant drug materials, especially those containing a large amount of mucilage. Therefore percolation battery cannot be used for materials containing mucilages. Percolators frequently exhibit 'nest formation', i.e. the formation of dry areas within the cake of drug plant material which are not reached by the solvent. The drug material in the nest is not extracted. Charging and emptying of the percolators is laborious. Conical percolators widening at the base can be emptied easily than the cylindrical percolators.

(b) Rotocel Extractor : Rotocel or Carousel extractor (Fig. 9.9) consists of a carousel fitted in a vapour-tight housing. The carousel divides the cylinder into number of chambers. The chambers have perforated bottom. The sieve plate at the bottom of the chamber is fitted with wires of trapezium shaped cross-section which widens downwards. The sieve slits run concentrically to the axis of rotation. The carousel rotates clock-wise. The first chamber comes at the feed point where it is fed with the fresh drug. Fresh solvent is normally introduced in the last chamber. The movement of the material takes place parallel to the axis of the sieve thus causes minimum sliding friction. During its movement in the cylinder the material in the cell is treated with solution in various stages of concentration. After extraction is completed, the cell passes to the discharge point where hinged bottom drops and discharges the exhausted material. The separating walls of the chambers become more widely spaced apart downwards, so that material can fall out easily.

Fig. 9.9 : Rotocel Extractor

Stationary compartments are present below rotating carousel (Fig. 9.10), these are liquid reservoir compartments. Pumps are used which take out the solvent from liquid reservoir compartment at one position and spray it onto the solids in the previous compartment. As shown in Fig. 9.10, the liquid reservoir compartment 7 is large to provide ample time for drainage of the material before discharge. The final extract is not drawn from the first compartment because it is turbid. The turbid extract of compartment 1 is filtered through the bed of solids in the second compartment and final concentrated extract is collected from second compartment.

Fig. 9.10 : Rotocel Extractor Stationary Compartment

The feed for the Rotocel extractor should not contain more than 5 – 10% of the particles having size less than 5 mm. This is important for frictionless extraction with suitable percolation rates. Therefore, generally the drug is comminuted in cutter mill or subjected to rolling process e.g. oil seeds.

Rotocel extractor is used for extraction of rauwolfia roots, fennel, cinchona bark, ergot, squill, valerian roots etc.

(c) Basket Extractor/Bollman Extractor : Basket extractor consists of a chamber with a contoured base, in which the baskets with perforated bottom are rotating with a chain loaded on sprocket wheels (Fig. 9.11). The feed is introduced in the bucket which moves downwards, at the end of the travel the bucket containing exhausted material is sprayed with fresh solvent. The solution collected at the bottom tank of the ascending portion of the chain is termed as 'half miscella'. This half miscella, a medium concentrated solution is pumped to the top and sprayed on the fresh material. The exhausted material is removed at the top. The solid liquid contact is co-current during the descending movement of the basket and counter-current during ascending movement.

Fig. 9.11 : Basket Extractor

(B) Continuous Absolute Extractors

  (a) **Screw Extractor :** In screw or helical extractor the drug material and the solvent are kept in continual motion in directions opposite to each other (Fig. 9.12). The extractor is a cylinder with screw conveyor, the sections of the cylinder can be heated or cooled. The feed is fed by the hopper and is conveyed by the screw. The screw conveying also causes mixing and partial compaction of the material towards the discharge end of the cylinder. The solvent flows from the discharge end against the drug material. Various factors affecting working of screw extractor include angle of inclination of cylinder, temperature of solvent, speed of rotation of the screw, feed charge and rise in pressure inside the cylinder.

Fig. 9.12 : Screw Extractor

Fig. 9.13 : Silver Continuous Diffusion Battery

In case of drug materials containing large amounts of mucilage, presence of large quantities of water swelling causes build-up of pressure. This hinders straight forward movement of the drug material. Mucilaginous material also have lubricating effect which causes slipping of the screw, thus stopping the extraction. Therefore, screw conveyor is not suitable for extraction of materials containing high proportions of mucilage. It is best suitable for hard barks and seeds. It is used for extraction of liquorice root, ginger and wild cherry bark.

Silver continuous diffusion battery (Fig. 9.13) is based on similar principle where number of screw / helical extractors (upto 20 – 24) are connected in series. Solids enter in the first unit and solvent enter the last unit. But in the extractor the flow of the solid and liquid is co-current.

(b) Hilderbrandt Extractor : Hilderbrandt Extractor (Fig. 9.14) consists of U-tube in which helical screws are fitted. The helix surface is perforated so that counter current flow is maintained. The screws are designed such that compaction of the solids occur during their passage through the unit. But in this extractor there is some solvent loss and feed loss. It is best suited for light and permeable materials.

Fig. 9.14 : Hilderbrandt Extractor

(c) Pulsation Column Extractor : In pulsation column extractor, the solid material is fed at the top of the column, through a hopper (Fig. 9.13) solvent is introduced at other end and flows in the upward direction. Plates and baffles in the column ensure intensive mixing of solid and liquid. The pulsations are induced in the liquid by rhythmic compression and expansion of the gas reservoir in the pulsation apparatus. The solid particles reaching the bottom of a pulsation column are conveyed by circulation pump to the solid-liquid separator. The extract is drawn off by the extract pump at the upper end.

The variables are particle size, contact time, density difference of the phases, height of column, pulsation, temperature etc. It can be used for 10 kg to several tons per hour output. It is suitable for extraction of leaves, roots, barks and seeds.

Fig. 9.15 : Pulsation Column Extractor

9.2.3.3 Extraction Centrifuges

For extraction of active constituents from the fine drug materials, a combination of equipments is used. It includes an apparatus for wet comminution of the material and a centrifuge (Fig. 9.16). Therefore, generally this combination of equipment is considered as extraction centrifuge. The wet comminution equipment produces the particles in the range of 5 – 50 µm. The centrifuges are discussed in details in section 6.5. The mills based on rotor-stator principle may be used for wet commination.

Fig. 9.16 : Centrifuge Extraction Plant

9.3 LIQUID–LIQUID EXTRACTION

Liquid-liquid extraction is a separation process in which separation is achieved on the basis of difference in affinity of the solute towards two liquids. It is a choice in separation technique where distillation is ineffective, e.g. when the two components have very low vapour pressure difference or component gets affected by high temperature. For example fast separation of penicillin from the fermentation broth with solvent butyl acetate is achieved by lowering pH to get favourable partition coefficient. In case of acetic acid dilute solutions, extraction of acetic acid is possible by distillation but extraction step reduces the amount of water to be distilled. Liquid-liquid extraction has disadvantage that the solvent used for extraction is to be removed again to obtain pure solute, which makes the process expensive and difficult. Therefore, generally distillation is the first choice of separation process between the two.

9.3.1 Principle

In liquid-liquid extraction the solute in solution is extracted with the use of another solvent which is immiscible / partially immiscible with the solvent in the solution. The solute diffuses from solution to the extracting solvent and equilibrium is achieved. The equillibrium or fashion in which the solute distributes itself between the two solvents, is indicated by the ratio of the concentration and is termed as distribution or partition coefficient of solute between two solvents. Distribution is termed ideal when the distribution coefficient is independent of the actual concentrations.

The solvent used for extraction may be completely miscible or partially miscible with the other solvent. The two extraction systems resulting from these are Type I system and Type II system. For example for extraction of acetone from water (diluent) using solvent methyl isobutyl ketone (MIK), the system is type I i.e. Acetone is completely miscible with diluent as well as solvent but diluent and solvent are completely immiscible with one another. In Type II system solvent is partially miscible with both other components i.e. solute and diluent e.g. extraction of n-heptane (solute) from methylcyclohexane (MCH) using aniline as a solvent. Aniline is only partially miscible with the other two components. The phase diagram for the two systems are shown in Fig. 9.17 (a) and Fig. (b)

As shown in Fig. 9.17 (a), when solvent MIK is added to a mixture of acetone and water, the composition of the resulting mixture lies on a straight line between the point for pure solvent and the point for the original binary mixture. When sufficient solvent is added such that the overall composition falls under the dome-shaped curve, the mixture separates into two phases. The points representing the phase compositions can be joined by straight tie lines. The tie line passes through the overall mixture composition (M) which separates into two phases (C) and (D). In the Fig. 9.17 (a), line ACE shows the compositions of MIK layer i.e. extract, and line BDE shows composition of water layer i.e. raffinate. As the proportion of solute i.e. acetone in the mixture increases, the compositions of the extract and raffinate layer approach each other and become equal at point E called 'plait point'.

(a) Type I System   (b) Type II System
Fig. 9.17 : Systems in Liquid-Liquid Extraction

The tie lines sloping upto the left indicate that the extract phase is richer in solute than the raffinate phase i.e. most of the acetone can be extracted using small amount of solvent. Therefore, a concentrated extract is obtained. The horizontal or rightward sloping tie lines indicate that large amount of solvent is required for extraction i.e. extract obtained will be dilute.

The number of ideal stages required for counterflow extraction may be obtained using triangular diagram as in case of leaching. A modified McCabe-Thiele method can also be applied.

9.3.2 Classification

Equipment for liquid-liquid extraction are divided into two classes stagewise extractors and differential extractors. The classification is shown in Fig. 9.18.

Fig. 9.18 : Classification of Liquid-Liquid Extractors

Following are the equipment commonly used for liquid-liquid extraction :

1. Mixer settler : A mixer settler is the simplest stagewise contactor, in which dispersion takes place in some form of vessel, using agitators, pump-mix or other devices. The settlers range from simple settling tanks, 2 to 3 times the size of the mixing vessel to more complex type containing packing, baffling or other devices to promote coalescence. Where rapid settling is essential, a hydrocyclone has been proposed which combines both the separation of phases and mass transfer. The basic mixer settler is shown diagramatically in Fig. 9.19.

Fig. 9.19 : Mixer Settler Design

The advantages of mixer settlers are as follows :

(a) Good contacting of phases.

(b) It can handle liquids over wide range of flow ratio with recycle.

(c) It has low headroom and low maintenance cost.

(d) It's efficiency is high.

Disadvantages :

(a) It has high liquid hold-up.

(b) Solvent requirements are large.

(c) Power cost is high.

(d) Large floor space requirement.

(b) In-line Static mixers : Kenic mixer is discussed in details in Chapter 8 (Sec.8.2.2).

2. Non-Agitated Columns : Non agitated columns carry out dispersion and coalescence of the phases on the basis of the density difference between them. Examples of this type of columns are spray column, packed column and tray column (Fig. 9.20)

In spray column the dispersed phase is sprayed either up or down the column. The size of the droplets injected into the column significantly affect the mass transfer. Smaller is the droplet size more is the mass transfer. The column has a main disadvantage that backmixing in the continuous phase occurs significantly. Therefore, the efficiency of the spray column is very low. It generally has only one or two theoretical plates.

Fig. 9.20 : Non-Agitated Columns

The backmixing in spray column is reduced by introduction of packings. In packed column various types of packings are used which include rings, saddles, meshes etc. The dispersed phase is maintained by the flow through the packing as droplets. The packings should be preferentially wetted by the continuous phase. Packed columns are easy to construct and inexpensive. Packings cause significant increase in the interfacial area, reduce backmixing thereby increase column efficiency.

A sieve-plate column also employs differences in gravity to interdisperse phases and produce counter current flow. Depending upon whether the continuous phase is light or heavy, the dispersed phase travels up or down the column, coalescing under or above the perforated plates. This continues until sufficient hydraulic head has been builtup to force this phase through the perforated plate into the continuous phase.

Therefore, overall advantages and disadvantages of the non-agitated columns can be summarised as below :

Advantages :

Simple construction, low initial as well as operating cost.

Disadvantages :

1. The output of the column is low especially when density difference is low.
2. These columns cannot handle wide flow ratio.
3. In general efficiency is low.
4. Head room is high.

3. Agitated Columns

Generally mechanical agitation is provided in the column e.g. Schibel, Mixco, reciprocating plates column and rotating disc contractor. But pulsation may also be used for agitation as in sieve-plate pulse column. Agitated columns cannot handle high flow ratio and emulsifying systems.

In Sieve-Plate Pulse Column energy in the form of pulse is supplied to the column to promote dispersion and coalescence. The dispersed phase will coalesce above or below the sieve plates and will be prevented by surface tension from flowing through the perforations until the pulse cycle forces the phase through the perforations to disperse it into the continuous phase. The continuous phase is drawn through the plate during the opposite pulse cycle. For most efficient operation the plate should be preferentially wetted by the continuous phase. By application of energy in the form pulse both turbulence and interfacial area are increased. This causes increase in the efficiency of mass transfer.

In reciprocating plate column, agitation is provided by the plate moving through the solution. The hole free area on a reciprocating plate is 50 – 75%. The two designs of the plate column are shown in Fig. 9.21. In Landau plates, the plate does not extend over the entire area of column shell. The plates are arranged in such a way that the continuous phase flow is in a cross-flow pattern. The plates are divided into two sets, with each plate of each set mounted alternatively on two shafts. The two shafts are driven in opposite directions. The plates with downcomers like Landau plates are superior to the plates with only small holes e.g. Karr plates.

Fig. 9.21 : Reciprocating Plates

Scheibel Column (Fig. 9.22) consists of ring-shaped baffles supported immediately above and below the impeller, in addition to the compartment baffles attached to the column shell. The internal baffling provides for more uniform mixing of the phases and optimum mass transfer. Settling occurs within the column as well as at the ends.

Fig. 9.22 : Schiebel Extractor

The Mixco column (Fig. 9.23) consists of an outer shell in which horizontal stage separation are constructed to form the desired number of processing stages each equivalent to a separate mixing operation. For counter current extraction, heavy and light phases are introduced at the top and bottom of the column respectively. A single drive with turbines at each stage provides the necessary turbulence.

Fig. 9.23 : Mixco-Extractor

Rotating disc contractor (Fig. 9.24), consists of a number of compartments formed by a series of stator rings. Each compartment contains a rotating disc in a central position supported by a common rotating shaft. Calming grids are placed at the ends of the top and bottom compartments, which separate the contacting zone from the settling zones. By suitable control of the interface level, the light phase and the heavy phase can each be made dispersed or continuous.

Fig. 9.24 : Rotating Disc Contactor

Pulsed packed column (Fig. 9.25), consists of a shell filled with a suitable packing material such as Raschig ring supported on a grid. The two liquid phase are fed into the column. The dispersed phase is dispersed in the form of droplets with the pulsating action. For proper function of the extractor, wetting of the packing by the dispersed phase must be prevented. The size of the droplets of the dispersed phase depend on the pulsating energy supplied.

Fig. 9.25 : Pulsed Packed Column

4. Centrifugal Extractors :

Centrifugal extractors utilize the centrifugal force to increase the specific gravity difference between the two liquids. Therefore the phase disengagement in enhanced.

Advantages :
1. These can handle phases with low density difference.
2. Liquid holdup volume is low.
3. Liquid holdup time is very short.
4. Space requirement is low.
5. The solvent inventory is low.
6. These can operate over a wide range of phase ratios and viscosities.

Disadvantages :
1. Initial cost, maintenance and operating cost is high.
2. Number of stages are limited per unit.

Tubular and bowl centrifuges are dealt in details in chapter 6. (Section 6.5.3).

Podbielniak extractor (Fig. 9.26), consists of a series of concentric, perforated bands. Counter current contact is produced as the liquid passes through the perforations. The liquid flow in and out occurs through the seals at the end of the shaft. The central rotating core has a number of cylindrical perforated plates. Heavy liquid flows from the centre outward, while the light phase flows from the outside towards the centre. Mass transfer occurs when both phases flows through the perforated plates. The rotational speed of the extractor is several thousand rpm. The liquid holdup volumes is only 0.7 to 7.5 litres. The flow capacities are between 3-19 lit./min. It has generally 10-12 theoretical plates. The contact time is as low as 10 sec.

Fig. 9.26 : Podbielniak Extractor

9.4 OTHER PHARMACEUTICALLY IMPORTANT EXTRACTIONS
9.4.1 Extraction with Supercritical Gases

Principle : Ideal gases obey relation

$$pV = nRT$$

where,
- P = Pressure in bars
- V = Volume in m^3
- n = Molar number of gas
- T = Absolute temperature in $°K$, and
- R = Gas constant (J/K mol)

Therefore, pV-p isotherms i.e. plots of pV versus p are lines parallel to the X-axis (Fig.9.27).

Fig. 9.27 : pV-p isotherms

Carbon dioxide does not obey equation, and pV-p isotherms at various temperature are not linear (Fig. 9.28). Ideal gas behaviour occurs when the number of gas molecules is low and their velocity is high. Therefore, as the temperature falls or pressure increases the gas behaviour changes from ideal to real and conversely gas behaviour is ideal at high temperature and low pressures. e.g. CO_2 behaves as a ideal gas above temperature 555 °C and low pressures. At temperature below this and high pressures behaviour tends to be real Isotherm is minimum below this temperature which decreases further with the temperature (Fig. 9.28).

Fig. 9.28 : pV-p isotherms of Carbon Dioxide

This is due to the increase in forces of attraction with temperature. Increase in pressure may cause molecules to come further closer and randomness in the motion is reduced. The curve of the isotherm is determined by the interaction of the forces of attraction and repulsion.

van der Waal equation is applicable to real gases,

$$\left(p + \frac{a}{V^2}\right)(V - b) = RT$$

where, $\frac{a}{V^2}$ is called as internal or cohesion pressure which is added to the external pressure and b is covolume i.e. the smallest volume to which a gas can be compressed.

The phase diagram (p Vs T) of a pure substance is shown in Fig. 9.29. The phase diagram shows sublimation curve, melting pressure curve and vapour pressure curve. The three curves intersect at triple point T_r, where all the three phases coexist. The vapour pressure curve which separates liquid and gas starts at triple point and ends at the critical point K_p. As temperature and pressure move towards critical point the difference in the densities of liquid and gaseous phase decreases reaching to the same density at critical point (Table 9.1).

Fig. 9.29 : Phase Diagram

Table 9.1 : Density of Carbon dioxide

T (°C)	P (bar)	Density of liquid (kg/m^3)	Density of gas (kg/m^3)
0	34.817	928.5	96.26
5	39.657	898.2	113.78
10	44.988	864.2	134.59
15	50.850	825.1	160.50
20	57.289	777.7	193.90
25	64.356	713.8	242.4
30	72.111	629.9	312.5
31.04	73.834	468.0	468.0

Thus only one phase exists above critical point termed as Supercritical fluid or supercritical phase shown by shaded region. For carbon dioxide, temperature of critical point is 31.04 °C and pressure P_c at critical point is 73.83 bar. Density at critical point is 468 kg/m^3. Above critical point density of fluid increases further. Therefore, physical properties of the gas vary significantly above the critical point. These gases attain the density of liquid at around 50 - 300 atm. Its density and dielectric constant are altered with temperature and pressure in this range.

Due to these changes in the physical properties carbon dioxide can dissolve many substances in the super critical phase. Apart from carbon dioxide other gases can also be considered which are given in Table. 9.2.

Table 9.2 : Gases suitable for 'Supercritical' extraction

Gas	T_c (°C)	P_c (bar)

Nitrogen	− 147.00	33.934
Methane	− 82.49	46.407
Carbon dioxide	31.00	73.836
Ethane	32.25	48.839
Ethylene	9.21	50.313
Nitrous oxide	36.45	72.549
Sulphur dioxide	157.50	79.841
Propane	96.85	42.557
Propylene	91.60	46.103
Ammonia	132.40	112.998

The extraction with supercritical gases can be carried out at low temperature. Therefore, gases carried out at low temperatures. Therefore, gases with low critical temperature are suitable for extraction. Fig. 9.30 indicate the binary mixture of a volatile extraction solvent and a non-volatile substance to be extracted. Extraction can be carried out outside the first order critical curve where one phase exist i.e. both components are in critical stage or in two phase region inside this curve.

Fig. 9.30 : Pressure–Temperature Diagram for Binary Mixture

Equipment :

As shown in Fig. 9.31, the extraction agent passes through heat exchanger and a filter. It's pressure is raised by a pump. It is then loaded to a vessel containing the drug material. The loaded supercritical gas under pressure leaves the vessel under pressure and then passes to the separating vessel through a valve. The extract is removed from the bottom of the separating vessel and gas under pressure is recycled to extraction vessel through the pump.

Fig. 9.31 : Super Fluid Extraction Equipment

Advantages of Super critical extraction :

1. Processing is carried out at low temperature, therefore suitable for thermolabile materials.
2. It has very high selectivity.
3. The extract is completely free from the solvent.
4. The extracting agents are relatively cheap.

Applications :

Supercritical fluid extraction has been used in the following areas :

1. Preparation of coal tars.
2. Processing of edible oils and fats and separation of fatty acids and triglycerides.
3. Extraction of above constituents from coffee.
4. It is used in the analysis of active constituents from various natural sources (Table 9.3).

Table 9.3 : Drug constituents extracted

Drug	Main constituents found bin extract	Molecular weight	Extractable at (bar)
Caraway seeds	Limonene	136	70
	Carvone	160	70
	Triglycerides	> 600	90

Peppermint leaves	Menthol	158	70
	Menthone	156	70
Coffee	Caffeine	194	80
	Triglycerides	> 600	90
Cannabis	Cannabidiol	314	85
	Cannabinol	310	90
	Tetrahydrocannabinol	315	90
Sesame seeds	Sesamine	354	85
	Triglycerides	> 600	90

2. Enfleurage :

Volatile oils from the natural drug sources can be separated by steam distillation, enfleurage and rarely by expression. Steam distillation is discussed in details in Chapter 13 (Section 13.8). Enfleurage is a process of extraction, in which volatile oils are extracted using fats and fatty oils. The volatile oil is absorbed, dissolved or bound to the fats and fatty oils.

There are two types of enfleurage process.

(a) Enfleurage à froid or cold flower extraction

In this process purified pork fat and beef tallow are used as extraction agent. The mixture of these two in different proportions are used because pure pork fat is too soft and pure, beef tallow is too hard. The mixtures in the ratio of 1 : 1 for high temperature and one part beef tallow and two part pork fat for low temperature conditions.

The mixture of fats is applied to the both sides of the glass plates; the material to be extracted is spread over the fatty material. Surface area is increased by making furrows. The glass plates are placed in wooden racks and stated one above the other (~ 30 – 40) with layers of material to be extracted above and below. After 24 – 72 hrs. the material is replaced by fresh material. This is continued several times and fats become concentrated with respect to the volatile oil. The fats enriched with volatile oil is known as 'pomade'. The material to be extracted are generally flowers. The ratio of weight of flowers to weight of fat mixture is called 'flower number' e.g. Pomade no. 20 means pomade obtained by treatment with 20 times flowers. Purity of fats affects the quality of the extract.

(b) Enfleurage à Chaud or Hot flower extraction

In this process molten fats and oils are used. The oils like olive oil, paraffin oil or molten paraffin wax may be used. The extraction is carried out at 50 - 70 °C. The material and oil is contacted 5 - 10 times. But this is less preferred than cold method because chances of degradation of volatile oil are higher.

The volatile oil is further extracted from pomades using solvents like ethanol, propanol or butanol.

***

CRYSTALLIZATION

10.1 INTRODUCTION

A crystal may be defined as a homogenous particle of solid which is formed by solidification under favourable conditions, of a chemical element or a compound, whose boundary surfaces are planes symmetrically arranged at definite angles to one another in a definite geometric form. In other words, a *crystal* is one in which the internal atomic or molecular arrangement is regular and periodic in three dimensions over intervals which are large compared with the unit of periodicity. The smallest arrangement of atoms and molecules which repeats regularly and is a true representation of crystal structure is known as *'unit cell'*.

Crystal lattice is defined as a three dimensional network of imaginary lines connecting the atoms. The distance between the centre of two atoms is called as the *length of unit cell* and angle between the edges of a unit cell is called as *lattice angle*. A unit cell is shown in Fig. 10.1.

Fig. 10.1 : Crystal lattice and unit cell

Crystallization is a complex unit operation widely used in the industry for the production of pure solid substances. Most of the drugs are obtained in their crystalline form. Recent advances in crystallization technology have made it possible to use it as a particle design technique to change the micromeritic properties, compressibility and wettability of pharma– ceutical substances. As a separation technique, crystallisation is a comparatively inexpensive process ; though it involves cooling and cooling energy is costlier than heating energy. For example, in desalination of sea water, crystallization requires only $1/7^{th}$ quantity of energy as compared to distillation.

Crystallization differs from precipitation which is generally referred as fast crystallization. Precipitates are insoluble substances produced by a chemical reaction, therefore, it is an irreversible process. But the products of crystallization can be redissolved if the original conditions of temperature and solution concentrations are restored. Secondly, precipitation is initiated at very high supersaturation which results in fast nucleation and thereby large number of very fine particles may be generated. But crystallization and preci-pitation both involve supersaturation, nucleation and growth of the particles.

10.2 CRYSTAL FORM

In crystal there is repetitive arrangement of constituent atoms in a three–dimensional network. There are only finite number of symmetrical arrangements possible for a crystal lattice, and these may be termed as crystal forms. It is described by the relationship among the crystal axes and angles between them. The various types of crystal forms are given in
table 10.1 and shown in Fig. 10.2. But in these crystal forms the ratio between the lengths of the axes existing in a given crystal must be constant. The ability of a compound to exist in different crystal form is known as polymorphism. Different polymorphs have shown significant differences in their properties such as melting point, solubility rate, compressibility etc. For example, paracetamol shows two polymorphs monoclinic and orthorhombic. The monoclinic form is stable and commercially used is not directly compressible, whereas orthorhombic form is directly compressible.

Fig. 10.2

Table 10.1 : Different forms of crystal

System	Description
Cubic	Three axis of identical length intersect at right angles. i.e. $a = b = c$, $\alpha = \beta = \gamma = 90°$
Hexagonal	Four axis lie in a horizontal plane, and they are inclined to one another at $120°$. The fourth axis, c, is different in length from the others, and it is perpendicular to the plane formed by the other three. ($a = b \neq c$, $\alpha = \beta = 120$, $\gamma = 120°$)
Tetragonal	Three axes intersect at right angles. The third axis, c, is different in length with respect to a and b ($a = b \neq c$, $\alpha = \beta = \gamma = 90°$)
Orthorhombic	Three axes of different lengths intersect at right angles. The choice of the vertical c axis is arbitrary. ($a \neq b \neq c$, $\alpha = \beta = \gamma = 90°$)
Monoclinic	Three axes of unequal length intersect such that a and c lie at an oblique angle, and the b axis is perpendicular to the plane formed by the other two. $a \neq b \neq c$, $\alpha = \gamma = 90°$, $\neq \beta$.
Triclinic	Three axes of unequal length intersect at three oblique angles. $a \neq b \neq c$, $\alpha \neq \beta \neq \gamma \neq 90°$.

10.3 CRYSTAL HABIT

Crystal is a polyhedral solid with number of planar faces. The arrangement of these faces is termed as habit. The crystal faces are identified by Miller indices. Depending on the arrangement of faces different crystal habits are as given in table 10.2 and shown in Fig. 10.3. The crystal habit of compound may change due to changes in rate of deposition, shielding of certain faces, presence of impurities in mother liquor.

Table 10.2 : Different Crystal Habits

Descriptor	Description
Avicular	Needlelike particle having a similar width and thickness. If the crystals are very thin, the term *fibrous* is used.
Columnar	Rodlike particle, having a width and thickness exceeding that a needle-type particle. The term *prismatic* may also be used.
Blade	Long, thin, and flat particle, which can also be referred to as being *lath-shaped*.
Plate	Flat particles of similar length and width. These may also be denoted as being *lamellar* or *micaceous*.
Tabular	Also flat particles of similar length and width, but possessing greater thickness than flakes.
Equant	Particles of similar length, width and thickness.

Plate   Tabular

Equant   Columnar

Blade

Avicular

Fig. 10.3 : Different crystal habits

We will discuss the crystallization phenomena as per the steps involved :

(A) Supersaturation

(B) Nucleation and

(C) Crystal growth.

10.4 SUPERSATURATION

When a solid is brought in contact with the solvent, the attractive forces of the liquid tend to break apart the surface of the solid and disperse its ions or molecules into the liquid in the form of discrete mobile units. This process is known as *solution*. The extent to which the solute dissolves is defined as its solubility. The *solubility* is the term to denote equilibrium - limit value of solution concentration, at which point the solution becomes saturated. A saturated solution is one in which the solid is in equilibrium with its solution at a given temperature. It is a step of thermodynamic equilibrium at a specified temperature.

If we analyse the solution process on the basis of hole theory then a three steps are involved :

(i) a solute is separated into its molecules or ions

(ii) formation of hole or cavity in the solvent and

(iii) solute occupies hole in the solvent.

First two steps require input of energy and energy is released in third step. A saturated solution is one, where all cavities of the solvent are occupied by solute molecules. If the solution which is saturated is cooled or evaporated slightly then some solute molecules are thrown out of the solvent cavities as energy is reduced in first and solvent hole number reduction in the later case. Thus at this instant the solvent holes are completely occupied by solute molecules and there are few molecules which are out of solvent hole but not out of solution. Such solution where concentration of solute is greater than the saturation concentration is known as *supersaturated solution*.

Supersaturation (S) may be expressed as :

$$S = \frac{C}{C^*} \qquad \ldots (1)$$

where,   C = Concentration of solution

C^* = Equilibrium saturation concentration at given temperature.

It can also be expressed in terms of Relative Supersaturation (σ).

$$\sigma = \frac{\Delta C}{C^*} = S - 1 \qquad \ldots (2)$$

where, ΔC = Concentration driving force = $C - C^*$

10.4.1 Mier's Theory of Supersaturation :

Fig. 10.4 : Supersolubility curve and regions

Mier and Issac proposed a theory explaining a relationship between supersaturation and spontaneous crystallization. The theory can be explained with the help of solubility - supersolubility diagram (Fig. 10.4), where curve AB represents a typical saturation or solubility curve of an inorganic salt with normal solubility. Each point on this curve represents an equilibrium condition between a solution and solid phase. Curve CD represents a supersolubility curve, it is an imaginary region which represents temperature and concentrations at which spontaneous crystallization occurs. These two curves divide the diagram into three zones viz. stable zone, metastable zone and unstable zone.

Stable zone : It is a well defined zone below the solubility curve where unsaturation prevails, therefore, crystallization is impossible in this zone.

Metastable zone : It is the region between the solubility and supersolubility curve. Spontaneous nucleation occurs in this region. But crystal growth is favoured. It is a variable zone which changes as per the conditions.

Labile or Unstable zone : It represents conditions of high relative supersaturation where only nucleation is favoured.

Mier's theory states that *"in a solution completely free from any foreign particles spontaneous nucleation occurs at supersaturation and not near the saturation concentration."*

If a solution completely free from foreign particles represented by point E is cooled without loss of solvent, spontaneous crystallization will occur only when conditions represented by point G are reached. In some cases of very soluble substances like sodium thiosulphate further coding upto point H is necessary so as to induce crystallization. The difference between the temperature at which the solution is saturated (point F) and that at which first crystal begins to form is known as *maximum supercooling* or *maximum supersaturation concentration*. The time period which elapses between the achievement of supersaturation and appearance of crystals is referred as *induction period*. Induction period is affected by degree of supersaturation, state at agitation, presence of impurities, etc. Once crystallization occurs the solution concentration follows path as shown by GM.

Fig. 10.5 : Mier's Theory of Supersaturation

Mier has explained this behaviour on the basis of molecular collisions. Ions or molecules in a solution can interact to form short lived cluster which develops into embryos or sub-nuclei, many of which failed to achieve maturity. They redissolve due to their extreme unstability. When these aggregates attain the size at which cohesive lattice forces exceed the force which tend to return them into the solution, a stable or critical nucleus is formed. Statistical probability of formation of such aggregates is very low in the vicinity of solubility curve and attains significant value near the supersolubility curve.

Thus, from Mier's theory we can conclude that the crystallization must be carried out in meta stable region. A plot of rate of nucleation as a function of supersaturation (Fig. 10.6) shows that increasing supersaturation beyond the boundary of the metastable zone, rapid increase in nucleation rate takes place and large number of crystals are formed causing steep drop in supersaturation. Hence it is difficult to attain supersaturations beyond metastable region boundary.

Fig. 10.6 : Effect of supersaturation on nucleation

But Mier's theory has *limitations* as follows :

1. Mier has proposed the theory with the basic requirement that the solution is completely free from foreign particles. But in practice it is very difficult to occur ; because many contaminants are added from the atmosphere.

2. It is reported that the large volumes of a given system nucleates spontaneously at lower degree of supersaturation than small volumes. This effect of volume has not been considered in Miers theory. This effect of volume may be attributed to greater chances of contamination as well as greater chances of collisions in larger volume.

3. Similarly, it was observed that spontaneous nucleation may occur, if the solution at lower degree of supersaturation is kept for longer period of time. This may again be attributed to higher chances of contamination and collisions with increase in time.

4. Mier has proposed that supersaturation occurs at a particular concentration. But formation of a nucleus is due to chance of collision and it cannot be specified by any particular concentration but it should be range of concentrations over which chances will be maximum. This will give the zone of supersaturation instead of a curve.

5. Miers theory is based on ideal conditions which will never exist in practice. It has not taken into consideration any external stimulus e.g. level of supersaturation which can exist and is inversely proportional to the mechanical shock or stimulus in the solution. The entire metastable zone can be made labile by producing sufficient mechanical shock.

Hence Mier's theory is of no significant use in practice.

10.5 NUCLEATION

Once supersaturation is achieved, nucleation is a next essential step for crystallization to occur. Nucleation may occur spontaneously or it may be induced artificially. Nucleation is classified as primary nucleation and secondary nucleation.

Primary nucleation is the nucleation in the systems that do not contain any crystalline matter.

Secondary nucleation represents the condition where nuclei are generated in the vicinity of crystals present in a supersaturated solution.

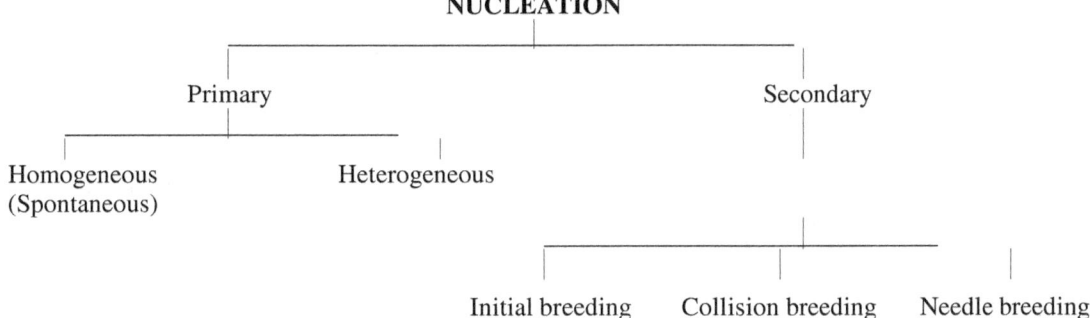

10.5.1 Primary Nucleation :

This is the mode of nucleation which occurs mainly at high levels of supersaturation and is most prevalent during unseeded crystallization or precipitation. Primary nucleation is further divided into homogeneous and heterogeneous nucleation.

Homogeneous Nucleation : Formation of stable crystal nuclei within a homogeneous fluid is called homogeneous or spontaneous nucleation. During nucleation molecules / ions forming nucleus should come together, for which they have to overcome the tendency to redissolve. They also have to get orientated in a fixed lattice structure. Around 10 to 1000 such molecules are necessary to form a stable nucleus. This cannot happen by simultaneous collisions of molecules which will be a rare chance. Hence it is expected to take place by a sequence of bimolecular additions as :

$$A + A \rightleftharpoons A_2$$

$$A_2 + A \rightleftharpoons A_3$$

$$A_{n-1} + A \rightleftharpoons A_n \text{ (critical cluster)}$$

Further additions of molecules to this critical cluster results in a nucleus.

The classical theory of nucleation by Gibbs and Volmer is based on the concept of solute clustering prior to nucleation. It proposed that the cluster may grow or redissolve. Of these two processes, that process will be favoured which results in decrease in the free energy of the particle. Therefore, particles smaller than critical nucleus size dissolve, because only in this way the particles can achieve reduction in its free energy, whereas, particles larger than critical size will grow. Although energy of a fluid system is constant at constant temperature and pressure there will be fluctuations in the energy about a constant mean value. In the supersaturated region, energy level rises temporarily and nucleation will be favoured. The rate of nucleation i.e. number of nuclei formed per unit time, per unit volume is given by Arrhenius equation as follows :

$$J = A \exp(-\Delta G / kT) \quad \ldots (3)$$

where,
- J = Rate of nucleation
- A = Activation energy
- k = Boltzmann constant
- ΔG = Overall excess free energy between the solid particle of solute and solute in solution

and T = Temperature in $^\circ K$.

The homogeneous nucleation occurs in perfectly clean systems without stirrer. Therefore, it cannot occur in stirred vessels and hence generally the nucleation in industrial vessels is of heterogeneous type.

Heterogeneous Nucleation :

True homogeneous nucleation is a very difficult event because the supercooled system unknowingly get seeded by the atmospheric dust which contain active particles or heteronuclei. The most active heteronuclei in liquid solution lie in the range of 0.1 to 1 µm. The overall free energy change associated with the formation of critical nucleus under heterogeneous condition is less than the corresponding free energy change associated with homogeneous condition. Similarly, in the presence of heteronuclei, nucleation can be induced at degrees of supercooling lower than those required for spontaneous nucleation.

10.5.2 Secondary Nucleation

Secondary nucleation involves nucleation in presence of existing crystals. The possible mechanisms of secondary nucleation involve; Initial breeding, Needle breeding and Collision breeding.

Initial breeding occurs if crystallization has been started by seeding the crystallizer. *Needle breeding* is associated with the growth of imperfect crystals and would not be expected under the regular crystal growth. *Collision breeding* involves collision of crystal, with moving parts such as stirrer, pump, impeller or crystal wall contact, under centrifugal force.

The rate of secondary nucleation is highly dependent on growth rate of parent crystals and in turn on the level of supersaturation.

10.6 CRYSTAL GROWTH

As soon as stable nuclei or the nuclei above the critical size are formed in a supersaturated solution, they begin to grow. During growth of the crystal from solution following steps are involved :

(i) Solute molecules break whatever bonds it has with the solvent.

(ii) These solute molecules migrate to the solid-liquid interface.

(iii) Adsorption and orientation of solute molecules in the crystal lattice.

This total phenomenon of crystal growth has been explained on the basis of various theories as follows.

10.6.1 Surface Energy Theory

Gibbs and Curie postulated the surface energy theory for crystal growth. It states that *"the crystal assumes that shape, which has minimum surface energy"*. It suggests that the crystal faces would grow at rate proportional to their respective surface energies.

But this theory cannot explain the surface energy changes during crystal growth to influence crystal habit. The theory also failed to explain the effect of supersaturation and solution movement on the crystal growth rate.

Gibbs considered that there is a possibility that kinetic factors dominate in the initiation of crystallization and they would probably become insignificant in growth.

10.6.2 Diffusion Theory

Noyes and Whitney in 1897 proposed the theory for dissolution of solid which was applied for the reciprocal process of growth. Nernst elaborated the Noyes – Whitney theory stating that the diffusion of solute takes place through a film of saturated solution at the surface of immersed crystal. This diffusion is followed by an infinitely rapid reaction at the surface. Nernst presented the modified Noyes and Whitney equation as :

$$\frac{dx}{dt} = \frac{DS}{\delta}(C_s - C)$$

where, $\frac{dx}{dt}$ = Rate of crystal growth

D = Diffusion coefficient

S = Surface area of the crystal exposed

C_s = Saturation concentration

C = Concentration in the bulk phase

δ = Thickness of the laminar film through which diffusion takes place.

The thickness of diffusion layer (δ) varies between 20 – 50 µm. The Noyes – Whitney – Nernst equation is applicable when the rate of growth or dissolution of different faces of the crystal is equal. This theory assumes that reaction at the surface is infinitely fast. i.e. incorporation of building units into the crystal lattice is rapid. This will be observed in cases of ionic crystals where bond energies and forces are very high, but in cases where surface reaction will be slower due to weak interaction it will be rate limiting instead of diffusion rate.

Diffusion theory is vague and cannot explain change in crystal habit due to change in supersaturation. Marc has pointed out that crystal growth differs from dissolution in many ways as follows :

(i) It is slower than dissolution.
(ii) Rate of growth is independent of rate of stirring if it is vigorous.
(iii) Many substances when adsorbed, considerably reduce growth rate but do not influence the rate of solution.

10.6.3 Adsorption theory

It was observed that when a supersaturated solution is inoculated with seed crystals, there is initially a very rapid addition of material to this base, after which normal activity is established. Considering this Marc postulated the adsorption theory and suggested that the interface of a growing crystal is better described in terms of adsorbed layer than a saturated film. It is considered that a adsorbed layer is first formed and then addition occurs to crystal lattice. Growth occurs at a measurable rate by addition to the substrate lattice from this layer, and the abstracted molecules are replaced from the surrounding solution.

10.6.4 Dislocation Theory

Kossel elaborated the process of crystal growth with crystal model as shown in Fig. 10.7. In a growing crystal, new molecules are added only at kink or repeatable step. Many positions are shown at which the building unit can be incorporated in the crystal lattice. Of these positions the one which involve maximum work of separation is the most stable site called "Kossel site" and favoured for addition of building unit. Thus the corners, edges and faces are in order the preferred building sites.

Fig. 10.7 : Kossel's crystal

The path taken by soluble molecules from solution to the kink site is not certain. Deposition may either occur directly at the step via volume diffusion or solute molecules may become adsorbed on the surface and migrate to the steps by surface diffusion. Once the layer is formed it is important to have a new kink site. For generation of kink there are two possibilities :

(i) Nucleation is taking place at the surface is called *two-dimensional nucleation*.

(ii) Surface do not grow perfect and takes helical path, it is known as *screw dislocation* (Fig. 10.8).

Fig. 10.8 : Screw dislocation

Two-dimensional nucleation require very high supersaturations. Therefore, Frank proposed screw dislocation provides the kink site in solutions of low supersaturations. According to screw dislocation theory, the steady state growth rate is proportional to the square of concentration.

10.7 CRYSTALLIZERS

The basic requirement in crystallization is achievement of supersaturation. The crystal-lizers are classified into following types on the method of achieving supersaturation :

1. Supersaturation by cooling
2. Supersaturation by solvent evaporation
3. Supersaturation by adiabatic solvent evaporation
4. Supersaturation by salting out
5. Supersaturation by chemical reaction.

Fig. 10.9 : Methods of achieving supersaturation

Fig. 10.9 shows the concentration - temperature relationships in all the methods of achieving supersaturation. Of the above mentioned methods, first three methods are commonly used.

10.7.1 Crystallization by cooling :

This method is used when the solubility of substance is strongly temperature dependent i.e. the solute has a steep solubility curve, e.g. KNO_3, urea etc. Cooling may be carried out by direct or indirect heat exchange between a hot solution of solute and a cooling medium which may be a gas like air or ammonia, or a liquid as water, brine etc.

Generally, water is used as a cooling medium. It's temperature is between 5 °C in winter and 20 °C in summer. The temperature achieved in the crystallizer is around 2 °C higher than the water temperature. At this temperature, considerable amount of solute may remain in the solution giving low yields. Therefore, cooling should be carried out at temperature of 10 °C or below.

But at low temperature following factors should be taken into consideration :

(a) Viscosity of solution reduces significantly at low temperature which may cause decrease in mass transfer rates and in turn crystal growth rate.

(b) Due to increased viscosity heat transfer rates also decreases, thus heat exchange surface area has to be increased.

(c) Mother liquor may remain adhered to the crystal surface due to high viscosity. It is not easily removed without washing; hence it may contaminate the crystals. Similarly, if washing has to be carried out the washing liquid has to be cold so as to avoid dissolution of crystals which is less effective in removal of adhered liquid.

(d) During cooling, maximum supersaturation is attained by solution near the cooling surface and deposits of crystals will be developed. Heat transfer through such surfaces is very low.

Batch Operation :

The batch type crystallizers have many advantages and limitations as given below :

Advantages :

(i) It uses simple equipment with very low mechanical troubles.

(ii) Maintenance cost required is less, similarly, the quality and skill of the operator required to operate a batch crystallizer is not very high.

(iii) It can produce large crystals.

Limitations :

(i) Variation may occur from batch to batch in crystal size.

(ii) It requires large head room.

(iii) Long operation time and more manual work is required.

The crystallizers of cooling batch type are :

(i) Tank crystallizer and

(ii) Agitated tank crystallizer.

(i) Tank Crystallizer :

It consists of a simple rectangular tank made up of material which is resistant to any corrosive effects of the solution. Glass enamelled or stainless steel vessel of 0.5 m diameter is generally used to produce certain pharmaceutical products such as potassium bromide.

In this crystallizer, a hot saturated solution is allowed to cool naturally by contact with air or cooling medium. There is no control of nucleation or crystal growth. The product obtained is mass of interlocked crystals. The product is obtained by draining completely the mother liquor.

Fig. 10.10 : Tank crystallizer

As the rate of cooling is very slow it requires several days to obtain the product; during which crystals reach to very large sizes as interlocked masses. These interlocked crystals masses entrap considerable quantity of mother liquor. Entrapped mother liquor may act as impurities source, but in the pharmaceutical industry where the starting solutions are very pure for the last-stage crystallization, the problem of contamination does not arise.

The product obtained by this method show wide crystal size distribution. Similarly, labour and space requirements are very high. But still it is considered as an economical method for the production of large crystals on small scale. The method is obsolete.

(ii) Agitated Tank Crystallizer :

In this crystallizer, the cooling is carried out by cooling tubes. The cooling tubes are placed internally and arranged in the form of helically wound tube or as a vertical tubular basket. A propeller type agitator is used. The tank may be open or covered.

The agitator in this crystallizer has following functions :

(a) It carries out mixing and enhances heat transfer and helps in achievement of uniform temperature distribution.

(b) Due to agitation, thickness of the diffusion layer surrounding the crystal surface is reduced, hence rate of mass transfer and crystal growth is increased.

(c) Faster cooling due to agitation results in the formation of a large number of small crystal nuclei, which are retained in the suspension and grow to uniform size. At the same time agglomeration of crystals is prevented.

The agitator should supply adequate energy so that movement of crystals takes place in the solution. The angular velocity of the agitator should be such that the crystal suspension is well carried by the upward flowing stream.

Fig. 10.11 : Agitated tank crystallizers

Higher supersaturations exist near the cooling tube surface and crystals may become trapped between the turns of a helix. The crystals attached to the cooling tubes reduce heat transfer. It is recommended that the temperature difference between the tube wall and the solution should not exceed $10°C$ so as to prevent crystal deposition. The combination of high liquor velocities in tubes, and a low temperature difference across the heat exchanger reduces the tendency for crystal deposition. The crystal deposits over the tube surface may be removed by a mechanical scraper or it may be removed by introducing steam into the tubing for a short time. The cooling tubes may also act as a diffuser. The pitch of the helix is $1/3^{rd}$ of the tube diameter and distance of the tubes from side wall as well as bottom is not more than 3 tube diameters.

Swenson - Walker Crystallizer :

It is a continuous crystallizer based on supersaturation by cooling. It consists of a semicylindrical open trough about 60 cm wide and 5 m long. It is around 67.5 cm in depth. This trough has jacket from outside through which a water is circulated for cooling
(Fig. 10.12). It contains relatively low-speed, long pitch spiral agitator placed horizontally as close as possible to the semicylindrical bottom. The angular velocity of the agitator is
5 – 10 r.p.m. The cooling water generally flows in the direction of the crystallizing solution, hence it is also classified as parallel flow crystallizer. Counter current contact is also possible in some cases. The jacket is divided into different sections in such a way that the cooling rates over different sections of the trough can be different.

The low speed spiral agitator functions,

(a) to prevent accumulation of crystals on the cooling surface,

(b) to lift the crystals and shower down through the solution to grow in free suspension,

(c) to move the crystals mechanically towards the discharge of the cylinder.

The gap between the crystallizer wall and the agitator should be optimum. If the gap is large then there is tendency of crystal deposit formation on cooling surface. On the other hand, if the agitator blades are very close to the trough wall then it acts as a scraper and fines will be produced due to crystal attrition.

Thus, the solution enters the crystallizer, the slurry is agitated gently in the crystallizer, which provides excellent conditions for crystal growth and crystals overflow with mother liquor leaving at the discharge end.

But this crystallizer tends to produce a product with relatively wide crystal size distribution because larger particles tend to stay more at the bottom of the crystallizer near the cooling surface where supersaturation is intense, whereas smaller crystals are suspended more easily by the movement of the agitator and less exposed to the region of high supersaturation.

Heat transfer in this crystallizer is limited. The overall heat transfer coefficients which can be obtained in this crystallizer are in the range of 30 to 50 kcal/m² hr °C.

Advantages of Swenson–Walker crystallizer include less floor space, small volume in process, low labour costs and cheap cooling medium.

Fig. 10.12 : Swenson - Walker Crystallizer

This is used for trisodium phosphate, oxalic acid, milk sugar, naphthaline etc.

10.7.2 Crystallization by Evaporation :

In this method, crystallization takes place mainly due to the removal of solvent by evaporation. It is used for those substances where there is very small change in solubility with temperature e.g. sodium chloride, ammonium sulphate. It is also used for substances having negative effect of temperature on solubility. e.g. sodium sulphate anhydrous. Evaporators are discussed in details in chapter 11.

10.7.3 Crystallization by Adiabatic Evaporation :

If a hot saturated solution is introduced into a chamber maintained at a lower pressure than that corresponding to the vapour pressure of the feed solution, part of the solvent will immediately flash off, and the liquid will be cooled to a temperature which is equivalent to the vaporising pressure. Hence solution becomes supersaturated due to combination of evaporation of solvent and some cooling. In adiabatic crystallizer, there is no external source of heat. Sometimes, heat may be supplied externally just to flash the solution or dissolve the nuclei or crystals.

Adiabatic evaporation or vacuum crystallization has following advantages :

(a) As heat exchange surfaces are absent it can be built in rubber lined or plastic lined steel or glass reinforced plastics.

(b) Region of greatest supersaturation is at the vapour-liquid interface, therefore, problem of crystal deposition does not arise and heat transfer remains high.

(c) Moving parts are less, therefore, maintenance of crystallizer is cheap and easy.

(a) Vacuum Crystallizer : As shown in Fig. 10.13, vacuum crystallizer consists of a conocylindrical vessel to which vacuum is applied by means of a vacuum pump. The feed which is a preconcentrated solution, enters at a convenient point and flashes into vapour. Flashing causes ebullition in the crystallizer and this natural agitation of the solution keeps the crystals in suspension. Once the crystals are grown they settle into the discharge pipe and are removed by means of a pump. In batch–wise operation, the entire slurry is discharged to the centrifugal or continuous vacuum filter.

Fig. 10.13 : Vacuum crystallizer

If liquid level in the crystallizer increases slightly the flashing of the liquid may not occur and the liquid may leave the crystallization chamber without flashing, this is known as 'short circuiting' of feed. So as to avoid this, propeller may be situated at the corners which will drive the liquid to the surface where the hydrostatic pressure will be less and it can flash. A sight glass is provided to check the liquid level.

As there is no mechanical stimulus or agitation provided in this crystallizer, unwanted nucleation due to attrition is minimised.

(b) Circulating Magma Crystallizer : It is a modification of vacuum crystallizer in which growing crystals are brought intentionally to the zone of the crystallizer where supersaturation is being created. The zone of generation of supersaturation is the boiling surface. The presence of growing crystals in the zone where supersaturation is created immediately utilizes this driving force, and the real super-saturation level is therefore considerably lower than other types.

Circulating magma crystallizer (Fig. 10.14) consists of a crystallizer body (A) where liquid is flashed and gets supersaturated. The crystals are deposited at the bottom. The pipe (B) contains crystals of varying sizes. From the baffles (C) situated on the lower side, a saturated stream of liquid free from crystals is taken out and pumped at the bottom up the pipe containing crystals. The upward force of the stream of saturated liquid washes the bed of crystals free of very fine crystals. This separation of particles by the liquid force is 'elutriation' and the pipe (B) is known as 'elutriation pipe or leg'. The stream of liquid carrying fine crystals carries out mixing of liquid at the bottom. The liquid containing fine crystals (magma) present near the bottom is taken out from side-pipe (D) and pumped through pump (E) to the top of crystallization chamber; during which the liquor passes through heater (F). The heater supplies small amount of energy if required, so as to increase the temperature of liquor to flashing temperature. But the negligible amount of crystals are dissolved. Thus fine crystals are available at the liquid-vapour interface where maximum supersaturation generates.

Fig. 10.14 : Circulating magma crystallizer

Advantages :

1. Generation of nuclei is minimised by reduction of supersaturation by recirculation of large volumes of liquor.

2. As large seed surface is available in the zone of generation of supersaturation, the tendency of material to precipitate on the equipment surface is eliminated.
3. The time interval between generation of supersaturation and it's liberation is very short due to which nucleation is reduced. This also allows operation at higher supersaturation levels.
4. It can give product from 200 – 10 mesh.
5. Suspension of solids in the zone of supersaturation leads to narrow size distribution.

Major drawback of this crystallizer is that the magma has to be pumped against high hydrostatic head.

Operating variables in circulating magma crystallizer :

In the operation of a circulating magma crystallizer, magma density and cycle time are important process variables.

Effect of magma density :

Fig. 10.15 : Effect of magma density

The magma is taken out for circulation from side pipe D. Magma density is the number of particles suspended per unit volume of magma. Fig. 10.15 is a plot of saturation of solution versus time. Points on X axis denote saturation concentration below which is a unsaturation region and above is region of supersaturation. SS' represent the region of spontaneous nucleation. It slants downwards because lower supersaturation is sufficient to cause nucleation as time proceeds. i.e. if molecules are given more time to colloid then lesser number may also cause spontaneous nucleation. The magma entering the flashing chamber is nothing but a saturated solution with fine crystals denoted by point A. As this solution flashes in the chamber the supersaturation is achieved upto level denoted by point B. This supersaturation is simultaneously liberated on the surface of fine crystals in magma. Supersaturation is completely liberated before solution leaves the crystallizer. (as denoted by point C).

Consider that Magma density is high. When solution flashes, two simultaneous processes are taking place, firstly liberation of solute molecule from solvent cavity causing supersaturation and secondly deposition of some of these molecules on the surface of magma particles.

The supersaturation achieved will be

$$\begin{pmatrix}\text{Supersaturation} \\ \text{achieved}\end{pmatrix} = \begin{pmatrix}\text{Solute molecules liberated} \\ \text{from solvent cavity}\end{pmatrix} - \begin{pmatrix}\text{Molecules deposited on} \\ \text{magma particles}\end{pmatrix}$$

Magma density is high i.e. more number of particles per volume and in turn more surface available for deposition of molecules. Therefore, due to more surface area available the second phenomenon of deposition is favoured and supersaturation achieved is reduced. Thus, the curve $A'B'C'$ always lies below the medium magma density curve ABC.

When the magma is thin i.e. contain less number of particles per unit volume, then the surface for deposition decreases and maximum supersaturation achieved also increases. The higher degree of supersaturation thus achieved in the process cannot be liberated in the cycle time which is set $(A''B''C'')$. Therefore, the solution leaves the crystallizer in supersaturated condition C''. This continues for few cycles and degree of supersaturation continuously goes on increasing in each cycle. It becomes so high that it reaches the region of spontaneous nucleation, and large number of nuclei are generated producing fine product. Thus a dilute magma produces fine product.

Effect of cycle time : One cycle in the crystallization process is the time taken by the solution from leaving the chamber and again reaching that point. It is volume of solution in the process divided by rate of circulation. As the cycle time is increased, the time available for the supersaturated solution to release the supersaturation becomes less and the solution leaves the crystallizer with higher degree of supersaturation (Fig. 10.16). Thus degree of super-saturation of magma entering next cycles goes on increasing till it reaches spontaneous nucleation zone, producing fine product.

Fig. 10.16 : Effect of cycle tome

Draft Tube Baffle (DTB) Circulating Magma Crystallizer :

To overcome the high pumping cost encountered in circulating magma crystallizer, DTB crystallizer is designed, where a baffle tube and a propeller is introduced which carry out internal circulation under lower hydrostatic head. The propeller circulates liquid alongwith crystals from the bottom to the top of the vessel. On the outer side of the closed vessel is a settling area which maintains magma density and controls nuclei removal.

Fig. 10.17 : DTB Crystallizer

Advantages :

1. It brings more effectively and frequently the growing particles to the boiling surface where supersaturation is most intense.
2. Due to large internal circulation within the body, it reduces the supersaturation at the boiling surface.
3. This internal circulation is achieved against extremely low hydrostatic heads, therefore, the power consumption for circulation is very low as compared to external circulation.
4. The appropriate seed surface present at the boiling surface allows effective liberation of supersaturation and minimizes nuclei formation. It gives uniformity of product.

Crystallizers for Large Crystals :

For some selected processes, crystals of large size are required. For this purpose some modifications of the vacuum crystallizer are carried out. It includes growth type vacuum crystallizer and Krystal or Oslo crystallizer. These crystallizers favour crystal growth and supress nucleation.

1. Growth Type Vacuum Crystallizer :

It consists of a flashing chamber (A) in which the solution is flashed. Flashing is controlled so that supersaturation is achieved but nucleation does not take place in chamber A. The supersaturated solution is transferred to chamber B where already grown crystals are present. The supersaturated solution is allowed to remain in contact with the bed of crystals; where it liberates its supersaturation on the surface of these already formed crystals. Thus crystal growth is favoured. The overflow from chamber B containing fine nuclei and particles are passed to heater D by pump C. The feed is added before entering the heater. The heater D adds energy so that temperature of liquid raises to flashing point in vacuum and at the same time all suspended fine particles are dissolved. Thus in contrast to circulating magma crystallizer, where the heater only raises the temperature and hot magma passes to flashing chamber, in growth type the solution enters the flashing chamber. The crystal product is taken out when developed to desired size.

Fig. 10.18 : Growth type of vacuum crystallizer

The basic limitation of this process is, it requires very long contact times between crystals and supersaturated solution. Similarly, generation of some fine crystals and again their dissolution in heater, these two exactly opposite processes are carried out continuously. Long contact times and crystallization - dissolution makes the process expensive.

The time required for/of supersaturated solution from chamber A to chamber B is an important operating variable in growth type vacuum crystallizer.

The concentration – time curve will be as shown in Fig. 10.19. The solution at just before entering the flashing chamber is denoted by point A, which indicates that solution is unsaturated. In the flashing chamber the solution flashes and gets supersaturated as indicated by point B. This solution is immediately transferred to crystal bed, during which time BC has elapsed. Point C thus indicates the concentration of solution and time at which it has come in contact with bed. On contact with crystal bed, the supersaturation is liberated on crystal bed and degree of supersaturation decreases to point D. The magma gets mixed with feed and passes through heater, where increase in temperature makes the solution unsaturated again as shown by point E, ready for flashing in next cycle. It was observed that increased fraction of undersized particles are obtained when time of transfer BC has increased. It can be explained on the basis of Mier's theory that as the time allowed increases, the lesser number of collisions may cause spontaneous nucleation. Thus, it is most important to prevent nucleation by keeping the transfer time as low as possible.

Fig. 10.19

2. **Krystal or Oslo Crystallizer :**

Fig. 10.20 : Krystal or Oslo Crystallizer

A Krystal or Oslo crystallizer consists of two different chambers. Chamber A is a flashing chamber where controlled supersaturation is achieved. The supersaturated solution under gravitational force to chamber C through pipe B. Chamber C contains a bed of already formed crystals. The solution enters the chamber C under pressure causing opening of the bed. Once the crystal bed opens it gets fractionated on the basis of size and density. The fine crystals containing supernatant is taken out from side pipe as a magma for further treatment. The feed gets added to magma and then mixture passes to heater H, where its temperature is increased sufficiently so that all the magma particles get dissolved and flashing can occur. Crystals when grown to desired size, the product is taken out from bottom.

The Krystal crystallizer offers advantages as, the time required for transfer of supersaturated solution on the crystal bed is minimised. Secondly, size separation is also achieved due to hydraulic separation in the bed. The geometry of the down pipe is such that potential energy is converted to kinetic by constriction and again to pressure energy by expansion. Thus it has low percentage of fines generation and size separation advantage.

10.8 CAKING OF CRYSTALS

Caking of crystals is an undesirable effect, which generally occurrs during storage. This involves formation of a saturated film on the surface of the crystals either by absorption or by migration of mother liquor incompletely removed in the separation of the crystals. This saturated solution will concentrate at the contacts of the crystals due to capillary forces and subsequently crystallize to form a solid bridge upon cooling or evaporation. The continuation of this surface recrystallization produces a hard cake or cement which creates difficulties in manipulating and handling both bulk and packaged materials. Various factors should be considered in caking of crystals.

1. **Humidity** : A crystal tends to be in continuous equilibrium with the moisture in the surrounding atmosphere, and the ratio of the vapour pressure of the moisture around the crystal to that of the saturated solution will determine whether the crystal is going to lose or absorb water. The humidity of the atmosphere in the storage space should not exceed a critical value (ϕ_k).

$$\phi_k = 100 \frac{P_s}{P_o}$$

where, P_s = Vapour pressure of the saturated solution

P_o = Vapour pressure of pure solvent at given temperature.

2. **Contact Area** : The cakability of a material is directly proportional to the contact area between individual crystals. The more are the gaps between the crystals less is the chance of caking. This can be achieved with uniform crystals of as large size, preferably of shapes close to spherical. Contact area between spheres is much less than between platelets and needles of similar volume. But uniformity of particle size is also necessary.

3. **Temperature** : Temperature fluctuations are undesirable so as to prevent caking ; because they cause variations in the solubility of the material. In absence of solvent also high temperature have undesirable effect, especially on low melting substances. If the product is at a

temperature equal to or in excess of a quarter of the melting temperature, some surface activation of the particles occurs.

4. Particle size : Particle size determines the upper limit of storage pressure. At a certain 'adhesive' pressure, fusion of the particles occurs.

$$P_a \propto \frac{1}{r}$$

Thus caking tendency can be reduced by :

(i) Production of stable modification of the product, so that it has suitable habit, size and uniformity.

(ii) Reduction of moisture content to lowest possible level, storage under steady temperature, low stacking pressure and lower air humidities.

(iii) Powdering or impregnation of surfaces with surface active and water repellant materials e.g. $Ca_3(PO_4)_2$ on NaCl and starch on sugar and confectionaries.

***

EVAPORATION

11.1 INTRODUCTION

Evaporation is the *process of removal of the liquid by vaporization below boiling point of the system*. Though, theoretically it should be carried out below boiling point, evaporation may be carried out at boiling point, with aim to increase rate of vaporization.

Evaporation is generally adopted to obtain concentrated solutions, extracts. It may be a preliminary stage for the preparation of dry extracts.

11.2 THEORY

The liquid to be evaporated is subjected to heating and rate of evaporation is dependent on rate of heat transfer from the heating medium to the liquid. Generally, heating is carried out using heating fluid and rate of heat transfer is given by as equation given below,

$$Q = U A \Delta t \qquad \ldots (1)$$

where, Q is rate of heat transfer, A is area across which heat transfer occurs, Δt is temperature difference between heating fluid and liquid and U is overall heat transfer coefficient.

From equation (1), it is clear that rate of evaporation can be increased by increase in surface area, overall heat transfer coefficient and by maintaining temperature difference high.

Surface Area : The area is maintained high by use of long tubes or coiled tubes.

Overall heat transfer coefficient : Overall heat transfer coefficient is a measure of resistance given by metal wall and liquid films (condensed steam film and liquid side film) present on either side of the wall. The material for wall construction should have high thermal conductivity and sufficient strength, so that wall thickness can be kept minimum. The condensed liquid on the steam side should be removed immediately, as soon as it is formed. This can be achieved by use of a suitable steam trap. The resistance on the liquid side can be minimized by maintaining the liquid turbulent or continuously moving, so that boundary layer (film) thickness is maintained low. Viscosity of the liquid should also be maintained low so as to keep the rate of evaporation high.

Temperature Difference (Δt) : Difference between the steam temperature and the apparent saturation temperature of vapour leaving the evaporating mixture is called as apparent temperature difference. It is the temperature difference between the temperature of the condensing steam in the steam space and the temperature of the boiling solution of the liquid-vapour interface in the evaporator body.

Thus boiling point of liquid is the factor which mainly controls Δt. It is important to maintain the boiling point of liquid low, which rises due to material in solution and hydrostatic head.

The boiling point rise due to material in solution is the actual surface temperature of the mixture minus the temperature of the pure solvent if it exerted the same vapour pressure as the mixture. For dilute solutions boiling point of solution may be obtained by Raoult's law. *Duhring rule* was developed for determining boiling point rise due to material in concentrated solution. Duhring rule states that *the ratio of the temperatures at which two solutions exert the same vapour pressure is constant*. Therefore, a plot of the temperature of a constant concentration solution versus the temperature of a reference substance, where the reference substance and solution exert the same pressure, results in a straight line. Pure water is generally used as the reference material (Fig. 11.1). Duhring line can be drawn by knowing two vapour pressures and temperature points required for solution to boil. Thus using Raoult's law or Duhring lines boiling point of the solution may be obtained, depending on its strength.

Fig. 11.1 : Duhring lines of sodium chloride

In the evaporating system, the liquid which is at the bottom is subjected to the pressure of liquid column above it. Due to this, hydrostatic head boiling occurs at the bottom at higher temperature than the surface. The difference between the boiling point of the solution under pressure and solution at the evaporating surface is boiling point rise due to hydrostatic head. It can be calculated if average density and concentration of the solution is known.

Thus hydrostatic head should be kept minimum, so as to keep high evaporation rates. Proper correction should be made for boiling point rise due to material in solution in the calculation of Δt.

Economy and Capacity of Evaporator :

Economy of an evaporator is the total mass of water vaporized in the evaporator per unit mass of steam input to the evaporator.

Capacity of an evaporator is the amount of water vaporized in the evaporator per unit time.

Different types of evaporators are as follows :

(A) Pan Evaporator

(B) Tubular Evaporators

    (a) Horizontal Tube Evaporator

    (b) Vertical Tube Evaporators

        1. Short tube (Standard) evaporator.

        2. Multiple effect evaporator

        3. Long tube evaporator.

            (i) Climbing film evaporator

            (ii) Falling film evaporator

            (iii) Forced circulation evaporator

(C) Wiped Film Evaporator

(D) Centrifugal Rotary Evaporator.

11.3 PAN EVAPORATOR

These are simple jacketed pans (Fig. 11.2). Steam is generally used as a heating medium. The pan evaporators are generally used for removal of small amount of moisture present in the extracts or semisolid ayurvedic dosage forms like avleha etc. Shallow pans are commonly used, they have capacity of around 90 – 100 litres. The agitation is manually provided to the material. The product may be removed at the end of the cycle by tilting the pan. The pans are made of copper, stainless steel, aluminium or enamelled iron. The jacket and vessel should be constructed in such a way that it should withstand the high pressure of the steam. The steam pressure is generally 40 lb/in^2 and the evaporation rates are usually 100 litres/m^2/hr.

Fig. 11.2 : Pan Evaporator

The pans should be operated under properly ventilated conditions so that rate of evaporation can be maintained high. These evaporators are simple and low in capital cost, but they are expensive in their running costs as heat economy is poor.

11.4 TUBULAR EVAPORATORS

11.4.1 Horizontal Tube Evaporator :

Horizontal tube evaporator consists of four to six horizontal tubes mounted in concentric manner. The butt ends of the tubes may be connected in such a way that it forms a hairpin like structure (Fig. 11.3). It is available in two models i.e. heating medium inside and outside the tubes. The liquid enters the tube at bottom and passes upwards and steam enters the top, so as to maintain counter-current contact. Baffles may be provided so as to increase heat transfer coefficient. The tubes are made up of stainless steel. It has been used to concentrate extracts e.g. cascara extract.

Fig. 11.3 : Horizontal tube evaporator

Liquid circulation is poor in this type of evaporator. Fouling i.e. build up of semisolid layer on the evaporating surface reduces heat transfer rates.

11.4.2 Vertical Tube Evaporators :

1. Short Tube Evaporator :

The Standard type evaporator (Fig. 11.4) is an example of short tube evaporator. It consists of vertical tubes having 5 – 8 cm diameter and a central large downcomer. The liquid is present inside the tubes and steam outside in the steam space of the calendria. The length to diameter ratio of the tubes is of the order of 15 : 1. The liquid boils inside.

Fig. 11.4 : Calendria type evaporator

There are four important controls in the evaporator :

(i) Feed control is provided to control the feed level. The control is achieved through feed valve (F).

(ii) A vent valve(V), is provided to remove any residual air in the steam space of the evaporator.

(iii) Steam valve(S) is provided to control the steam input to the steam space. As soon as the steam space gets saturated with steam, the valve gets closed.

(iv) A condensate valve(C), is provided so as to remove the condensate as soon as it is formed so as to maintain the heat transfer rates high.

The feed enters the evaporator. The tubes are submerged in the liquid where liquid is heated by steam. Boiling of liquid takes place and the vapours are separated. The liquid at the bottom is subjected to hydrostatic head of the liquid above it, hence its boiling point may not be reached. This may cause the liquid to leave the chamber without complete evaporation i.e. this liquid may "short-circuit".

As the high liquid levels are required to be maintained, hydrostatic head is a critical variable in this evaporator. Slight increase in the liquid level in the chamber, may cause significant rise in boiling point of liquid at the bottom and capacity of evaporator may decrease.

2. Multiple Effect Evaporator (MEE) :

Principle : It is an arrangement of short tube evaporator to achieve economy. In this arrangement, vapours formed in the evaporator are used as the heating medium for the next evaporator. In this way, the energy associated with the vapours produced during evaporation is used many times to achieve economy. Each evaporator used in this arrangement are termed as effect and hence arrangement as Multiple Effect Evaporator (MEE). Therefore, a short tube evaporator is termed as Single Effect Evaporator (SEE).

Economy of MEE and SEE :

Economy of an evaporator is the amount of vapours produced per unit steam input. To compare economy of MEE and SEE, we will assume that

(a) Feed is at boiling point i.e. heat will not be required to raise the temperature of feed and

(b) Loss of heat is negligible.

Therefore, when steam condenses, the heat which is liberated i.e. heat of condensation will be completely transferred to the liquid. The liquid does not need heat, to raise its temperature, hence all energy is utilized for conversion of liquid into vapours i.e. as latent heat of vaporization (LHV). According to this discussion, all energy supplied if utilized as LHV, then, heat liberated during condensation of unit mass of vapours will vaporize unit mass of liquid. Therefore,

$$\text{Economy of SEE} = \frac{\text{Mass of vapours produced}}{\text{Mass of steam used}}$$

$$= \frac{1}{1} = 1 \quad \ldots (2)$$

In MEE, the unit mass of vapours produced in 1st effect will produce unit mass in the 2nd effect and this continues. Therefore, if N number of effects are used, mass of vapours produced will be N kg and economy becomes

$$\text{Economy of MEE} = \frac{N \text{ kg of vapours produced}}{1 \text{ kg of steam input}} = \frac{N}{1} = N \quad \ldots (3)$$

Therefore, economy of MEE is N times SEE.

Fig. 11.5 : Multiple effect evaporator

Working : Consider an evaporator containing three effects (Fig. 11.5). The three effects denoted by I, II and III are connected to each other, where, F denotes feed valve, V denotes vent valve, S denotes steam valve and C denotes condensate valve. Subscripts 1, 2 and 3 correspond to the effect number I, II and III respectively.

Feed is introduced in all three effects. Steam enters the first effect and residual air is removed through vent valve V_1. The steam condenses on the outer surface of the tube; liquid inside the tube will be heated to its boiling point and vapours are formed. The vapours from effect I, pass to the steam space of the effect II. These vapours remove the residual air and vent value V_2 gets closed. Heat transfer takes place between the condensate film and liquid in II effect. Rate of heat transfer is high at initial stages, but it decreases slowly as the temperature of liquid in the tube rises causing decrease in temperature difference between vapour and liquid. As rate of heat transfer decreases, rate of utilization or condensation of vapours decreases. The rate at which vapours are utilised in effect II is less than rate at which they are produced in effect I. Therefore, the vapours get accumulated in the vapour space of effect I. Due to pressure of these accumulated vapours, boiling point of liquid in effect I is elevated.

Similar compression of vapours will occur in the effect II as they are not utilized as fast in the effect III. Due to this vapour accumulation, the temperature and pressure in three effects are different. P_1, P_2, P_3 and t_1, t_2, t_3 are pressure and temperature in effects I, II and III respectively. $P_1 > P_2 > P_3$ and $t_1 > t_2 > t_3$. The concentrate of previous effect acts as feed for next effect.

Capacity of MEE and SEE :

Capacity i.e. mass of vapours produced per unit time, is dependent on the rate of heat transfer given by UA Δt. Consider a SEE, then capacity is given by UA Δt, where U is overall heat transfer coefficient, A is area of heat transfer and Δt is difference in temperature of steam and liquid. For MEE consider that A_1, A_2 and A_3 be the areas of three effects I, II and III respectively. Δt_1, Δt_2 and Δt_3 be the temperature difference and U_1, U_2 and U_3 are overall heat transfer coefficient. Rate of heat transfer q_1, q_2 and q_3 will be given as :

In   Effect I : $q_1 = U_1 A_1 \Delta t_1$

     Effect II : $q_2 = U_2 A_2 \Delta t_2$

     Effect III : $q_3 = U_3 A_3 \Delta t_3$

Therefore, total heat transferred in three effects will be :

$$q = q_1 + q_2 + q_3$$

$$= U_1 A_1 \Delta t_1 + U_2 A_2 \Delta t_2 + U_3 A_3 \Delta t_3$$

If all effects have same area i.e. $A_1 = A_2 = A_3 = A$ and if we consider average overall heat transfer coefficient U_{av}. then,

$$q = U_{av} A (\Delta t_1 + \Delta t_2 + \Delta t_3)$$

Now if total temperature difference (i.e. temperature of steam entering the effect I and vapour leaving effect III) Δt is same as in SEE, then equation becomes,

$$q = U_{av} \, A \, \Delta t$$

same as that for SEE. According to this capacity of MEE is equal to SEE.

The capacity of MEE will be equal to SEE, when apparent temperature difference is considered. The apparent temperature difference Δt, for single effect is equal to multiple effect.

But net temperature difference (i.e. temperature difference between the temperature of condensed film in steam space and temperature of boiling liquid) ; in MEE is less than SEE. It is because the vapours are produced under pressure, and condense in the steam space of next effect at lower pressure. Hence the temperature of condensed film is lower than that of the vapours. For example, if vapours are produced in effect I at 200°C, these condense in the steam space of effect II at 170°C where pressure is lower. Therefore the net Δt will be less than apparent Δt by 30 °C. Such loss of Δt occurs in each effect in multiple effect, hence capacity of MEE is less than SEE.

Methods of Feeding : In MEE vapours always pass from first to third effect. The feed may be fed by different methods as follows : (Fig. 11.6).

(a) Forward feed arrangement for feeding multiple effect evaporator system

(b) Backward feed arrangement for feeding multiple effect evaporation system

(c) Mixed feed arrangement for feeding multiple-effect evaporator system

Fig. 11.6

(i) **Forward feed method :** In forward feed, the feed moves from effect I to II and II to III. The advantage of this method is, feed moves from high pressure to low pressure chambers, therefore, pumping is not needed. The product is obtained at lowest temperature (t_3).
[Fig. 11.6 (a)].

Forward feed method is not suitable for cold feed because the steam input in the first effect is used mainly for increasing the temperature of feed and amount of vapours produced in
I effect is low. The lower amount vapours in the first effect results in lower vapour production in

subsequent effects and hampers economy. The method is suitable for scale forming liquid as concentrated product is subjected to low temperature.

(ii) Backward feed method : In backward feed, the feed enters the last effect and moves from III ∅ II ∅ I. As the liquid moves from low pressure to high pressure pumping is required. The product is obtained at highest temperature (t_1) [Fig. 11.6 (b)].

It is suitable for cold feed, as the heat used for increasing the temperature in III effect, is already used for heating for N – 1 times. This will give more economy.

The method is suitable for viscous product as highly concentrated product is at highest temperature, hence lower viscosity. At lower viscosity, heat transfer and in turn capacity will be maintained high.

(iii) Mixed feed method : The feed enters in the intermediate effect, moves forward and then to the initial effects i.e. Feed ∅ II ∅ III ∅ I. It is advantageous as liquid moves from high pressure to low pressure II to III and then product is obtained at high temperature and low viscosity. [Fig. 11.6 (c)]

(iv) Parallel feed method : In this method, the separate feed enters the effect and product is taken out from each effect. The method is suitable where the feed has to be concentrated slightly.

Optimum number of effects : The optimized number of effects can be obtained by analyzing the operating cost and capital equipment costs of multiple effects. It involves changes in steam cost, labour charges, cost of equipment with change in number of effects. It can be calculated using equation

$$N_{opt} = \left\{ \frac{B}{C} \left[\frac{U(T_s - T_N)}{\lambda} \right]^m \left[(1 - f_N) W_o \right]^{1-m} \right\}^{1/2}$$

where,
- B = Cost of steam per kilogram
- T_s = Temperature of input steam in effect I
- T_N = Temperature of vapours generated in N^{th} effect
- λ = Latent heat of vaporization of water
- W_o = Amount of water in feed solution
- f_N = Fraction of water remaining in concentrate leaving N^{th} effect
- C & m = Constants

3. Long Tube Evaporators :

These are the evaporators which use tall and slender tubes. The tubes having a length to diameter ratio of the order of 100 : 1, pass vertically inside the steam chest.

(i) Climbing film evaporators :

The long tubes with diameter of about 2.5 to 5 cm and height 6 – 7 m are used (Fig. 11.7). The feed enters at the bottom of the evaporator. Steam enters into the steam space through the inlet at the top. The height of liquid column is maintained low. In the tube the liquid at the bottom is cold and subjected to pressure of column above it. As it moves in the upward direction temperature increases and pressure decreases. Convection occurs near bottom, as the liquid progresses upwards boiling occurs. The phases in the liquid boiling inside tube i.e. bubbly region, plug or slug flow, annular flow and mist flow are explained in chapter Heat Transfer (Fig. 3.5). The mist flow emerging at the top of the tube is then passed to the cyclone separator. The liquid concentrate and vapours are separated.

Fig. 11.7 : Long tube vertical evaporator

As the film is moving in tube, high velocity vapour core propels it in the upward direction. Therefore, it is called as climbing film evaporator. The film moves at high velocity and the turbulence increases the heat transfer rates to the film. The heat transfer occurs at low temperature difference. The convection zone near the bottom where heat transfer rates are low, can be reduced by preheating the feed. The feed may be preheated using the vapours separated from the cyclone separator of the same process. This increases process economy.

Advantages :

1. High surface area is provided by the tubes causing higher heat transfer rates. Heat transfer coefficients are about five times horizontal tube evaporator.
2. Larger surface area and turbulent film keeps the residence time of the liquid very low about 5 – 10 sec. This short exposure of liquid to the high temperature make it suitable for handling of thermolabile substances, such as insulin, hormones etc.
3. It is suitable for foam forming liquids because the foam is broken when the high velocity mixture is subjected to separator action.
4. High velocity of fluid reduces scale formation and fouling inside the tubes.

Disadvantages :

1. Large head space is required.
2. It is not suitable for viscous liquids.

(ii) Falling film evaporator :

Fig. 11.8 : Falling-film evaporator

In falling film evaporator, the feed flows downward along the heated walls of a column (Fig. 11.8). The tube diameter is around 8 –10 cm. These are suitable for viscous liquids, where climbing film evaporator cannot be used. The major problem with this evaporator is even distribution of the feed; therefore suitable spreading techniques may be used. Thickness of the falling film depends on properties of the solution, temperature of solution, heating medium and on their flow-rates. It can develop 'hot spots', because the laminar films created during the descent down the tube surfaces develop large temperature differences through the film. The liquid residence time is about one minute. It is suitable for separation of volatile from non-volatile materials, where the feed material is of low viscosity. There may be climbing-falling combination possible (Fig. 11.8), in which liquid moves upwards in one section and falls in the another section. Falling film evaporator is used for concentration of yeast extract, manufacture of gelatin, extracts of tea and coffee.

(iii) Forced circulation evaporator :

Climbing film and falling film evaporator uses natural circulation of the liquid. The low viscosity liquid flows are satisfactorily treated by natural circulation but liquids having significantly high viscosities can not be handled efficiently in the natural circulation evaporators. Therefore, long tube evaporator is modified to work under forced circulation conditions.

The forced circulation evaporator consists of two parts :

(i) a heat exchanger and

(ii) a vapour separation chamber.

The heat exchanger may be placed internally [Fig. 11.9 (a)] or externally [Fig. 11.9 (b)]. The liquid to be concentrated is pumped through the heat exchanger at the velocities of 2 – 6 m/s (in natural circulation it is 0.3 to1.2 m/s) where it is heated. The pressure drop and hydrostatic heat on the fluid is maintained in such a way that liquid does not boil in the tube. The superheated liquid flowing in the tubes, flashes just while entering the vapour separation chamber as static heat is reduced. The spray of liquid and vapours collide with the deflector and separation occurs. The vapours are subjected for further separation of entrained droplets if any. The concentrate is collected at the bottom.

(a) Forced circulation evaporator with horizontal external heating element

(b) Forced circulation evaporator with vertical heating element

Fig. 11.9 : Forced circulation evaporator

External heating system has following advantages over the internally heated system :

1. Cleaning and replacement of tubes is simpler.
2. Compact and requires less heat room.
3. Boiling of liquid can be easily suppressed just by changing the relative position of the heat exchanger, relative to the vapour space.
4. It has less chances of solids deposition.

The forced circulation evaporators are suitable for handling viscous, foam forming and thermolabile materials. The residence time of material in the evaporator is very low in the range of 1 – 3 secs. But pumping cost makes the operation expensive.

11.4.3 Wiped Film Evaporator :

Wiped film evaporators (Fig. 11.10) were developed to overcome the limitations of falling film evaporator. The large temperature difference and hot spots can be reduced by use of wipers or other suitable rotory device.

As with the falling-film evaporator the feed enters onto a heated wall from the top but a fast rotating wiper element spreads it mechanically. The vapours produced flow counter currently into the upward direction into the separator. The concentrated solution is drawn off at the bottom of the evaporator. It can handle solutions with viscosities upto 3000 centipoise. The rotor speed is 200 – 500 r.p.m. Residence time is 5 – 25 sec.

The wiper blades are available in various designs such as scraper, solid wiper (Fig.11.10). The clearance between the wall and blade is about 0.75 - 4 mm. But as there is friction between the wiper blade and the fluid, there are chances of contamination of end product with the traces of impurities from the wiper material.

Sambay evaporator (Fig.11.10 (c)) is a special design of wiped film evaporator where the heating jacket is divided into number of separately heated segments. Due to this the temperature conditions in each segment can be adjusted separately. The rotor blades are in contact with the heating jacket, therefore, it is suitable for highly viscous materials (upto 5 pascal) and materials having tendency to form crust or coatings on the wall.

(a) The wiped-film evaporator

(b) Rotary wipers for thin layer vaporizers

(c) Multisegmented rotary thin layer vaporizer (Sambay system)
Fig. 11.10 : Wiped film evaporator

11.4.4 Centrifugal Rotory Evaporator :

Fig. 11.11 : Principle of operation of a thin layer vaporizer system

If consists of a steam heated bowl rotating at high speeds of about 400 to 1600 r.p.m. (Fig. 11.11). The solution is fed at the centre of the bowl. The solution is carried upwards on the heated surface by the centrifugal forces; where evaporation occurs. The concentrate is taken out at the top, the condensate is drawn by the side tubes. The residence time of material is about one sec. It is used in pharmaceutical industry.

11.5 VAPOUR RECOMPRESSION

Vapour recompression is a technique adopted to achieve economy in the heat transfer processes. The vapours generated by boiling the liquid are subjected to compression so that they can be used as heating medium. The vapours can be recompressed by mechanical compressors or thermal compressors.

Mechanical compression of vapours by positive displacement or a centrifugal compressor. The saturation temperature of these compressed vapour is higher than the boiling point of the liquid from which they are produced. Therefore, these vapours may be used to heat the liquid from which they are produced. These compressed vapour may be mixed with small quantities of fresh steam if required. Recompression gives economy equivalent to that given by 10 to 15 effects of multiple effects.

Thermal recompression involves compression of vapours using high pressure steam in a jet ejector. The high pressure steam is at around 8 to 10 atm. pressure. It is suitable for handling of large volumes of low density vapours.

The recompression has following limitations :

1. Compressor cost is very high.
2. It is useful for very low Δt operations. The cost increases with increase in Δt.
3. Cost of recompression becomes very high if liquid has very high boiling point elevation.

11.6 SCALE FORMATION

Scales are the solid deposits which accumulate on the heat transfer surface during evaporation. The scale have very low thermal conductivity. As evaporation proceeds, there is gradual increase in the resistance to heat transfer due to deposition of scales. The scale formation problem is severe while handling solutions containing 'inverse solubility' i.e. the solutes of which solubility decreases with increase in temperature. As the liquid temperature is high near the heating surface, the solubility of such substances decreases in the localized area and scaling occurs. Inorganic substances such as calcium sulphate, calcium hydroxide, sodium carbonate, sodium sulphate and calcium salts of organic acids have scaling tendency.

The scale formation can be minimized by :

(a) Maintaining high circulation velocities so that scales does not deposit e.g. forced circulation evaporator.

(b) Manipulating the process, so that highly concentrated solution near completion of process is subjected to low temperature e.g. forward flow feeding in MEE. Periodic removal of scales should be done. The period after which operation should be stopped i.e. cycle time, so that the scales are essential to be removed can be determined by following equation :

$$\frac{1}{U^2} = a\theta + b$$

which shows linear increase in the resistance or reciprocal of U due to scale deposit with time (θ), a and b are constants. The operation is stopped when $\frac{1}{U}$ reaches the critical resistance value.

***

DRYING

12.1 INTRODUCTION

Drying is a widely used unit operation in pharmaceutical industry. Proper knowledge of drying mechanisms and equipments will help to resolve the drying problems in the industry. In pharmaceutical industry, drying of granulation for tabletting, heat sensitive materials and continuous drying of powders need special attention.

The term drying refers to the removal of liquid from a solid by thermal means. It also includes removal of volatile liquids or water from another liquid or gas or a suspension. Process of evaporation involves removal of much larger quantities of liquid per hour and per unit plant than in the drying process. The product obtained from an evaporator is either concentrated solution or suspension or a wet slurry, whereas that from a dryer is substantially dry.

Significance of Drying :

Drying is an important operation in pharmaceutical industry :

(i) It enables the product to be presented in the form, suitable for subsequent processing or marketing. For example, tablet granules are dried to the extent suitable for further compression; liquid extracts are dried to a dry form.

(ii) Transportation costs are reduced as drying reduces weight as well as volume of the material.

(iii) Physical and chemical stability of the product is affected in presence of moisture. Removal of moisture significantly reduces rate of chemical reactions, chances of microbial attack or enzymatic actions and thus imparts better stability to the product.

(iv) Adoption of a suitable method of drying enables to obtain a product with desired physical properties, e.g. spray dried lactose is free flowing and compressible.

12.2 MECHANISM OF DRYING

Drying involves heat transfer and mass transfer simultaneously. Heat transfer takes place from the heating medium to the solid; except in dielectric or high frequency electric drying, where heat is generated within the solid and flows to exterior surface. Mass transfer involves movement of the moisture to the surface of the solid and it's subsequent evaporation from the surface. Movement of moisture depends on physical characteristics of the solid and moisture content. The transfer of vapours from the surface to the surrounding is affected by external conditions like temperature, humidity, air flow rate, pressure and evaporating surface exposed.

In a solid moisture is present in two forms; bound and unbound moisture. The bound moisture in a solid exerts equilibrium vapour pressure lower than that of the pure water at the same temperature. Water retained in small capillaries in the solid, adsorbed at the solid surfaces, water of crystallisation, solution in cell or fibre walls is bound moisture. The unbound moisture exerts an equilibrium vapour pressure equal to that of pure water. Various theories have been proposed to explain the internal movement of the moisture. They are as follows :

(a) Diffusion theory

(b) Capillarity theory

(c) Pressure gradient theory

(d) Gravity flow theory

(e) Vaporization and condensation mechanism.

Of the above mentioned theories, first two theories predominate in the drying of pharmaceutical substances.

Diffusion theory suggests two ways of moisture movement :

(i) Water diffuses through the solid to the surface and then diffuses into the air surrounding the solid.

(ii) Evaporation of water occurs at an intermediate zone much below the solid surface and then vapours diffuse through the solid into the air.

Diffusion theory assumes that the effect of capillarity, gravitational and frictional forces is too small and the rate of flow of water to the surface is proportional to the moisture gradient. But the diffusivity decreases with decreasing moisture content and temperature and increases with pressure. Due to this limitation, the theory can not predict drying rate and moisture gradient over a range. Hence, capillarity theory was put forward.

Capillarity theory applies to the air drying of porous granular solids. A porous material contains a complicated network of interconnected pores and channels which are not circular or straight. The cross-section of these capillaries at the drying surface forms various sizes of pores. As evaporation proceeds at the surface, a miniscus is formed across each pore. Due to interfacial tension between water and solid, the miniscus formed sets the capillary force. These capillarity forces act as driving forces for the movement of water through the pores towards the surface. The curvature of the miniscus which depends on pore diameter, determines the strength of capillary forces. Greater capillarity forces are developed in small pores as compared to larger ones. Thus small pores can pull more water than large pores and larger pores are emptied first. In this emptied pore, air enters readily and the moisture concentration near the surface can remain relatively high. But in a tightly packed wet material air replacement is not possible and normal capillary flow cannot carry the liquid to the surface. Hence capillarity theory holds good only for free water in the bed and hygroscopic materials tend to agree with the diffusion theory. Capillary movement of the liquid takes place in the granules as well as in the spaces between the granules. As the pore diameter in the granules is considerably smaller than the surrounding capillaries, the liquid surrounding the granules is removed before the pore liquid.

12.3 THEORY OF DRYING

Depending on the external conditions and internal mechanisms of fluid flow solids show different drying patterns. A typical drying cycle of a solid can be divided into three distinct zones.

(a) Initial Adjustment Period
(b) Constant Rate Period
(c) Falling Rate Period.

These drying zones are shown in Fig. 12.1 (a) and (b).

(a)

(b)

Fig. 12.1 : Drying curves of solids

(a) Initial Adjustment Period : In the Fig. 12.1 (a) and(b) it is OA which is also called as 'Heating up period'. An wetted substance when kept for drying it absorbs heat from the surrounding and vaporization of moisture takes place which cools the surface. Heat flows to the cooled surface at higher rates, leads to rise in temperature and evaporation again. This continues and then an equilibrium is reached when the heat transfer to the material just balances the heat required for the vaporization of water. If all the heat transfer is taking place by convection, the material should attain wet bulb temperature. But if there is additional heat flow by conduction and radiation, then material attains higher temperature. If the initial temperature of the material is higher than WBT, then it reduces to WBT.

(b) Constant Rate Period : During this period there is a continuous liquid film over the surface of the solid. Evaporation from this film at WBT proceeds at a constant rate and the film is continuously replaced by moisture from inside. As long as the delivery of water from the interior to the surface is sufficient to keep the surface completely wet, the drying rate remains constant as shown by region AB. Drying rate in the constant rate period is given by :

$$\frac{dW}{d\theta} = \frac{A\, h_c\, (t_d - t_w)}{\rho\, L\, \lambda} \quad \ldots (1)$$

where, $\dfrac{dw}{d\theta}$ = Rate of drying in kg of water per kg of dry solid

A = Area exposed to drying

t_d = Dry bulb temperature

t_w = Wet bulb temperature

ρ = Bulk density of solid

L = Thickness of solid bed

λ = Latent heat of vaporization of water

h_c = Convection heat transfer coefficient.

Thus, particle size, bed height, air temperature and humidity of the air are important factors which affect the constant rate period.

From equation (1), it is clear that rate of drying can be increased by increase in surface area exposed e.g. in spray drying, due to atomization of liquid fine droplets are formed which expose high surface area for drying. Increase dry bulb temperature and WBT is maintained low, by continuously replacing the hot air. Convection heat transfer coefficient can be maintained high by agitating the solid and maintaining the film thickness on solid surface as low as possible. The solid bed thickness should be maintained low.

As drying proceeds, the coarse capillaries are completely depleted of water and solid fails to maintain a complete uniform film. The area over which moisture film is not present is known as 'dry spot'. Such dry spots start appearing and drying rate starts falling. The moisture content at which decrease in drying rate starts is called critical moisture content and the time as first critical point.

(c) Falling Rate Period : Due to dry spots on the surface, the area of constant mass transfer decreases and the heat transferred to the dry spots will be utilized to raise the temperature of solid to dry bulb temperature. Thus as number of dry spots increase, heat transfer and mass transfer rates fall which is called as first falling rate period. The solid surface becomes completely free of liquid film due to emptying of fine capillaries and now movement of moisture to the surface takes place by diffusion. The time at which fine capillaries are also empty and no film is present on surface is called as 'second critical point'. After second critical point the drying rate falls further as the rate of moisture movement by diffusion is very low. At the end, the drying rate becomes zero, and moisture content of solids at this point is called Equilibrium Moisture Content (EMC). EMC may be defined as *mass of water per unit mass of dry solid when the drying limit has been attained by use of air at any given temperature and humidity*. EMC will be determined by nature of the material, temperature and humidity of air.

A crystalline or granular material holds water near to the surface and hence show easy transport to the surface, by maintaining a continuous film over the surface. Therefore, constant rate period for such substances is long. An amorphous substance holds water in the interior and cannot maintain film for long times exhibit shorter constant rate and longer falling rate periods. At equilibrium moisture content, the exerted vapour pressure of water in the solid is equal to the partial vapour pressure of water in the air. The moisture in the bound conditions, entrapped in the interiors cannot exert complete vapour pressure. Therefore the substances with bound moisture or deeply entrapped water show higher values of EMC. Similarly, increase in humidity of air increases the EMC, whereas temperature has inverse relationship with the EMC. EMC plays an important role in residual moisture in granules for compression, gelatin capsule storage and preparation etc.

12.4 DRYING EQUIPMENTS

12.4.1 Tray Dryer :

Tray dryer is a batch dryer where forced convection heating takes place. It consists of a small cabinet or a large compartment in which the trays containing wet materials are inserted. The trays are either loaded onto the trucks in tiers or may be inserted directly into the dryer cabinet. The heating air is circulated by means of fans which also removes the humid air from the cabinet. The trays containing the load remain in the dryer until drying is complete, after which they are withdrawn, emptied and recharged for drying the next batch.

In tray dryers, the air travels very short distance around two to three stacks of trays. The operation involves recirculation of hot drying air with partial rejection of humid air and its replacement by fresh air. Thus, recirculation type tray dryer involves, use of large volumes of recirculated air with frequent heating, together with controlled introduction of fresh air into the cabinet and controlled exhausting of humid air. Stacks of trays when placed properly may act as horizontal partitions and permit recirculation. Thus recirculation and reheating facilitate drying at low temperatures than that possible with a single passage of heated air through a tray dryer.

The trays in a dryer are spaced in such a way that the pressure losses are low. The trays which are 1.25 to 1.5 inches deep are spaced around three inches apart. Air velocities upto 1000 ft/min. are commonly used. High air circulation ratio alongwith large quantities of fresh air are necessary in the initial stages of drying cycle so as to remove large quantities of moisture present in the material. Once solid reaches the falling rate period, the air recirculation ratio upto 90 – 95% without supply of fresh air is sufficient.

Fig. 12.2 : Tray dryer

Thermal efficiency of the dryer is very low for materials which are to be dried to a very low moisture content because in such cases, the falling rate period will be lengthy requiring longer drying time.

12.4.2 Tunnel Tray Dryer :

In a tunnel tray dryer, the trucks loaded with wet material at one end of the tunnel and dried product is discharged at the other end of the tunnel. The tunnel is comprised of number of units each of which is thermostatically controlled. Throughout the length of the tunnel fresh air inlets and humid exhausts are suitably spaced.

Fig. 12.3 : Tunnel Dryer

The movement of the air from inlet to outlet may be parallel or countercurrent in relation to the movement of the trucks. Thermal efficiency of the dryer is higher with countercurrent flow of air and the material.

12.4.3 Turbo-Tray Dryer :

It is a continuous tray dryer (Fig. 12.4) in which wet material is continuously introduced onto a series of trays and is discharged continuously in a dried form. It consists of a cylindrical or hexagonal vertical housing with internal or external compartment having heating coil. In the housing several tiers of segmented trays rotate slowly at around 0.1 r.p.m. In the central area centrifugal fans are fixed on a vertical shaft. This facilitates high air flow rates over and above the trays and through the heating coil.

Fig. 12.4 : Turbo-tray dryer

12.4.4 Fluidized Bed Dryer :

Fluidized bed dryer enjoy widespread popularity for drying of pharmaceuticals and many other industrial products. It has maintained popularity due to high thermal efficiency, gas - solid contact, low capital and maintenance cost with high reliability.

In fluidized drying, the wet material on a suitable perforated plate is subjected to a stream of hot air at a certain temperature. The material is removed from the dryer when it is sufficiently dry.

Principle : Consider the solid material like tablet granulation is resting on distributor plate in a tube. Now, if a vertically rising stream of gas is introduced at the bottom, the difference in pressure across the granular bed (ΔP) is linearly proportional to the flow rate of air. As per Kozeny – Carman equation, this pressure drop across the porous bed will be :

$$\Delta P = \frac{150 \, V_g \, \eta \, (1 - \varepsilon)^2 \, L}{(D_p)^2 \, \varepsilon^3}$$

where
- V_g = Velocity of gas
- η = Viscosity of gas
- ε = Porosity
- L = Bed height

D_p = Diameter of particle

ΔP = Pressure drop across the bed.

Now, the behaviour of the bed can be visualised as follows :

(i) For gas velocities below minimum fluidizing velocity (V_{mf}) i.e. $V_g < V_{mf}$; the bed behaves like a packed bed and pressure drop increases from A to B as shown in Fig. 12.5.

(ii) When gas velocities are increased and past V_{mf} i.e. $V_g > V_{mf}$ as shown by point B, the granular bed expands (L increases), the particles move apart and are able to slide past each other. This expansion of bed causes considerable increase in voids with consequent reduction of pressure drop as shown between points B and C.

Now the entire particle - gas mass behaves like a fluid and the system is called to be fluidized. Here onwards, the pressure drop increases only slightly with increase in air flow rates.

Fig. 12.5 : Pressure drop - air flow rate relationship

(iii) If the velocity is further increased, the bed becomes more and more expanded and the solid content becomes more and more dilute.

Construction : Horizontal F.B.D. is used for continuous process and vertical F.B.D. is for batch process. The fluidized bed dryer whether used for continuous or batch process incorporate similar features regardless of their design. The dryer consists of :

(A) **Air Handler :** Which is a source of fluidizing air. It is also attached by a means of heating and dehumidifying air, if necessary.

(B) **Plenum :** It consists of a screen or plate to distribute the incoming air as it enters the dryer.

(C) **Product container :** This container holds the product which is subjected to drying.

(D) **Expansion chamber :** This chamber is situated above the product container and holds the suspended material.

(E) **Filter :** The upper part of the expansion chamber has filters. It prevents fines from escaping into the atmosphere or collecting on the blades of fan which pulls the air through the drier.

(F) **Explosion Relief Duct :** It helps to avoid the explosion which may occur due to rapid pressure build up due to organic solvents.

Fig. 12.6 : Fluidized bed dryer

Applications :

1. **Coating of tablets :**

The fluidized bed dryer can be used in coating process as well. The technique is called as Wurster technique. The design is modified slightly. It has three basic designs.

1. Top spray : It is similar to the fluid-bed granulation process.
2. Bottom spray.
3. Tangential spray.

         (a) Top spray   (b) Bottom spray   (c) Tangential spray
                    Fig. 12.7 : Three basic types of fluid-bed coating processes

During normal operation, production is accelerated by fluidizing air through the inner partition that defines the spray zone. Deceleration occurs in the region of expansion chamber and the product is dropped back in the coating chamber. The product coated by the Wurster technique is typically characterized by uniform distribution of coating and high gloss. Also the process also exhibits excellent drying qualities.

The parameters which need to be controlled are the

1. Batch size
2. Fluidizing air volume
3. Inlet air temperature
4. Inlet air humidity
5. Spray rate.

2. Wet granulation

Fluidized Bed Dryers are used as wet granulators. Powders are agglomerated in the drying chamber and liquid binder is sprayed over it, while hot air flow simultaneously dries the agglomerates by vaporizing the liquid phase. This is advantageous due to reduction in handling and reduction in contamination by dust.

Advantages of fluidized bed drying :

1. Efficient heat and mass transfer facilitate high drying rates. Heating time of thermolabile materials is minimized.
2. Individual particles of the bed get dried in the fluidized state. So, most of the drying will be at constant rate and the falling rate period is very short.
3. Temperature can be controlled uniformly.
4. A free-flowing product is obtained.

5. Since the bed is not static, free movement of individual particles eliminates the risk of soluble materials migrating.
6. Containers can be mobile, so handling is simple and labour cost is reduced.
7. Short drying time yields a high output from a small floor space.

Disadvantages :

1. Turbulence of fluidized state may produce fines due to attrition.
2. Fine particles lead to segregation, so they must be collected by bag filters.
3. Static charges may be produced due to vigorous movement of particles in hot dry air.

12.4.5 Spray Dryer :

Spray drying is a one step continuous drying process which involves transformation of feed from a fluid state into a dried particulate form by spraying the feed into a hot drying medium. The feed may be either a solution, suspension or paste. The feed is atomized into a spray and contact between the spray and drying medium takes place resulting in moisture evaporation. This is continued until a dried product is obtained.

In pharmaceutical industry, spray drying is successfully used for drying of antibiotics, enzymes, vitamins, yeasts, vaccines, plasma, hormones, plasma substitute etc.

In spray drying, moisture flow through a droplet is by diffusional mechanism, supplemented by capillary flow.

Construction and Working :

Fig. 12.8 : Spray dryer

The spray drying process involves four basis stages :
(i) Atomization of feed into a spray.
(ii) Contact of spray and air.
(iii) Evaporation from droplet.
(iv) Separation of dried product from air.

(A) Atomization of feed into a spray :

Atomization is carried out by an atomizer which produces from liquid bulk a spray of individual small droplets having uniform size. Small individual droplets offer high surface to mass ratio ensuring quick evaporation, short drying times and low surface temperature. Uniform droplet size ensures uniform dried product characteristics.

Atomizers are classified as follows on the basis of different energy forms applied to break up the bulk of liquid.

(a) Centrifugal Atomizers : e.g. Rotary Atomizer. In rotary atomization technique, the feed liquid is centrifugally accelerated to high velocity before it is discharged into the drying chamber. The liquid is distributed centrally on the wheel disc or cup. The liquid extends over the rotating surface as a thin film. Maximum centrifugal energy is imparted to the liquid when the liquid acquires the peripheral speed of the wheel or disc before discharge. Then the liquid film disintegrates to give droplets. Centrifugal wheel atomizer is commonly used for pharmaceuticals. Slurries or pastes having either heat sensitive, thermoplastic, abrasive, corrosive or high viscous properties can be successfully atomized. Rotary atomizers are used to produce fine to medium coarse product having size 30 – 150 μm.

(b) Pressure Atomizer : e.g. Centrifugal pressure nozzle. The pressure nozzle is based on the principle of conversion of pressure energy within the bulk of the liquid into kinetic energy of a thin moving liquid sheet. The feed concentrate is fed to the nozzle under pressure. Pressure energy is converted into kinetic energy, and feed issues from the nozzle orifice as a high speed film, that readily disintegrates into a spray as the film is unstable. The feed rotates within the nozzle, resulting in cone shaped spray patterns emerging from the nozzle orifice. The pressure nozzles have pressures of about 10,000 lb/in^2. Mean droplet size of the spray is directly proportional to feed rate and viscosity, and inversely proportional to pressure. Pressure nozzles are used to obtain coarse particle powders of 120 –250 μm.

Fig. 12.9 : Atomizers

(c) Pneumatic Atomizer : e.g. Two fluid Nozzle atomizer. This atomizer is based on utilisation of kinetic energy of one fluid to break another fluid into droplets. It involves impact of liquid with a high velocity gas or air. The high velocity gas creates high frictional forces over the liquid surfaces leading to disintegration of liquid into droplets. The stream of gas is rotated within the nozzle and may come in contact with liquid either within the nozzle or after emerging of liquid from the orifice.

It can handle high viscosity feed producing medium coarse spray with less uniformity. But for low viscosity feeds, product having low size between 15 – 20 μm and high degrees of homogeneity are obtained.

(B) Spray – Air Contact

The spray and air can flow through the dryer in *counter-current flow* i.e. the product and air pass in the same direction. Counter-current contact is preferred for heat sensitive products, because the spray evaporation is rapid, as fresh droplets contacts with hottest air and drying air cools accordingly. Thus drying time is short. The product is not subjected to heat degradation. Product temperature is maintained low when bulk of the evaporation takes place and droplet temperature is at wet bulb temperature. Temperature of dried product does not rise as it is in contact with comparatively cool air. Counter-current contact minimizes the bulk density of product.

In *counter-current* contact the spray and air enter at the opposite ends of the dryer. It has advantage of better heat utilisation. But the dried powder comes in contact with hottest air, and temperature of dried product is high. Thus, it is more suitable thermostable substances. This is widely used when high product temperature is required to obtain case hardening effect. Counter-current contact gives product with high bulk density.

(C) Droplet Drying :

Heat is transferred by convection from air to droplet. Vapours formed by evaporation of moisture get transported to surrounding air by convection. The moisture from the interior at the droplet migrates to the surface maintaining the surface wetness. But generally the air temperature is so high that moisture migration is incapable of maintaining the surface wetness and a dried layer is formed at the surface of the droplet.

Now, this dried layer is the main resistance for mass transfer of moisture to the surface. The rate of heat transfer exceeds the rate of mass transfer and evaporation of moisture takes place below this solid layer. Vapours set up pressure inside the droplet. The effect of pressure depends on the nature of the surface layer.

	Layer porous and Rigid	No change
Dried surface layer	Less porous and Rigid	Broken particle
	Non-porous and Plastic	Expanded particle

Formation of expanded and hollow particles is a main feature of spray drying. The hollow particles are formed by mechanisms mentioned below.

(a) The surface layer is semi-impervious to vapour flow. The droplet puffs out as vapours are formed in the droplet and it expands with increase in droplet temperature.

(b) In crystalline products, rate of moisture evaporation is more than the diffusion of solids back into the droplet interior. This leads to formation of air voids.

(c) Due to capillary action, liquid flows with the accompanying solids to the droplet surface, creating void at the centre of the droplet.

(D) Separation and Recovery of Dried Product :

This process recovers solids and exhausts dust free air. Majority of dried product falls to the base of the chamber where primary separation takes place. A small fraction of product passes out entrained in the air, which is recovered by a suitable separation equipment. This secondary product separation is carried out by cyclone separators, bag filters, electrostatic precipitators and wet scrubbers.

Advantages of spray dryers :

1. Operation is continuous, easy and adaptable to automatic control.
2. It can be used for both heat sensitive and heat resistant materials in solution, slurry, paste or melt form.
3. Flexibility in design allows drying of toxic materials, organic solvent containing feed, feed forming powders explosive with air. It can also be used for aseptic conditions.
4. Product quality remains constant all over the process when other conditions are kept constant.

Disadvantages of spray dryers :

1. Due to it's larger size, fabrication and installation cost is very high.
2. Thermal efficiency is very poor or large amount of heat is wasted in exhaust air.

Applications of Spray drying :

Spray drying is used successfully for drying of pharmaceutical infusions, extracts, digitalist, adrenaline, etc. Spray driers for pharmaceuticals are of three types :

(a) Standard open cycle type.

(b) Aseptic open cycle type.

(c) Closed cycle type.

First two types use atmospheric air as a drying media while the third type which is commonly used to remove organic solvent uses inert gas like nitrogen.

Blood plasma, serum, bacitracin, vitamins, penicillin, yeast, chloramphenical succinate, dextran, harmones, enzymes, etc. are dried using aseptic or closed type spray direct. In aseptic type sterile air is obtained using 'HEPA' filters.

Closed cycle drier : Closed cycle drier is used when : (a) Solvent system is flammable, (b) Drying of toxic substances, (c) To prevent atmospheric pollution, (d) If powder forms explosive mixture with air and (e) For complete solvent recovery.

Spray Congealing : In this process a melt of certain substance comes in contact with a stream of air, and gets cooled to form fine solid particulate product. When a slurry of some insoluble material in a molten mass is spray congealed, the product obtained is insoluble particle coated with congealing substance. This is mainly used in chewable formulations to mask the taste or improve stability of drugs. e.g. 1 part of vitamins like riboflavin, pyridoxine hydrochloride, niacinamide and thiamine monohydrate is mixed with 2 parts of fatty acids or mono and diglycerides of fatty acids and spray congealed to get free flowing powder. The taste of vitamins is also masked. Spray congealing is also used in sustained release formulations.

Spray coating and spray encapsulation involves evaporation of solvent from solution forming a coat on the substance to be coated. For coating of liquids, an emulsion is prepared, where, the liquid to be coated is present in the internal phase and the coating material in the external phase. After spray drying, solvent from continuous phase evaporates leaving a coat over the dispersed particles. Similarly, a suspension is prepared and spray dried to the solids.

It is also used for micro-encapsulation by interfacial polymerization, where the dispersed phase contains liquid to be encapsulated and first reactant and solution of emulsifier and second reactant as continuous phase.

Fig. 12.10 : Spray congealing

12.4.6 Freeze Drying :

Freeze drying is a method of drying where the liquid in the solid - liquid mixture is frozen by cooling and is subsequently caused to sublime. Generally, the liquid to be evaporated is water. It is also termed by lyophilization i.e. "made solvent loving". Freeze drying is widely used for drying of pharmaceuticals which are highly heat sensitive e.g. blood proteins, vitamins, antibiotics, human protein hydrolysates and animal vaccines, penicillin. Freeze drying consists of freezing of the material followed by sublimation of ice or frozen moisture under vacuum of 100 to 300 micron at temp. $-10\ ^\circ C$ to $-30\ ^\circ C$. The sublimated water vapours are then condensed. For sublimation heat is supplied at a controlled rate so that sublimation of ice takes place avoiding melting of the material. As drying proceeds, ice surface recedes gradually within the body of the material, leaving behind a porous structure in the dried product through which water vapour moves to the surface. All the original constituents of the material remain frozen in their original positions. Thus dried product usually retains its original shape and size with considerable porosity resulting in ready solubility in water. The freeze drying operation consists of :

(a) Preparation and pretreatment.
(b) Pre freezing to solidify the water.
(c) Primary drying (sublimation of ice under vacuum).
(d) Secondary drying (removal of residual moisture under high vacuum).
(e) Packing.

(a) Preparation and pre-treatment : In some cases pre-treatment is given before pre-freezing e.g. protein solutions take eight to ten times longer period than pure water. Therefore in such cases, it is desirable to pre-concentrate the solution under normal vacuum tray drying unless a very highly porous product is required.

(b) Pre freezing to solidify the water : The aqueous solutions packed in vials, ampoules or bottles are cooled by using cold shelves (around – 50 $^{\circ}$C), alcohol baths, (around – 50 $^{\circ}$C) or liquid nitrogen bath (– 195 $^{\circ}$C). Normal cooling rates in pre-freezing stage is around 1 to 3 $^{\circ}$K/min. Thickness of the frozen material affects the rate of drying, thinner is the layer, higher is the drying rate. The thickness is usually maintained between 1/2 to 3/4 inch. During this stage cabinet is maintained at low temperature and atmospheric pressure.

The freezing rate during this stage is important to be controlled, large ice crystals are formed at low freezing rate resulting in relatively large holes on sublimation of ice. Dextrin solution when lyophilised at freezing rate between 3 to 25 $^{\circ}$K /min resulted in a product having pore size 1 to 4 micron.

(c) Primary drying (Sublimation of ice under vacuum) : Once the solution is frozen, during primary drying vacuum is applied of the value of about 0.5 m bar. The temperature is linearly increased to around 30 $^{\circ}$C. in a span of 2 hr. and temperature is maintained constant during primary and secondary drying. As a necessary condition of sublimation temperature of subliming surface should be below its eutectic point. Thus subliming surface is maintained around 1 to 8 $^{\circ}$K below the eutectic point. The supply of heat controls movement of ice layer inwards and it has to be controlled in such a manner so as to get highest possible water vapour pressure at ice surface without melting material. Primary drying stage removes easily removable moisture. During this stage around 98 to 99% water is removed. This is followed by secondary drying.

(d) Secondary drying (Removal of residual moisture under high vacuum) : This stage removes (sublimes) the moisture which is difficult to remove during primary drying. Temp. is maintained constant at 30 $^{\circ}$C. But now vacuum is lowered to 0.07 m bar. The rate of drying is very low it takes around 10 to 20 hours.

(e) Packing : Closing of vials or bottles occurs in the drying plant after the vacuum has been broken by dry inert gas. Removal of residual moisture takes considerable time. In drying sera containing 10% of solid has shown that 80% of the total drying period is required to remove 95% of the total moisture, whereas 90% of total drying period is required to attain 1% residual moisture and remaining 10% of the drying time is required to remove next 0.5%.

Fig. 12.11 : An industrial freeze-dryer for pharmaceuticals

A freeze dryer (Fig. 12.11) consists of :

1. A drying chamber in which the trays are loaded.
2. A heat supply in the form of radiation source, heating coil.
3. Vapour condensing or adsorption system.
4. Vacuum pump or ejector.

Types of Freeze dryers :

1. Batch dryers : As the name implies it deals with one fixed quantity at a time and that usually completed. The product is arranged to be static, while the whole process is performed, environment, variables being altered around it to suit.

2. Continuous dryers : These are large freeze dryers refers to sequence batching in the main where trays or dishes rest throughout the stages of the process, each stage being in an assigned part of the dryer where the environment is set principally by the heating temperature. Physical entery and discharge are affected by means of locks, capable of dealing with carrods or single tray.

Factors affecting the process rate :

The greater the depth of the product more will be the time required for drying process. Therefore, product to be frozen by placing the container on refrigerated shelf (plug freezing) should be filled to planned limited depth. If the large volume of the solution must be processed, the surface area may be increased and the depth decreased by freezing the solution on a slant or while rotating the container at an angle in a liquid refrigerant bath such as dry ice and alcohol.

The passageway between the product surface and the condenser surface must be wide open and direct, far effective operation. Evacuation of system is necessary to reduce the impending effect that collisions with air molecules would have on passage of water molecule.

The amount of solids in the product, their particle size and thermal conductance will affect the rate of drying. Fluidized beds were more popular where vibration is used to shuffle and gently throw the material onwards. Both vertical and horizontal forms have been used. Because of short drying times, particle size distribution has to be very close. (1 – 2 or 1.5 – 2.5 mm) recycling of fines occur far more than in static dryers.

Advantages :

Freeze drying as a result of the character of the process has certain special advantages :

1. The solution is frozen such that the final dry product is a network of solid occupying the same volume as the original solution. Thus, there is no case-hardening and the product is light and porous.
2. Drying takes place at very low temperatures, so that enzyme action is inhibited and decomposition, particularly hydrolysis is minimized.
3. The porous form of the product gives ready solubility.
4. There is no concentration of the solution prior to drying, hence salts do not concentrate and denature proteins as occurs with other drying methods.
5. Under high vacuum, there is no contact with air and oxidation is minimised.

Disadvantages :

There are two main Disadvantages of freeze drying :

1. The porosity, ready solubility and complete dryness yield a very hygroscopic product. Unless dried in the final container and sealed in suitable packing, it requires special conditions.
2. The process is very slow and uses complicated plant, which is very expensive. It is not a general method of drying, therefore, is limited to certain types of valuable products that can't be dried by any other means.
3. It is difficult (but not impossible) to adopt the method for solutions containing non-aqueous solvents.

Applications :

1. It is utilized in maintenance and preservation of microbial culture.
2. The solution of penicillin must be kept at 0 – 2 °C and used within two-three days. If freeze dried and stored in hermetically sealed ampoules, full activity is retained for several months.
3. Fibrinogen is dissolved in sodium chloride injection and whipped into a foam, which is them clotted by addition of human thrombin. The foam is then freeze dried.
4. A solution of gelatin containing traces of formaldehyde is foamed, freeze dried, sterilised and used as a surgical dressing.
5. Freeze dried Haemoglobin formulated with sucrose to minimise inprocess degradation.
6. In general, a product is freeze dried if aqueous solution does not have any sufficient stability and if the product can't be crystallized in bulk. Compared to spray drying, freeze

drying is a low temperature process and is normally regarded as being less destructive to the product, particularly for proteins.

This technique is mainly used for drying immune serum, blood products, certain enzymes, a variety of viral and bacterial preparations, plant extracts, diagnostics as well as mammallian tissues useful in skin and bone graft surgery.

Also employed for preservation of products like several antineoplastics, vaccines, toxoids, hormones, vitamins and many food–stuffs.

12.4.7 Pnuematic or flash dryer :

Fig. 12.12 : Pneumatic dryer

Pneumatic drying process can be considered as a cross between fluidised bed dryer and the spray dryer. In pneumatic drying process, there is a continuous flow of particulate matter which is dried with warm or hot air while being transported by air stream. The free flowing medium size particles when introduced to a flow of hot air at adequate velocity become totally dispersed and entrained in such a way that it will be dried and pneumatically conveyed from the fill point to the point of delivery. The dried product is separated from air by reduction in velocity. Generally cyclone is used for this separation purpose. It is suitable as a pneumatic conveyor also to convey the moist material from point of production to a convenient post where it can be stored or packed in its dry form.

In flash drying gas velocity is appoximately ten times as compared to fluidised bed dryer and thereby requires large cyclones. The exit gas velocity is around 10 to 30 metres/sec. Some important points to be considered are as follows :

1. Particle size : The maximum particle size of the material is about 1 to 2 mm because the particles larger than this are not entrained by the air and require longer drying period than that achieved by flash dryer. If the material in its initial condition is not suitable for entrainment, it may be subjected to preliminary disintegration in cage mill to disintegrate it while the drying gas is passed through the mill. Sometimes the feed is made suitable by backmixing it with the product.

2. Gas velocity : The velocity of the air stream must be above the terminal velocity of fall of heaviest particle, so that general movement of all the particles is upwards without any fallback. The gas velocity for pneumatic handling is around 40 to 80 feet/sec. The high gas velocity may cause abrasion or dust formation. Dust formation is promoted by gas velocity, when the smaller particles are eroded from the feed particles. The ratio of weight of air to weight of material should not be less than 2 : 1. It may exceed in some cases like drying of relatively coarse material containing 2 to 3 per cent (low) moisture of elevated temperature.

The flash dryer essentially consists of

(a) Source of hot gas

(b) A material feeding device

(c) A drying column or duct with ventury section at material feed point.

(d) Cyclone for solid air separation.

(e) Air exhaust fan for discharging humid air.

The main drying duct is circular having well finished internal surface so as to avoid any interference to gas flow. The drying duct is around 1 metre in diameter and 10 m to 30 m in length. A ventury may be fitted at the feed point. As the heat transfer from hot gases to the material is instantaneous, material although subjected to very high gas temperature period of contact is very short.

Advantages :

1. Time of contact between the material to be dried and hot gas is very short only few seconds. Therefore it is suitable for drying of heat sensitive materials having good drying characteristics which helps in complete local entrainment of the material and also produces point of suction for filling without necessity of other mechanical feeding device.

Thus in a pneumatic dryer there is small particle size, high gas velocity, high temperature difference, between gas and material provides optimum drying condition with minimum drying period. During drying the material remain at weight bulb temperature of the gas and never exceeds the outlet gas temperature. For drying of materials, containing explosive or inflammable solvents earthing all parts of dryer is necessary.

Limitations :

1. It is not suitable for materials which are sticky and greasy in nature or where attrition may cause damage to the dried product.
2. For materials having high moisture content about 60% and above flash dryer is ineffective as high air velocities provide insufficient residence time so as to release all the moisture.

Drum or Roller Dryer (Film Drum Dryer)

It is a conduction dryer where heating medium generally steam is present inside a rotating cylinder. Heat is transferred by conduction to the metal surface of cylinder to the film of liquid to be dried (Fig. 12.13).

Fig. 12.13 : A double-drum dryer for low-viscosity solutions

(a) Single drum   (b) Multiple drum dryer

Fig. 12.14 : Roller Dryer

It is used for drying solutions, slurries, like liquid products and suspensions. The drum rotates at the speed of 5 – 20 revolutions per min. The time of contact between material and heating surface is very short around 3 to 12 sec. These dried material attains the temperature of heating surface for a very short period. Hence, film drum dryer dries material without significant thermal degradation.

Drying in film drum dryer involves transfer of heat from condensing steam within the drum through the metal of the drum to the thin film of liquid on the outer surface of the drum. The overall heat transfer rate during this drying process depends on solid content and it's physical properties, film thickness, steam temperature, metal thickness and it's thermal conductivity. The temperature drop through the metal drum is about 65 to 35 °F.

The roller dryer may be encased in a vacuum tight chamber for drying of materials which are heat sensitive, are subject to oxidation or where solvent has to be recovered.

Film drum dryers are extensively used in chemical and pharmaceutical industries yeast, pigments, meat extracts, distillery by products, antibiotics, glandular extracts, insecticides, D.D.T, calcium and barium carbonates and other organic and inorganic salts.

Disadvantage :

Maintenance cost of film drum dryer is higher than the spray dryers.

***

DISTILLATION

13.1 INTRODUCTION

Distillation is an unit operation which involves separation of a vaporisable component from a multi-component system and subsequent condensation of vapours. It has been practised as early as 3500 B.C. for isolation of odoriferous principles from flower petals, leaves etc. In eleventh and twelfth century it was widely used in Southern Italy for isolation of alcohol from wines.

Distillation differs from evaporation mainly in three aspects :

(i) In evaporation process, the vaporization takes place at the free surface of the liquid below its boiling point. Whereas, in distillation vaporization occurs from the bulk of the liquid at it's boiling point. Although, evaporation should be carried out below boiling point generally, it is carried out at boiling point so as to increase the rate of operation.

(ii) The vapours in evaporation process diffuse through the space above the liquid whereas, vapours in distillation has sufficient pressure to push away the molecules of air or gas present above the surface.

(iii) In evaporation, concentrated residue is a desired product, in contrast distillate is generally a desired product of distillation.

13.2 RELATIVE VELOCITY

The real basis for separation of two components of distillation is the difference in their volatilities (i.e. relative volatility of the system). The volatility of a liquid is indicated by its vapour pressure. Higher is the vapour pressure of the substance more volatile it is. If a mixture of two liquids A and B is heated, the vapours in equilibrium with the liquid mixture will contain more proportion of the more volatile component A, than in the liquid. The degree of enrichment of vapours with respect to A depends on its relative volatility (α_{AB}) with respect to component B. Relative volatility can be mathematically defined as :

$$\alpha_{AB} = \frac{Y_A/X_A}{Y_B/X_B} = \frac{Y_A X_B}{Y_B X_A} \qquad \ldots (1)$$

where, Y indicate the mole fraction of component in the vapour phase and X indicate the mole fraction of component in the liquid space.

Subscripts A and B denote more volatile and less volatile component respectively.

13.3 VAPOUR - LIQUID EQUILIBRIUM

Thus, to understand the process of distillation it is necessary to have a clear concept about the vapour-liquid equilibrium conditions. The vapour liquid equilibrium relations of binary systems can be studied for three different classes of systems viz. Miscible, immiscible and partially miscible systems.

13.3.1 Miscible System :

The miscible binary system may have ideal or non-ideal behaviour.

(a) Ideal Systems :

Ideal binary mixtures obey Raoult's law. According to Raoult's law "a component's vaporising tendency depends on it's concentration in the mixture and its vapour pressure at that temperature." In such system, the components have no effect on each other except dilution. In these systems each component acts independently for a binary system of components A and B Roult's law can be mathematically expressed as :

$$P_A = P_A^o X_A \quad \ldots (2)$$

$$P_B = P_B^o X_B \quad \ldots (3)$$

where, P = Partial pressure of the component

P^o = Vapour pressure of pure component at that temperature.

Subscripts A and B denotes component A and B. The total vapour pressure of the mixture is given by,

$$P_{total} = P_A + P_B \quad \ldots (4)$$

The vapour pressure composition relationship at a constant temperature for a binary system is shown in Fig.13.1.

Fig. 13.1 : Vapour pressure - composition curve for an ideal binary system

$$\therefore \quad \alpha_{AB} = \frac{P_A}{P_B} \qquad \ldots (5)$$

The vapour-liquid equilibrium pattern at constant pressure can be exhibited by the equilibrium curve and boiling point diagram for a particular system.

Fig. 13.2 : Boiling point diagram

'Boiling point diagram' is obtained by plotting boiling points of various mixtures at atmospheric pressure against composition. A typical boiling point diagram is shown in Fig. 13.3. It shows two curves, the boiling curve which indicates the boiling points of various compositions. The second is a dew curve which gives the composition of the vapours in equilibrium with the boiling mixture. The ends of the two curves coincide at the boiling points of the pure components. Above the dew curve the mixture is completely vapour, whereas below the boiling curve the mixture is completely a liquid. The area between the two curves represents a system which consists partly of liquid and partly of vapours. As shown in Fig. 13.2, if we start heating a system containing X_A mole fraction of component A (denoted by m), it starts boiling at temperature t_A to produce vapours in equilibrium with Y_A mole fraction of A. These vapours on cooling will naturally produce a liquid phase with Y_A mole fractions of A. As A is more volatile than B, Y_A is always greater than X_A.

'Equilibrium curve ' is a plot of mole fraction of a more volatile component in vapours against it's mole fraction in the liquid phase. A typical equilibrium curve is shown in Fig. 13.3. It shows that for an ideal binary mixture at all compositions the more volatile component is always present in higher concentrations in the vapour phase than the liquid phase.

Fig. 13.3 : Equilibrium curve

Although there is slight change in the relative volatility of an ideal mixture ; concept of average relative volatility was introduced for theoretical construction of an equilibrium diagram. This may introduce a deviation in equilibrium concentration upto the level of 1.7% only.

The average relative volatility is calculated as the root mean square of the relative volatilities of the system at the boiling point of each component :

$$\therefore \quad \alpha_{AB\,(avg)} = \sqrt{\alpha_{AB\,(at\,b.p.\,of\,A)} \infty \, \alpha_{AB\,(at\,b.p.\,of\,B)}} \quad \ldots (6)$$

By assuming average relative volatility, an equilibrium diagram can be developed as follows,

As we know

$$\alpha_{AB} = \frac{Y_A/X_A}{Y_B/X_B} \quad \ldots (7)$$

But, $Y_B = 1 - Y_A$

and $X_B = 1 - X_A$

By substituting these values in eqn. 7, we get

$$\alpha_{AB} = \frac{Y_A/X_A}{(1-Y_A)\,.\,(1-X_A)} \quad \ldots (8)$$

By solving this,

$$Y_A = \frac{\alpha_{AB}\,X_A}{1 + (\alpha_{AB} - 1)\,X_A} \quad \ldots (9)$$

By assuming various values for X_A in eqn. 9 corresponding values of Y_A are calculated and an equilibrium diagram is plotted.

Example 1 : Construct an equilibrium diagram for binary system of benzene – toluene.

(a) Calculation of average relative volatility

Data	V.P. of Benzene (P_A)	V.P. of Toluene (P_B)	$\alpha_{AB} = \dfrac{P_A}{P_B}$
Boiling point of C_6H_6 80.1 °C	760 mm	270 mm	2.81
Boiling point of Tolulene 110.6	1,780 mm	760 mm	2.34

$$\therefore \quad \alpha_{AB\,(avg.)} = \sqrt{2.81 \infty 2.34} = 2.52$$

(b) Calculation of Y_A

For increment of 0.1 X_A we will calculate Y_A

$$Y_A = \frac{\alpha_{AB}\,X_A}{1 + (\alpha_{AB} - 1)\,X_A}$$

$$\therefore \quad Y_A = \frac{2.52\, X_A}{1 + 1.52\, X_A}$$

X_A	$2.52\, X_A$	$1 + 1.52\, X_A$	Y_A
0.1	0.252	1.152	0.201
0.2	0.504	1.304	0.386
0.3	0.756	1.456	0.519
0.4	1.008	1.608	0.637
0.5	1.260	1.760	0.717
0.6	1.512	1.912	0.791
0.7	1.764	2.064	0.855
0.8	2.016	2.216	0.911
0.9	2.268	2.368	0.957

Now Y_A is plotted against X_A as shown in Fig. 13.4.

Fig. 13.4 : Equilibrium curve

(b) Non-Ideal Systems :

In non-ideal binary system there is an interaction of one component upon the other. It may be attraction or repulsion of molecules. The increase in adhesive interaction between the two components over the cohesive interaction of each component leads to decrease in escaping tendency and in turn partial vapour pressure of each component and the total vapour pressure of the system than expected by Raoult's law. This is negative deviation from Raoult's law as shown in Fig. 13.5 (a). Acetone-chloroform system exhibits negative deviation from Raoult's law.

(a) Vapor pressure of a system showing positive deviation from Raoult's law

(b)

(c)

Fig. 13.5 : System showing positive deviation from Raoult's law

Repulsion between two components causes cohesive force to exceed the adhesive force. This causes increase in escaping tendency and partial vapour pressure of each component along with total vapour pressure greater than that expected by Raoult's law. This is called as positive deviation from Raoult's law. Benzene ethyl alcohol system exhibits positive deviation from Raoult's law as shown in Fig. 13.6 (a).

(a) Vapor pressure of a system showing negative deviation from Raoult's law

(b)

(c)

Fig. 13.6 : System showing negative deviation from Raoult's law

In case of an ideal binary mixture the escaping tendency of any component is a function of its concentration (X) in the system. But in case of non-ideal mixtures deviations from ideality is shown due to the molecular interactions. Thus in non-ideal system the effective concentration or activity (a) of the component is a real function instead of actual concentration (X).

From non-ideal mixture Raoult's law will be modified as :

$$P_A = P_A^o \, a_A \qquad \ldots (10)$$

where, a_A = Effective concentration or activity of component A.

The ratio of activity to the actual concentration of a component is known as activity coefficient.

∴ Activity coefficient of A ; $\gamma_A = \dfrac{a_A}{X_A}$ ... (11)

By substituting value of a_A we get

$$P_A = P_A^o \, \gamma_A \, X_A \qquad \ldots (12)$$

Thus, relative volatility of a non-ideal mixture is given by

$$\alpha_{AB} = \dfrac{\gamma_A \, P_A^o}{\gamma_B \, P_B^o} \qquad \ldots (13)$$

From the eq. 13, we can say that the relative volatility in non-ideal system differs from introduction of an activity coefficient.

For an ideal system the activity coefficient is equal to one. In case of systems showing negative deviation from Raoult's law $P_A^o \, X_A > P_A^o \, \gamma_A X_A$ i.e. activity coefficient γ_A is less than one.

Whereas, for a system showing positive deviation γ_A is less than one. Whereas, for a system showing positive deviation γ_A is greater than one and $P_A^o X_A < P_A^o \gamma_A X_A$.

In non ideal system the change in the relative volatilities of both components with the composition of mixture is such that reversal of relative volatility occurs at certain composition. Such mixtures which shows reversal in relative volatility are termed as azeotropic mixtures and the composition of which reversal in relative volatility takes place is known as azeotrope or constant boiling mixture.

In Greek azeotrope means to boil unchanged. It is a constant boiling mixture which has maximum or minimum boiling point than any other composition or pure components [Fig. 5 (b) and 6 (b)]. An azeotropic mixture behaves like a pure component i.e. when distilled we get the distillate of the same composition. At some composition intermediate between the two pure components reversal of relative volatility takes place. Over one portion of the composition range one component is more volatile, while over the remaining of the range the other component is more volatile. Fig. 13.5 (c) and 13.6 (c) shows the equilibrium diagrams of azeotropic mixtures. The condition of the azeotropic composition can be given by,

$$\frac{\gamma_A P_A^o}{\gamma_B P_B^o} = \alpha_{AB} = 1 \qquad \ldots (14)$$

At this composition the difference in the inherent volatility of two components is overcome by the deviations from ideal behaviour. Therefore such mixture cannot be separated completely by simple distillation procedures and a modified method has to be adopted.

13.3.2 Immiscible Systems :

In the mixture of two immiscible liquids, each component will tend to vaporize independently hence their vapour pressures are additive. Thus the system starts boiling at temperature when the summation of two vapour pressures is equal to the atmospheric pressure i.e. at boiling point of a mixture,

$$P_A + P_B = 760 \text{ mm. Hg}$$

Vapour pressure - temperature relationship for an immiscible system is shown in Fig. 13.7.

Fig. 13.7 : Vapour pressure relationships for an immiscible system

Naturally, this temperature is below the boiling points of either of the individual components.

During distillation of such a system the composition of vapours produced will be in proportion of the relative vapour pressures of the two components. Therefore in vapour phase,

$$\frac{\text{Moles of A}}{\text{Moles of B}} = \frac{P_A}{P_B} \quad \ldots (15)$$

$$\therefore \quad \frac{\text{Weight of A in vapour phase}}{\text{Weight of B in vapour phase}} = \frac{P_A M_A}{P_B M_B} \quad \ldots (16)$$

This forms the basis of distillation of an immiscible system.

13.3.3 Partially Miscible System :

Partial miscibility is exhibited by some mixtures like water and n-butanol. Such partially miscible system is a special case of minimum boiling azeotrope. In this type of system over a range of liquid composition, the vapour composition and boiling point are constant as shown in Fig. 13.8 (a) and (b). Over the liquid composition range z, there are two immiscible liquid phases of compositions C and D, each having equilibrium vapour composition E.

(a)   (b)

Fig. 13.8 : Partially miscible system

13.4 DISTILLATION METHODS

Distillation methods for miscible liquid system are as follows :

1. Equilibrium or Flash distillation.
2. Simple or Differential distillation.
3. Fractional Distillation.
4. Distillation under reduced pressure.
   Molecular Distillation.

5. Special Distillation Methods for non-ideal mixtures
   (a) Azeotropic Distillation
   (b) Extractive Distillation

13.4.1 Equilibrium or Flash Distillation :

It is a single stage operation where a liquid is partially vaporized, the vapours are allowed to come in equilibrium with the residual liquid and the resulting vapours and liquid are separated. This is used only when the difference between the volatilities of the components is very large.

Material Balance for flash distillation will be as follows :

Consider the equilibrium distillation of a mixture containing components A and B.

Component A is more volatile. If we consider :

W_o = Total moles in distillation pot at the starting stage

X_o = Mole fraction of component A at start

V = Moles of vapours produced

X and Y = Mole fraction of A in liquid and vapours respectively.

As, Moles of A at start= Moles of A in vapour phase + Moles of A in liquid phase

∴ $\quad W_o x_o = V_y + (W_o - V) x$ ... (17)

The values of x and y are such that they satisfy both equilibrium curve and eqn. 17.

13.4.2 Simple or Differential Distillation :

In simple distillation, vapours from the boiling liquid is removed from the system as soon as it is formed. This method is commonly used on laboratory scale, but in industry, it is used only for systems with high relative volatilities. The assembly for distillation consists of a boiler, condenser and a receiver as shown in Fig. 13.9.

Fig. 13.9 : Simple distillation unit

In simple distillation there is continuous change in the distillate composition. It is necessary to know the composition of distillate at every instant during operation so as to control it.

In 1902, Rayleigh analysed the simple batch distillation mathematically. Consider that simple distillation was started with total W_o moles of system containing components A and B. If at any given instant W moles of liquid are present in the still which contains X mole fraction of component A.

∴ $\qquad$ XW = moles of component A present in the pot at given instant

Now, if a small amount dW is vaporized then total moles change from W to (W – dW) ; and suppose it's mole fraction changes from X to (X – dX). The vapours produced by vaporization of dW moles contain Y mole fraction of component A. Therefore material balance will be

∴ $\qquad$ XW = (W – dW) (X – dX) + Y dW $\qquad$ ... (18)

$\qquad$ XW = XW – dX W + dX dW – X dW + Y dW $\qquad$ ... (19)

dX dW is a second order differential which will be over Y small, hence if neglected we get

$\qquad$ dX W = (Y – X) dW $\qquad$ ... (20)

∴ $\qquad$ $\dfrac{dX}{Y - X} = \dfrac{dW}{W}$ $\qquad$ ... (21)

As simple distillation is a continuous operation, integration function is used. Equation 21 is thus integrated between initial and final conditions of total moles as well as mole fractions of more volatile component in the liquid.

∴ $\qquad$ $\displaystyle\int_{X_1}^{X_o} \dfrac{dX}{Y - X} = \int_{W_1}^{W_o} \dfrac{dW}{W} = \ln \dfrac{W_o}{W_1}$ $\qquad$ ... (22)

Left hand side of the equation can be integrated graphically. This equation (22) is known as Rayleigh's equation. It relates the amount of material distilled with instantaneous com-position of the liquid at that moment.

Application of Rayleigh's Equation :

This equation finds application in determination of cut-off point in batch distillation. We will apply the equation for two purposes as follows :

1. As we know simple distillation is industrially used only for systems where relative volatility is high. By using Rayleigh's equation we can predict the effectiveness of simple distillation for a given system.

2. In determination of cut-off point ; by using Rayleigh's equation we can stop operation as soon as the overhead composition falls below the required purity of the product.

The applications are illustrated below :

Let us consider that we started simple distillation of two ideal systems. M and N both containing 70 mole % of a more volatile component. if,

Average Relative volatility of system M = 1.5

Average Relative volatility of system N = 6.

Let us now analyse the systems for increments of x = 0.1.

For each value of x, corresponding value of y is calculated using equation (9).

(a)   (b)

Fig. 13.10 : $\dfrac{1}{y-x}$ Vs. X plots

The $\dfrac{1}{y-x}$ was plotted against X. The area under curve was calculated by integration by graph as shown in Fig. 13.10 (a) and (b). This integrated area is nothing but represents left hand side of Rayleigh's equation. i.e. $\ln \dfrac{W_o}{W}$.

Now,   Antilog $\left(\dfrac{\ln W_o/W}{2.303}\right) = \dfrac{W_o}{W}$ ... (23)

Suppose, $\dfrac{W_o}{W} = a$, then percent distilled is given by

per cent distilled $= \left(\dfrac{W_o - W}{W_o}\right) \times 100 = \left(1 - \dfrac{1}{a}\right) \times 100$ ... (24)

After following above discussed method, Tables 13.1 and 13.2 are prepared for $\alpha_{AB} = 1.5$ and $\alpha_{AB} = 6$ respectively.

Table 13.1

System M ($\alpha_{AB} = 1.5$)

X	Y	$\dfrac{1}{Y-X}$	Integral area	$\dfrac{W_o}{W}$	$\dfrac{W_o - W}{W_o} \times 100$

0.1	0.143	23.256	7.30	1448.00	00.930
0.2	0.273	13.699	5.50	244.30	99.590
0.3	0.391	10.989	4.30	73.64	98.640
0.4	0.500	10.000	3.25	25.77	96.120
0.5	0.600	10.000	2.25	9.482	89.450
0.6	0.692	10.869	1.20	3.319	67.870
0.7	0.773	12.821	0.00	1.000	00.000

Table 13.2

System N ($\alpha_{AB} = 6.0$)

X	Y	$\dfrac{1}{Y-X}$	Integral area	$\dfrac{W_o}{W}$	$\dfrac{W_o - W}{W_o} \times 100$
0.1	0.400	3.33	1.720	5.582	82.08
0.2	0.600	2.50	1.430	4.178	76.07
0.3	0.720	2.38	1.185	3.270	69.42
0.4	0.800	2.50	0.940	2.560	60.94
0.5	0.860	2.78	0.675	1.963	49.57
0.6	0.900	3.33	0.370	1.447	30.89
0.7	0.933	4.29	0.00	1.000	00.00

Now distillate composition(y) in terms of more volatile component is plotted against percent distilled as shown in Fig. 13.11.

Fig. 13.11 : Distillate composition as a function of percent distilled

From Fig. 13.11, we can conclude the following :

(a) If we start simple distillation with 70 mole % of a volatile component in a pot and if relative volatility of system is 6 (system N) we can get a distillate containing above 90 mole % also. But in case relative volatility be 1.5 (system M) we will never get distillate composition above 80 mole %. Therefore, in the later case we will not suggest simple distillation as it cannot enrich the component significantly.

(b) In case of system N i.e. $\alpha_{AB} = 6$, if we want the strength of the distillate to be minimum 80 moles % ; then stop the operation when 60% of the original system is distilled.

Aromatic spirit of Ammonia I.P. is prepared by simple distillation process. Nutmeg oil and other aromatic principles are introduced to the required degree in the final preparation when 2/3 of the original solution is distilled.

13.4.3 Fractional Distillation (Rectification) :

In fractional distillation, the vapours rising from the still come into contact with a condensed but not further cooled portion of vapours. The part of the condensate which is returned to the system is known as reflux. This is used for systematic separation of a mixture into relatively pure fractions.

Fig. 13.12 : Fractional distillation unit

The fractionation equipment as shown in Fig. 13.12, consists of :

(a) A still for generation of vapours.

(b) A fractionating or rectifying column for vapour liquid contact.

(c) A condenser for condensing overhead vapours.

The vapours are generated in the boiler or still. These vapours pass through the fractionating column, where they come in contact with the descending stream of liquid which is reflux from the condenser. Thus counter-current contact takes place between vapours and liquid. During this contact mass transfer and heat transfer takes place. The more volatile component from the liquid phase passes into the vapour phase and the less volatile component from the vapour phase condenses and passes into the liquid phase. Thus, the vapours rising from top to bottom get enriched in a more volatile component (MVC), whereas, the descending liquid stream becomes richer in a lower volatile component (LVC). Thus fractionating column assists heat transfer and mass transfer by bringing two phases in intimate contact. As MVC is larger at the top and LVC increases towards bottom, the top of the column is relatively cooler than the bottom of the column.

Fractionating columns are classified as :

(A) Plate columns :

    (a) Sieve plate column ;

    (b) Bubble cap column ;

    (c) Valve - plate column ;

(B) Packed column.

(A) Plate Columns :

A plate column is a stage wise contacting device. A plate column consists of plates or trays on which the liquid is retained for certain length of period when it is moving down the column. The vapours rising from the bottom are bubbled through this liquid when intimate contact is achieved between two phases. Thus contact between vapour and liquid occurs on the plate. Heat and mass transfer occurs between vapour and liquid phase. The liquid phase passing below becomes richer in LVC and vapour phase richer in the MVC from the plate above it. This occurs in all parts of column except the top plate where the concentration of MVC is maintained by returning part of the condensate from the last stage to the top plate. This is known as reflux return. Reflux ratio is the ratio of the condensate returned to the column and the amount withdrawn as product. Liquid flow patterns over a plate differ with the requirements. In crossflow pattern, Fig. 13.13 (a), the liquid flows across the plate and passes over a weir into the downcomer. In Reverse flow pattern Fig. 13.13 (b), the liquid passes across the plate and again direction of flow is reversed, thus liquid stays on a plate for longer period of time. In split flow, Fig. 13.13 (c), liquid passes on one plate from center to the sides, whereas on next plate the flow is from side of the plate to the centre. A crossflow may be modified to a cascade cross flow Fig. 13.13 (d) where plate is again divided in stages on which liquid flows in crossflow pattern.

(a) **Cross-flow**

(b) **Reverse flow**

(c) **Split flow**

(d) **Radial flow**

Fig. 13.13 : Flow patterns in rectification column

Very low liquids levels on plate will be unable to cover the holes, whereas excess liquid heights will increase the pressure drop. Therefore optimum liquid heights should be maintained over the plates. The liquid height is governed by liquid flow rate and weir height.

Entrainment i.e. carryover of liquid droplets with the vapours from the plate above ; is undesirable as it reduces the efficiency of the column. This may occur at high gas flow rates in such cases entrainment may be reduced by increasing diameter of the column. Thus higher is the gas flow rate larger is the diameter of the column. Thus higher is the gas flow rate larger is the diameter of the column. When gas at high velocity passes through the liquid over the plate there is formation of froth which increases gas-liquid surface area and increases rate of mass transfer but excessive foaming or frothing may increase entrainment. Excessive entrainment or if excessive gas or liquid is passed through the column results in *flooding*. Thus column diameter and spacing of trays of column should be carefully chosen to avoid entrainment. A smaller tray spacing increases entrainment whereas, larger tray spacing decreases entrainment but increases column height and cost.

The vapour-liquid contacting devices of plate type are :

(a) Perforated or sieve plate.

(b) Bubble cap plate and

(c) Valve plate.

Bubble cap and sieve plate are the old and commonly used devices.

(i) Bubble Cap Plate

Typical bubble cap plate is illustrated in Fig. 13.14. Here the vapour passed through short vertical pipes called riser ; on the top of which a cap is mounted. The caps force the vapour to bubble through the liquid ; for this purpose the edges of cap are perforated with slots which break the vapours into bubbles. The liquid flows across the plate and then downward from plate to plate through downcomers. The level of liquid on the plate is maintained in such a way that the slots of the cap remain submerged in the liquid. The caps are spaced evenly over the entire plate with the distance between two caps at about 1 to 3 inch. The gas bubbles coming out from the slots are projected around 1 inch from the cap. The caps have diameter of around 6 inches and riser has diameter of 4 inches.

Fig. 13.14 : Bubble cap plate

Thus vapours pass from one plate to the riser then trough the bubble cap slots in the liquid and then leave the plate. During this flow, the pressure of the gas decreases due to
(i) contraction of gas as it enters the riser, (ii) friction in the annualar space of a bubble cap,
(iii) friction due to change in direction of gas flow, (iv) during passage through slots, (v) liquid head above the slots.

When a liquid is flowing over a bubble cap plate column due to the resistance to flow by the caps and risers, there is decrease in liquid depth as the liquid passes across the plate, thus liquid height gradient is produced on the plate. Due to this gradient, vapour is not uniformly distributed among the caps.

(ii) Sieve Plate

It consists of a flat plate perforated with small holes having size 1/8 to 1/2 inch in diameters. The liquid flows across the plate. The upward flow of vapour keeps the liquid from flowing through the holes. The size of holes is optimum : As large holes give low pressure drop but low gas velocities and at low gas velocities some or all the liquid may drain down through the holes so that weeping takes place, causing some of the contacting areas to be by passed.
$3/16$ inch is the common hole size on a sieve plate. The liquid head on a sieve plate is around 2 to 4 inch. The downcomer velocity of liquid is around 0.4 ft./sec.

In a sieve plate column the pressure drop is significantly reduced. The major pressure drop in a sieve plate is due to contraction of gas at sieve opening, liquid head over the opening and friction at the sieve opening. But liquid head in a sieve plate is significantly less.

The gas when passing through the holes passes in the vertical direction forming a spray or froth, there is no change in direction, thus there is no lateral movement of the gas. Thus mass transfer takes place in the vicinity of the holes but as there is no lateral movement i.e. less mixing or agitation concentration gradient will be developed over the plate.

A modification of sieve plate is a *turbogrid plate*. It is a plate on which there are slots instead of holes, it has a flat grid with parallel slots. It gives counter flow without downcomers.

Fig. 13.15 : Sieve Plate

(iii) Valve Plate Column :

In a valve plate, the hole is covered with a disk type valve which acts as a cap. As the velocity of vapour rises the cap is slowly lifted up and provides an increasing opening ; and finally reaches the maximum. The vapours flow in a lateral direction. This type has an advantage of lateral flow of vapour with very low pressure drop, as larger area is available for it and contraction losses in a bubble cap are also reduced. (Fig. 13.16).

Fig. 13.16 : Common types of valves

A fractionating column plate is expected to carry out equilibrium achievement between the gas and liquid phases. A plate where the vapour leaving the plate is in equilibrium with liquid leaving the plate when the plate is called as theoretical plate. There are many approaches for determination of number of theoretical plates.

Many Scientists analysed the process of fractionation for predicting the number of theoretical plates required for fractionation process. The various methods can be classified on two approaches :

1. Mc Cabe – Thiele Approach
   (a) Mc Cabe Thiele method
   (b) Smoker's method
   (c) Gilliland correlation
2. Ponchon - Savarit Approach

13.4.3.1 Mc Cabe-Thiele Approach

(a) Mc Cabe – Thiele Method : This method is based on the following assumptions :

(i) Both components have *equal molal* heats.

(ii) There is not heat of solution and

(iii) The operation is adiabatic.

Fig. 13.17 : Material balance diagram for continuous fractionation

Thus according to these assumptions of equimolal overflow we can say one mole of incoming vapours condense on the plate to release enough heat to vaporise a mole of material from the liquid. Therefore, the rate of *vapours rising from plate* to plate and *rate of liquid descending* from plate to plate will both be constant.

The material balance for the column can be as follows :

For this purpose the two sections are considered in the column, above the feed plate is rectification zone and below feed plate is the stripping zone. The feed having composition X_f enters the feed plate at the rate of F moles per hr.

V and L denote vapour flow rate and liquid flow rates in moles per hr. above feed plate respectively.

V' and L' are vapour flow rate and liquid flow rate respectively below the feed plate in moles per hr. D and X_D are flow rate in moles per hr. and composition of overhead product respectively.

W and X_w are flow rate in moles per hr. and composition of bottom product respectively.

Therefore, above the feed plate

$$V(Y_{n+1}) = L X_n + D X_D$$

or
$$Y_{n+1} = \frac{L}{V} X_n + \frac{D}{V} X_D \qquad \ldots (19)$$

And, below the feed plate we can say

$$V'(Y_{m+1}) = L' X_m - W X_w$$

$$Y_{m+1} = \frac{L'}{V'} X_m - \frac{W}{V'} X_w \qquad \ldots (20)$$

X and Y denote mole fractions of the more volatile component.

Eq. (19) represents the rectification operating line which has slope $\frac{L}{V}$ which is internal reflux ratio. Eq. (20) represents stripping operating line with slope $\frac{L'}{V'}$.

The flow rates above and below the feed plate are related by the thermal condition of the feed as :

$$V = V' + (1-q) F \qquad \ldots (21)$$

and $L' = L + q F \qquad \ldots (22)$

where, q = heat necessary to convert one mole of feed to saturated vapour divided by the molal heat of vaporization of feed.

By simultaneously solving Eq. (18), (19), (20) and (21) we get,

$$Y_i = \frac{q}{q-1} X_i - (q-1) X_F \qquad \ldots (23)$$

This is the eqn. for q – line.

This can be analysed graphically as follows :

1. Draw equilibrium curve and on 45° line locate the points A, B and C corresponding to liquid compositions X_w, X_F and X_D respectively.

2. From point B, draw a line with slope $\dfrac{q}{(q-1)}$ (q – line).

3. From point C, draw a line of slope $\dfrac{L}{V}$ i.e. rectification operating line, intersecting with q-line at pt. D.

4. Join AD i.e. stripping operating line $\left(\text{Slope } \dfrac{L'}{V'}\right)$

5. Step off the theoretical plates.

Fig. 13.18 : Graphical analysis of continuous fractionation by McCabe-Thiele method

When two operating lines meet each other at 45° line ; at the time the no. of plates required is minimum and this occurs at the condition of total reflux.

When two operating lines intersect each other and q-line on equilibrium curve, it is the condition at minimum reflux ratio and, in such case it is difficult to determine the number of plates, as operating lines are too close to the equilibrium curve.

(b) Smoker's Method : When relative volatility of the system is low (i.e. equilibrium curve is close to 45° line) or when we require to keep reflux ratio minimum. In such cases it is difficult to calculate number of plates by graphical method. In such situations Smoker's method is useful which can operate graphically or mathematically.

(c) Gilliland Correlation : This is useful initial approximation, where first minimum reflux ratio R_m and minimum number of trays N_m are determined. Then for any reflux ratio calculate $(R - R_m)/(R + 1)$ and from this value graphically we get the value of $(N - N_m)/(N + 1)$ which will give us the value of N.

13.4.3.2 Ponchon – Savarit Method :

The basic limitation of Mc Cabe – Thiele method is that ; some binary systems do not meet the assumptions of McCabe – Thiele Method of equimolal heats of vaporisation.

Ponchon – Savarit method does not assume equimolal overflow. It uses Enthalpy–composition diagram. It considers both material and enthalpy balance of the system. After considering both it resulted in following equations.

Operating line eq. for rectification zone is

$$Y_n = \left(\frac{M - H_n}{M - h_{n-1}}\right) X_{n-1} + \left(\frac{H_n - h_{n-1}}{M - h_{n-1}}\right) x_D \qquad \ldots (23)$$

and stripping operating line equation is

$$\frac{Y_m - X_w}{H_m - M'} = \frac{X_{m-1} - X_w}{h_{m-1} - M'} \qquad \ldots (24)$$

where, H = Molal enthalpy of vapour

h = Molal enthalpy of liquid

M = $(V_t H_t - L_t h_t) / D$

M' = $h_w - Q_w/W$

where, V_t = Moles of vapours overhead

L_t = Moles of reflux

Q_w = Heat input to reboiler

For graphical analysis by Ponchon-Savarit method

Fig. 13.19 : Ponchon-Savarit method uses an enthalpy-composition diagram

1. Using enthalpy data plot enthalpy of vapour (H) and enthalpy of liquid (h) as a function of composition.

2. Locate rectification focus (X_D, M) ; stripping zone focus (X_W, M') and feed composition and it's enthalpy (X_P, h_F). These three points lie in straight line.

3. As lines originating from M connects the conditions of composition of two adjacent trays. Join x_D to rectification zone from $(X_D\ M)$, where it cuts H curve is the composition of vapours rising from top tray (Y_1). Now, using equilibrium curve find out composition of liquid which is in equilibrium with these vapour i.e. X_1. Locate X_1 on h–curve. Join X_1 to rectification focus which gives Y_2 on H–curve. Now, repeat the procedure same as for Y_1. Thus, we get no of theoretical plates.

4. Similarly, analyse the stripping zone using M' as the focus.

This method is used only when the molal heats of two components are considerably different. It can be used only when enthalpy data is available.

Plate Efficiency

In case of theoretical plate we have assumed that the liquid on a plate is completely mixed having uniform composition and the vapours reach perfect equilibrium with the liquid on each plate. But on actual plate such condition does not exist ; and plate efficiency is a factor which is introduced to express the performance of an actual plate in relation to the theoretical plate.

Plate efficiency is a ratio of calculated number of theoretical plates required to the actual member of plates in the column. This is known as Overall Efficiency (E_o).

Overall Plate Efficiency can be written as

$$E_o = N^*/N_A$$

where, N^* = No. of Theoretical plates

N_A = No. of Actual plates

Overall efficiency is smaller when relative volatility is higher. It is easy to use.

In contrast to the overall efficiency state efficiencies are defined for each stage. Most commonly used stage efficiency is *Murphee Plate Efficiency (MPE)*. It is the efficiency of a single plate as the ratio of the actual change in composition to the change that would occur if perfect equilibrium was achieved. Thus it can be written as :

$$E_{MV} = \frac{\text{Actual Change In Vapour}}{\text{Change in Vapour for Equilibrium Stage}}$$

The Murphee Plate Efficiency at n^{th} plate may be defined as in terms of vapour composition as :

$$E_{MV} = \frac{(Y_n)_{av} - (Y_{n-1})_{av}}{Y_n^* - (Y_{n-1})_{av}}$$

where, $(Y_n)_{av}$ and $(Y_{n-1})_{av}$ are average compositions of vapours leaving n^{th} plate and $(n-1)$ plate respectivelY.

Y_n^* = Composition of vapour in equilibrium

In terms of change in liquid composition MPE can be defined as :

$$E_{mL} = \frac{X_{(n+1)} - X_n}{X_{(n+1)} - X_n^*}$$

where, X_n^* = Composition of the liquid in equilibrium with the vapour Y_n

The operation on actual plate can be analysed if the MPE is known. In the Mc Cabe Thiele diagram (Fig. 13.20), on each vertical step AB a point C is located such that,

$$E_{mv} = \frac{AC}{AB}$$

The horizontal step is drawn from C to the operating line. Each step now represents an actual plate (except the lowest step i.e. boiler which is considered as one theoretical plate). By joining points C pseudoequillibrium curve can be constructed.

Fig. 13.20 : Pseudo equilibrium curve

Murphee has assumed that due to the turbulence created by vapour bubbling there is complete mixing of liquid on the tray. But mixing is not efficient on plates of larger diameter, and there exists a concentration gradient in the direction of liquid flow across the plate. Therefore, a concept of *Point Efficiency* (E_p) was introduced, which is the efficiency at any point on a plate. It can be defined in terms of the compositions at the point of the equation :

$$E_p = \frac{Y_n - Y_{n-1}}{Y_n^* - Y_{n-1}}$$

If the liquid is completely mixed on the plates then point efficiency is equal to Murphee Plate Efficiency. Due to the general existence of concentration gradient on large plates, Murphee plate efficiency is higher than the average point efficiency.

Packed Columns

Packed columns are also commonly used for vapour liquid contact in rectification operation. The liquid flows over the packings and where it forms a thin film exposing large surface area to the gas stream. The vapours flows in the void space inside and between the packings. The packed column thus provides intimate contact between the liquid and vapour phase, facilitating fast heat and mass transfer.

An Ideal packing material should have following properties :

(i) It should have a large surface area.

(ii) It should allow uniform distribution of the liquid over itself.

(iii) It should allow uniform gas flow.

(iv) It should have low pressure drop for gas flow i.e. should provide larger free space.

(v) It should be inexpensive.

(vi) It must be applicable over a wide range of pressure drop.

(vii) It must be corrosion resistant.

No ideal column packing is available. The column packing material is broadly classified as :

(a) Random or Dumped Packings.

(b) Structured or Grid Packings.

(a) Random or Dumped Packings :

Initially quartz or broken stone was used as a packing ; but now rings or saddles are the commonly used packings, which provide around 70 to 90% free space with larger surface area per unit size. Some typical packings of this type are as follows :

(a) Ring packings : Commonly used ring packings are Raschig ring, Lessing ring, Pall rings, etc. Fig. 13.21 (a) & (b) Raschig rings [Fig. 13.21 (a)] are hollow cylinders with the height equal to the diameter. On dumping they adopt random arrangement and facilitate uniform distribution of the liquid. These rings are available in ceramics and metals. They are also manufactured in glass and carbon. When Raschig ring is partitioned diametrically with a single wall, it is referred to as a Lessing ring [Fig. 13.21 (b)].

Efficiency of these packings are difficult to predict. Similarly, due to its geometric shape this packing tends to the maldistribute the liquid if it is not properly placed. Hence generally the packing size is less than $1/30^{th}$ the diameter of the column.

Uniform efficiency and increased capacity is obtained by modifying it as shown in Fig. 13.21 (c), it is known as Pall rings. Pall rings are available in ceramic. Its size is around 2 into 3 in.

(a) Raschig rings   (b) Lessing ring   (c) Pall rings

Fig. 13.21 : Ring packings

The ring packings are relatively inexpensive but have less efficiency than saddle packings.

(b) Saddle packings : Berl and Intalox saddles are commonly used saddle packings [Fig. 20 (a) and (b)]. These are shaped in such a way that they can be randomly packed with no line of contact between adjacent pieces.

Berl saddles [Fig. 13.22 (a)] are negatively wrapped surface, are available in ceramics, carbon, metals and some thermosetting plastics. Similar to Raschig ring it also give wide fluctuations in efficiency but maldistribution is not to the extent that in Raschig ring.

Intalox saddle is a inner half of a $180°$ sector of torus. It has somewhat higher efficiency than Berl saddles. It is available in ceramics, carbon and plastics. It is a packing of choice for distillation of highly corrosive chemicals or at conditions of very high temperature.

(a) Berl saddle   (b) Intalox saddle

Fig.13.22 : Saddle packings

Generally, random packings offer various different paths to the liquid and lateral flow takes place due to which single central field is adopted for such packings. But sometimes during lateral flow the liquid flow may follow some preferential path causing 'channelling'.

(b) Structured Packings :

Grid packing is a structured packing which consists of rows of thin slats laid on edge and held in place by spacer bars. The girds are stacked one on the another inside the column. The liquid flows as a film over the vertical sides of the slats and passes from one slat to the next at the points of contact.

Structured packing provides a continuous vertical path for the liquid thereby avoiding the lateral flow. Thus uniform distribution of the liquid should take place at the top of the packing.

Fig. 13.23 : Structured packing

Height Equivalent To Theoretical Plate (H.E.T.P.)

In a packed column there is no one definite plate upon which the vapour and liquid streams approach equilibrium before passing to the succeeding plate. But the interchange between vapour and liquid takes place gradually as they flow in counter-current manner. A definite length of packing is required to produce the same fractionating effect as one theoretical plate ; as measured by Mc Cabe Thiele diagram. Thus, height equivalent to theoretical plate (H.E.T.P.) is the height of packed section required to give the change in composition that would be provided by a theoretical plate. It is given by the equation.

$$\text{H.E.T.P.} = \frac{\text{Height of Column}}{\text{Number of theoretical plates}}$$

But the major limitation of this method is the calculation of number of theoretical plates in the Mc-Cabe Thiele diagram is a stepwise procedure, whereas the process in a packed column is continuous. Due to this, concept of Height of Transfer Units (H.T.U.) was developed ; which is based on an overall gas phase driving force. It's calculation is based on differential treatment of the column and defined by following equation :

$$\text{H.T.U.} = \frac{\text{Height of Column}}{\text{Number of Transfer Units (N.T.U.)}}$$

$$\text{N.T.U.} = \int_{Y_2}^{Y_1} \frac{dY}{Y^* - Y}$$

where,   Y = composition of vapour

Y* = vapour which is in equilibrium with the liquid at the point in column for which Y is taken.

Number of transfer units can be calculated by plotting $\frac{1}{(Y^* - Y)}$ Vs. Y and graphically integrating the area under curve. (Fig. 13.24).

Fig. 13.24 : Number of Transfer units

H.E.T.P. is proportional to the *packing diameter*. It varies with the nature of the liquid and it increases with increase in molecular weight of liquid. As packed height increases H.E.T.P. increases. It is proportional to the cube root of the packed height. Larger is the size of packing more is H.E.T.P.

H.E.T.P. varies from 0.5 inches to several feet. In normal industrial equipments the H.E.T.P. is between 1 ft to 4 ft. The smaller the H.E.T.P., the shorter the column and the more efficient the packing.

> Thus, Material Balances for Distillation
>
> **Equilibrium Distillation :**
>
> $$W_o X_o = V_Y + (W_o - V) X$$
>
> **Simple or Differential Distillation :**

$$\int_{\lambda}^{X_o} \frac{dX}{Y-X} = \int_{w}^{w_o} \frac{dw}{w}$$

Fractional Distillation :

(i) Above the feed plate

$$Y_{n+1} = \frac{L}{V} X_n + \frac{D}{V} X_D$$

(ii) Below the feed plate

$$Y_{m+1} = \frac{L'}{V'} X_m - \frac{W}{V'} X_w$$

13.5 DISTILLATION UNDER REDUCED PRESSURE

As we know, liquid boils at temperature when its vapour pressure reaches the atmospheric pressure. Thus, lowering of the external pressure will cause decrease in boiling point of a liquid. This is the principle on which process of distillation under reduced pressure is based.

Distillation under reduced pressure has many applications in separation of heat sensitive materials or when solvent recovery is desired. The simple applications include :

(i) to minimise chemical changes due to heat and

(ii) to change physical form of the material whereas, special application is molecular distillation.

13.5.1 To avoid chemical changes :

It is used to prevent destruction of enzymes in the preparation of extracts e.g. extract of Malt, or Pancreatin etc. where temperature has to be controlled below 70°C.

Extracts of Solanaceous drugs like belladona, hyosyamus contain hyosyamine which on exposure to temperatures above 60 °C may get converted to its isomer atropine which is less active therefore concentrated or dry extracts of such drugs are subjected to distillation under reduced pressure. Such extracts are Dry extract of Belladona, Dry extract of Hyosyamus, etc.

Glycosides like sennosides in Senna extract, many alkaloids undergo hdyrolysis at high temperatures therefore extracts containing such drugs should be subjected to distillation under reduced pressure during their concentration.

13.5.2 To change physical form :

Distillation under atmospheric pressure will provide a compact dry residue but if the same operation is carried out under vacuum then highly porous and friable mass will be obtained. e.g. Dry Extract of Cascara sagarada a purgative if prepared under vacuum and passed through sieve will provide granular powder which can be easily compressed as tablet.

13.6 MOLECULAR DISTILLATION

If a high vacuum distillation operation, where the material distills from an evaporating surface to a relatively cool condensing surface. The conditions are such that, the mean free path of the distillating molecules is greater than the distance between the evaporating and condensing surface.

13.6.1 Principles and features of the molecular distillation are as follows :

(a) The vacuum applied during this operation is about 1 micron or less.

As we know, mean free path is the average distance travelled by the molecule in a straight line without any collision. It can be calculated by Clausius' equation as :

$$\lambda = \frac{1}{\sqrt{2\pi \sigma^2 N}}$$

where,
λ = Mean free path in cm
σ = Diameter of molecules in cm
N = Number of molecules in 1 cc

It is clear from the above equation that mean free path can be increased by reducing the number of molecules per cc. At the vacuum of 1 micron the number of molecules in 1 mole of a gas have been reduced from $23 \infty 10^{24}$ at atmospheric pressure to around $23 \infty 10^{18}$. Therefore, now the substance if heated under these conditions of pressure, the molecules evaporate from the surface and travel few cm. without colloiding with the molecules of the residual gas in the space above. If now the condensing surface is placed within this distance, a major fraction of the molecules will condense and not return to the distilland. Thus each molecule distills by itself and hence called "Molecular Distillation".

(b) The molecular distillation is used or distillation of compounds with molecular weight between 300 – 1100. The compounds with molecular weight above 250 to 300 have sufficiently low vapour pressure at the conditions on the condenser surface (around 50°C) and therefore, the chances of re-evaporation from the condenser are avoided. The upper limit of molecular weight is on the basis of sufficient vapour pressure at 300 – 350°C (evaporating surface condition to which the material can be subjected without decomposition)

(c) The molecules of a distillation should get chance to reach the surface and evaporate. The molecules at the bottom of the distilland have to overcome the pressure of the layer above, to come to the surface. Hence, the layer should be thin and be in the state of turbulent movement so as to provide best chance to the molecules to reach to the surface.

(d) The material to be distilled by this method should be effectively degased before entering the still. As the volume of the dissolved gases at the very high temperature in the still increases many folds.

13.6.2 Falling Film :

In this still the distilland is made to spread over and fall down a vertically placed cylinder which is heated internally. The water cooled condenser is placed concentrically around this evaporator with the gap of few cm.

13.6.3 Centrifugal Still :

It has a spinning rotor as an evaporator. The distilland is fed to the centre of the rotor, and the centrifugal force spreads it out in a thin film which travels over the rotor in a very short time, generally fractions of a second. The condenser may be placed either opposite to the rotor or within the rotor.

1. It spreads the distilland in a thin layer over large area, therefore rate of evaporation is considerably increased.
2. The distilland is given a turbulent flow. Thus, it passes the heated zone in a very short time. Therefore exposure to high temperature for very short time.

Applications of Molecular distillation

1. Vitamin Concentrates :

Vitamin A, D, E, K and tocopherols are obtained from vegetable and fish oils.

The vitamin A concentrate produced by molecular distillation are very pure and have good stability. As no chemical is used in this method which could split the ester linkage, the vitamins are retained in the natural ester form, which is the most stable form of Vit. A. The stability of the concentrates is further enhanced by natural antioxidants distilling over from the original oil.

During distillation, oxidation products and traces of metals are non-distillable, remain in the residue.

The fractionation of oils into various components is carried out by molecular distillation.

	Component	Molecular wt.	Temperature
(a)	Fatty acids, unsaponifiable matter of low molecular weight.	150 – 300	50 – 140 °C
(b)	Unsaponifiable matter like steroles, vitamins, dyes, wax alcohols, monoglycerides	300 – 600	140 – 190 °C
(c)	Triglycerides, sterol esters, vitamin esters, resins, waxes.	600 – 900	Above 190 °C

Thus molecular distillation can be used for analysis of fat.

2. It can be used to investigate the degree of polymerization during drying of various drying oil. Similarly core oil obtained by molecular distillation of fish oils has drying oil properties comparable to linseed oil.
3. It is used for purification and fractionation of Lanolin into various fractions like, cetyl alcohol, cholesterol, ceryl alcohol, lanoplamitic acid, isocholesterol etc.

4. On laboratory scale, it is also used for separation of PEG according to the degree of polymerization.

13.7 DISTILLATION OF NON-IDEAL LIQUID SYSTEMS

13.7.1 Azeotropic Distillation :

As we have seen, in azeotropic mixtures one component is more volatile over one portion of composition range and the other component is more volatile in the remaining range. At the composition where reversal of volatility occurs, relative volatility is one, hence separation of azeotrope becomes difficult. Azeotropic distillation is a special class of multi-component distillation, where a new substance is added to alter the relative volatilities of the components of the mixtures. The added substance is called an 'entrainer'.

Azeotropic distillation is commonly employed :

(i) To separate a pair of closely boiling liquids.

e.g. Butyl acetate is used as an entrainer to separate a closely boiling pair acetic acid- water.

(ii) To separate an azeotropic mixture.

e.g. ethyl alcohol forms a minimum boiling azeotrope with water therefore, it is not possible to obtain absolute alcohol by rectification. Benzene is used as a entrainer. Benzene forms a minimum boiling azeotrope with ethanol and water, which boils at lower temperature (64.8 °C) then ethanol water binary azeotrope (78.15 °C) and also contains higher proportion of water to ethanol.

Benzene is added to the feed stream. The ternary azeotrope is collected as overhead product, while pure alcohol is withdrawn from the bottom. The overhead vapour forms two layers, upper benzene rich layer is returned to the column via reflux. The lower water rich layer is fed to a second column ; which also forms ternary azeotrope as the overhead product. The bottom product of a second column is a mixture of alcohol and water which split in the third column into a product of pure water and an overhead product is the ethanol water azeotrope. The overhead stream is recycled to the feed in the first column. Trichloroethylene can be used as an entrainer instead of benzene.

Fig. 13.25 : Azeotropic distillation

13.7.2 Extractive Distillation :

As in case of azeotropic distillation, a third substance is also added to a closely boiling pair or an azeotrope. The third substance added in extractive distillation is called as solvent. A solvent added in extractive distillation is a high boiling liquid and alters the relative volatilities of the components of boiling mixture. The solvent is introduced in extractive distillation column above the feed plate. The solvent used in extractive distillation has two features that, it is less volatile than the component of binary mixture and it is polar. e.g. propylene glycol can be used in extractive distillation of water-ethanol mixture and we will obtain alcohol as a top product and a mixture of water with propylene glycol as a bottom product.

13.8 DISTILLATION OF IMMISCIBLE LIQUIDS

We have seen in the vapour-liquid equilibrium relationship of immiscible systems that the vapour pressure exerted by the components is additive i.e. when sum of the vapour pressures of two component reaches atmospheric pressure the system will start boiling which will naturally be less than the boiling point of any of the components e..g at $80^{\circ}C$ component A exerts v.p. 500 and component B exerts v.p. 260 then mixture will boil at $60^{\circ}C$ (500 + 260 = 760) if A and B are immiscible. Boiling point of individual A and B is greater than $60^{\circ}C$. Similarly, moles of A and B collected as distillate is proportional to the ratio of their v.p. i.e. Moles of A/Moles of B = 500/260 as explained by eqn. 15, 16. Vacuum may also be applied in the process of steam distillation, so as to reduce further the temperature.

Applications : Based on the principle of distillation of two immiscible liquids ; important application developed is *'steam distillation'*. Steam distillation is a method widely used for

(i)   Separation of volatile oil and

(ii)   Preparation of some aromatic waters.

Volatile oils are the mixtures of high molecular weight compounds having low vapour pressure (i.e. high boiling point). To separate these from the natural sources like petals, barks etc. it is not possible to take them to their boiling points around $200^{\circ}C$. If these oils are distilled out with an immiscible component having low molecular weight and high vapour pressure (i.e. low boiling point) then distillation will occur at low temperature i.e. below the boiling point of low boiling component. Thus water is selected which has low molecular weight of 18 and high vapour pressure. Volatile oil when boiled with water will distilled out at temperature below $100^{\circ}C$ and the operation will be economical as molecular weight of volatile oil is very high as compared to that of water.

As $\dfrac{\text{Weight of volatile oil in distillate}}{\text{Weight of water in distillate}} = \dfrac{M_v \, P_v}{M_w \, P_w}$

Where, M_w and M_v are molecular weight of water and volatile oil respectively and P_w, P_v are v.p. of water and volatile oil at distillation temperature respectively.

The aqueous phase which is collected as distillate is not only water but water saturated with volatile oil i.e. Aromatic water.

Thus, steam distillation is used as a method for separation of volatile oils like eucalyptus oil, rose oil, clove oil etc. It is used as a method for preparation of Concentrated Rose Water. Steam is used for it's better penetration power and high energy content. Water may be used for distillation of fresh materials, then it is called as 'hydrodistillation'.

The assembly for steam distillation consists of a distillation still having a mesh near bottom as shown in Fig. 13.26. The steam is generated by boiling water below the mesh ; the steam passes through the material to be extracted over the mesh. The vapour containing volatile oil is then passed to the condenser. The distillate is collected in a special type of collecting device i.e. florentine receiver which separates the oil and water depending on their densities. The aqueous phase may be recirculated so as to avoid loss of volatile oil in water.

Fig. 13.26 : Steam distillation

On large scale the same operation may be carried out with centralised steam generation. In this method a separate boiler provide steam to different distillation tubes containing material to be extracted instead of generation of steam in distillation still itself. Centralised distillation units are commonly used in India in extraction of mentha oil and show better yields than decentralised method.

Steam distillation is also used in quality control of pharmaceuticals. The vegetable drugs like digitalis leaves require the leaves containing not more than 5% moisture. Thus, if these leaves containing water are distilled with toluene then distillate will contain water and toluene. Thus percentage of water can be determined.

***

PUMPS

14.1 INTRODUCTION

There is loss of pressure energy of the fluid when it is moving between two points. This loss is attributed to the friction with the pipe wall, energy loss due to sudden expansion and contraction or bending and fittings. Thus energy should be supplied to the fluid to make it flow. Pumps are the devices which supply mechanical energy to the fluid which is used as pressure energy of the fluid. Thus pumps are the devices necessary for flow of fluids against certain head.

14.2 TYPES OF PUMPS

The pumps are classified as :

(A) Positive Displacement Pumps :

Which deliver a definite quantity of fluid for each stroke or revolution of the device. These pumps are further categorised as :

(a) Reciprocating pumps

(b) Rotary pumps.

(B) Centrifugal pumps

The pumps deliver the volume of fluid which is dependent upon the discharge pressure or energy added.

14.2.1 Positive Displacement Pumps :

In a positive displacement pump, the fluid is drawn into the chamber and is then forced through the outlet with pressure.

(a) Reciprocating pumps : The reciprocating pump has an element which moves to and fro in a stationary cylinder.

Piston pump as shown in Fig. 14.1 has a piston moving in the cylinder. In a single acting piston pump during the backward (intake) stroke of a piston, negative pressure is developed and fluid flows into the chamber through inlet valve. This liquid is forced out during the forward (discharge) stroke of the piston. Thus in a single acting piston pump there is intermittent flow of liquid, the output is only during the discharge stroke and no discharge during intake stroke. Hence a double acting piston pump is developed, as shown in Fig. 14.1 which, intake stroke of piston in one section is an discharge stroke for the other section of the chamber. Thus there is continuous intake and continuous discharge of fluid from a double acting piston pump. We can say double acting piston pump delivers energy in it's forward as well as backward stroke. The

rate of delivery of fluid from the piston pump is zero at the beginning of a piston stroke and increases to a maximum value when piston reaches full
speed; and again reduces and comes to zero as the volume of fluid goes on reducing. Theoretically, a piston delivers the volume of fluid equal to the total volume swept by the piston. But in actual practice actual volume delivered is less than the expected ; this is due to leakage past the piston and valves, failure of the valves to close instantly. Thus ratio of the actual displacement to the theoretical one is known as volumetric efficiency. Volumetric efficiency of piston pump is about 70 to 95 per cent. The piston pumps discharge at pressures of about 50 atm.

Fig. 14.1 : Piston pump

A piston homogenizer used for production of emulsion and suspensions uses a piston pump which produces pressures in the range of 3000 – 10,000 psig and force the product through a specially designed restrictive valve where high shear forces are exerted. Thus energy required to cause the high shear rates in the homogenizing valve is derived using a piston pump.

For higher pressure, a *plunger pump* is used. In this pump, a heavy walled cylinder of small diameter contains a close fitting reciprocating plunger which is just an extension of piston rod. These pumps can discharge against a pressure of 1500 atm. or more.

In a *diaphragm pump*, the reciprocating part do not come in direct contact with the liquid. A diaphragm is placed which is a flexible disc generally made up of rubber which expands and contracts the pumping chamber causing intake and discharge of liquid. As there is no contact of liquid and reciprocating part, diaphragm pump is suitable for corrosive and toxic liquids.

Reciprocating pumps have following advantages :
(i) They can deliver fluids against high pressures.
(ii) They can be operated over a wide range of pressures.

The limitations of reciprocating pump include, unsuitability of piston and plunger pumps for pumping fluids containing large amounts of suspended solids. But diaphragm pump can be used for this purpose.

(b) Rotary Pumps : The basic principle of rotary pump is entrapment of fluid in an expanding chamber and convey it to the outlet point. They differ from reciprocating pump in a way that none of the rotary pumps have automatic inlet and outlet valves as that of reciprocating pump.

In gear pump Fig. 14.2 (a), as the intermeshing gears rotate in opposite direction, liquid is trapped in the spaces formed between a case and the consecutive teeth of two gears. Similar is the operation of a lobe pump Fig. 14.2 (b). In a vane pump Fig. 14.2 (c), the sliding vanes are mounted in the surface of an off-centre rotor. But the vane remains in contact with the case by centrifugal force. The fluid is entrapped in chamber formed between two vanes. The fluid is rotated with this chamber and discharged by contraction at the outlet.

(a) Gear pump   **(b) Lobe pump**

(c) Vane pump

Fig. 14.2

Fig. 14.3 : Working of Rotory pump

Rotary pumps are suitable for pumping of viscous fluids. They can deliver fluid at a constant rate upto high pressures. But these pumps are not suitable for fluids containing large amounts of solid particles.

14.2.2 Centrifugal Pumps :

A centrifugal pump (14.4) is based on a principle, where the rotational energy is converted into velocity and pressure energy. The fluid to be pumped is taken in at the centre of a high speed rotary element called the impeller and then passes out along the spinning rotor, thereby acquiring energy of rotation. This rotational energy is then converted into kinetic energy which is further converted into pressure energy.

Fig. 14.4 : Centrifugal pump

Volute pump (Fig. 14.5), is a centrifugal impeller type pump where an impeller containing series of curved vanes is used. The vanes may be open or closed between one or two supporting plates. The cross section of the pump increases towards the tangential outlet which causes decrease in acceleration of liquid and allows conversion of kinetic energy to pressure energy. Closed impeller reduces turbulence and thereby loss of energy.

Fig. 14.5 : Volute pump   Fig. 14.6 : Diffuser pump

Diffuser pump is a centrifugal turbine type pump, the liquid from the impeller passes through a series of fixed vanes which form diffusion ring. This use of diffusion ring reduces the turbulence at the point where the liquid path changes from radial flow to tangential flow thus giving more efficient conversion of kinetic energy to pressure energy than a volute pump.

In a centrifugal pump, rate of fluid discharge (Q) is proportional to the speed of the impeller (N) and, pressure difference (ΔH) produced by the pump is proportional to square of impeller speed. The power required by the pump is directly proportional to the product of the head and the flow rate :

$$Q \propto N$$
$$\Delta H \propto N^2 \text{ or } Q^2$$
$$\text{Power (P)} \propto N^3 \text{ or } Q^3$$

Advantages of centrifugal pump are :

(i) It delivers the fluid without any pulsation, at a uniform pressure.

(ii) No valves are involved in the pump operation.

(iii) It can handle liquids with large amounts of solids.

(iv) It is simple as it has only one rotating part and no valves. It is cheap and its maintenance cost is also low.

Disadvantages of a centrifugal pump are :

(i) It cannot be operated against high heads. If the liquid encounters a high resistance in the external circuit, the rate of flow may be quite small, as the external resistance falls, the rate of flow increases due to this it cannot handle viscous fluids efficiently.

(ii) If a centrifugal pump is full of air, then the increase in pressure which it can carry out is very low. This is due to difference in density of liquid and air. Due to this low pressure increase, liquid will be neither drawn into the pump nor it is discharged. Therefore it is necessary to remove all the air by the liquid to be pumped. This is known as priming of a pump.

Centrifugal pumps are subject to air binding and must be primed. In contrast, most of the positive displacement pumps are self-priming i.e. when they are first set to work they automatically suck the liquid upto suction pipe and begin regular delivery as soon as the liquid reactivates the pump.

14.3 Comparison of pumps :

(i) **Hydraulic consideration :** Centrifugal pumps give discharge at around 10 – 20 gal/min. with small units while the large sets may give upto 1,00,000 gal/min. but discharge pressure is very low of about 10 to 40 lb/in^2.

The piston or plunger pump give discharge upto 500 gal/min. but pressure generated is upto 10,000 lb/in^2. And the rotory pump gives discharge rate of about 1 gal/min. to 500 gal./min. at pressures of about 500 lb/in^2.

(ii) Effect of speed : The discharge from a positive displacement pump varies directly with speed. But in a centrifugal pump increase in speed will cause both an increase in head and an increase in discharge.

(iii) Effect of head : At a constant speed, the discharge of a positive displacement pump is nearly independent of the pressure. Thus a positive displacement pump will deliver nearly the same amount of liquid whether the resistance is large or small. The rotary pump shows a slight reduction in discharge.

But in a centrifugal pump slight increase in head causes considerable decrease in discharge. If the head rises beyond a certain limit, the pump will stop delivering the liquid completely, although its shaft rotates steadily. The point on a characteristic performance curve (Fig. 14.7) at which the pump efficiency is at its maximum is termed as 'duty point' or 'design point'.

Fig. 14.7 : Performance curve for centrifugal punp

(iv) Liquid properties : Due to increase in viscosity, the resistance in external circuit increases, the pump will be affected in the same manner as that of head. Thus for a positive displacement pump rise in external head will not affect efficiency to a great extent but at the same time there is increased resistance to flow within the pump when viscous liquid has to pass through valve opening or parts. Taking into consideration this increased internal resistance, it is necessary to run the pump slowly.

For centrifugal pumps increase in viscosity does not affect the efficiency initially but it falls eventually. The decrease in efficiency of a centrifugal pump is proportional to size and speed of the pump. Thus efficiency will be lowest if a small pump is used to lift a very viscous liquid against a low head.

Corrosive liquids may attack the internal components and ultimately destroy them. Although if the reaction between the internal parts and liquid is not severe it may cause damage to the parts and contaminate the liquid which will not be acceptable in pharmaceutical preparations. In such cases diaphragm pump is suitable but many times pumps are made up of highly resistant materials or give the lining of rubber, lead or stoneware.

***

CHAPTER 15

TRANSPORTATION OF SOLIDS

15.1 INTRODUCTION

Transportation or conveying of solids involves transportation of bulk solids and package. Transportation of bulk solids means the movement of materials in bulk e.g. powders, granules, etc. whereas in package transportation concern is about solid packaged goods or materials and components that can be considered as separate objects. There is some overlap between the equipments used for bulk and package solids.

Conveyors for transportation of bulk solids are classified as follows :

A. Pneumatic conveyors

B. Mechanical conveyors/elevators

   1. Belt conveyors

   2. Screw conveyors/elevators

   3. Chain conveyors

      (a) Apron slat conveyor

      (b) Bucket conveyor/elevator

      (c) Scraper conveyor.

   4. Roller conveyors

      (a) Gravity roller conveyor

      (b) Powdered roller conveyor

   5. Package elevators.

15.2 PNEUMATIC CONVEYORS

Pneumatic conveying may be defined as *transportation of dry bulk materials through a pipeline by either a negative or a positive pressure air stream.* Material is fed into the conveying system at a suitable location in the pipeline through a special feeding device known as injector or feeder, which is then carried on by the air stream to the point of discharge. For separation of the material from the air stream, separator or collectors are used. Thus, materials are conveyed from one place to another.

To obtain gas under pressure centrifugal fans, reciprocating compressors and blowers are used. The material feeding devices include blow tanks, venturi feeders, rotary feeders and stand pipes. For solid-gas separation, bag filters, cyclone separators or settling chambers may be used.

There are different types of pneumatic conveying systems, viz. pressure transport, suction transport and combination of pressure and suction transport.

In positive pressure system the material, in fluidized condition is conveyed through pipelines where positive pressure exists (Fig. 15.1). In suction transport negative pressure (vacuum) is created in the pipeline (Fig. 15.2). In suction pressure transport the material passes through two phases i.e. one under-pressure and the other at positive pressure (Fig. 15.3).

Fig. 15.1 : Positive pressure system

Fig. 15.2 : Suction system

Fig. 15.3 : Suction pressure

Pneumatic conveying may be used to transport the material horizontally or vertically. It is easier to convey materials in a vertical pipe than a horizontal one, because lower velocities may be used to float the material. In horizontal pipes too low velocities separation of material from the air stream may occur causing drifting and clogging of pipe, at the bends. But more power is required for lifting the materials than conveying an equal distance horizontally, at the same velocities.

The velocity of air at which satisfactory flow of material will occur in vertical as well as horizontal direction is dependent on specific gravity and diameter of the particles. It is given by following equation,

$$V = 0.41\ W^{1/3}\ d^{1/2} + 0.75\ W^{1/2} \qquad \ldots (1)$$

where, V is velocity of air (m/s), d is diameter of particle cross-section (mm) and W is bulk weight of material (kg/m^3).

It is economical to use lower air velocities and higher ratios of material to air. In the feeding device, material is fed from the top, while air enters from one side and passes through a narrow opening where the mixing of material and air takes place. Passage of air through a narrow opening create very high velocity which is necessary to give sufficient impulse to the falling particles to change their direction of motion.

Advantages :
1. It is a totally closed system, therefore, product contamination and atmosphere pollution is very low. The method is hence suitable for pharmaceutical and biological material handling. The closed system also reduces chances of mechanical accidents as well as fire and explosion hazards.
2. It is compact and space requirement is less than the conventional mechanical conveying systems.
3. The equipment is flexible, direction of flow can be changed easily.
4. Maintenance cost is low as compared to mechanical conveyors.

Disadvantages :
1. Material should be dry and free-flowing.
2. Excessive particle breakage could occur during conveying of friable materials.
3. For materials that oxidize easily, an inert gas should be used as the carrier fluid.
4. Abrasive materials may cause excessive wear and tear of the equipment.
5. Capital investment and power requirement is higher than mechanical conveyors.

15.3 MECHANICAL CONVEYORS / ELEVATORS
15.3.1 Belt conveyors :

Belt conveyor is most widely used conveyor for transport of bulk as well as package. It is suitable for almost any type of material from dry, free flowing solids to wet, sticky and lumpy powders. It is suitable for material handling upto temperature of 120 °C.

Fig. 15.4 : Belt conveyor

Belt conveyor is an endless belt which is friction driven at one end and carried on an idling drum at the other end. Generally, belts can convey materials at angles of inclination up to $22°$, which can be modified under special conditions.

The materials used for belts include rubber coated polyester, plain or coated canvas, woven wires or steel ribbon. For transportation of packages, belt is generally flat. The articles to be transported are placed uniformly and squarely on the belt. The belt width should be greater than the diagonal of the largest article. For transportation of bulk solids the belt may be troughed by using troughing rollers. Troughing rollers require periodic repair and replacement due to excessive wear. Therefore, air-supported belt conveyors are used. In air supported belt conveyor (Fig. 15.5), the belt travels on a cushion of air in a trough that forms the upper surface of a plenum. Small holes of intervals allow air to flow to create a frictionless layer of air between the trough and the underside of the belt. The power consumption of air-belts is low.

Fig. 15.5 : Air-supported belt conveyor

Belt speeds depends on the processes involved, and may be changed to suit the production rates. For general warehousing, it is 40 – 70 ft/min, and for sorting it is 20 – 40 ft/min. The capacity of belt conveyors varies from 20 tonnes/hour to 4500 tonnes/hour. The power requirement for belt conveying for lifting may be obtained using following equation,

$$\text{Power to lift} = \frac{\text{Capacity in tonnes per hour} \infty \text{ ht in ft. (for lifting)}}{884} \qquad \ldots (2)$$

Belt conveyors with woven metal wires are suitable for packages and can be used at temperatures ranging from sub-zero to 1150 °C.

15.3.2 Screw Conveyor/Elevator :

It is used for transportation of bulk material. The material is transported by the rotation of a helical screw, moving the material axially in a trough or tube. Screw conveyor (Fig. 15.6) is versatile and is used to convey, elevate, feed and discharge the bulk material. The screw is fitted in casing which may be a trough with square, rectangular or U-shape.

(a) (b)

Fig. 15.6 : Screw conveyor

The maximum size of the particle of the bulk to be transported should be smaller than the gap between the rotating blades and the inner walls of the casing. Smaller is the gap, higher is the conveying efficiency.

Generally, a single screw with a continuous flighting and a constant pitch to diameter ratio of unity is used (Fig. 15.7). For free flowing materials, pitch equal to $1\frac{1}{2}$ times the diameter is suitable, whereas for vertical movement of particles or for screw feeders, pitch to diameter ratio is $\frac{2}{3}$ to $\frac{1}{2}$. A continuous screw with constant diameter but increasing pitch is used for uniform discharge of fine powders; whereas for lumpy materials screw with variable pitch and tapering diameter may be used. The energy requirement and discharge rate from screw conveyor depends on speed of rotation, screw size, pitch, degree of fill and angle of inclination from horizontal. It has capacities upto 200 tonnes/hr.

(a) Constant-pitch   (b) Variable-pitch

(c) Variable-pitch, tapered

Fig. 15.7 : Typical screw flights

15.3.3 Chain Conveyors :

(a) Apron and Slat conveyors : Apron conveyor is the simplest form of chain conveyor used for handling of bulk solids and package. It is used for heavy loads and short runs. The slat conveyors are used for package transport. These are versatile and simple. Although slat conveyors are often used for light and medium duty package handling, they are also excellent for heavy loads and rough treatment.

The chains used for both the conveyors are malleable iron series with the wheels necessary to drive the chains. The attachment or slats of suitable size are used. The slat size and shape varies according to load requirements and the shape of the articles to be carried. Slats are bolted to the chains and can be replaced as per necessity. The conveyor speed is generally upto 70 ft/min to 100 ft/min. The advantages of slat and apron conveyors as compared to a belt conveyor are that not only it carry heavy loads at steeper angles but it can also easily be made to change slope for loading and unloading. The apron conveyor can handle many kinds of materials but are particularly suitable for those which are heavy, abrasive and lumpy.

(b) Bucket conveyor/elevator : In applications where bulk solids have to be elevated in an area where sufficient floor space is not available for inclined belts or screw conveyors, bucket elevator is a suitable alternative.

Bucket elevator consists of an endless chain of metal or plastic buckets mounted on a chain or double chain. The buckets are arranged in such a way that they are loaded at one end and discharge at higher level. (Fig. 15.8). The discharge from the bucket may be under centrifugal force or gravitational force. At high operating speeds of about 1.5 m/s, the material is discharged centrifugally. The material from the bucket is thrown to a discharge chute. Centrifugal bucket elevator has high capacity but maintenance problems due to wear and tear. In gravity discharge, the buckets are mounted very close to one another and operates at low speeds of about 0.5 m/s. The bucket discharges on the back of the preceding one.

    (a) Centrifugal   **(b) Gravity**

Fig. 15.8 : Methods of discharge from bucket elevators

The power requirement, discharge capacity and smooth operation of bucket elevators depend on speed of travel, bucket shape, size and spacing. It also depends on method of feeding and discharge and the physical properties of the bulk solid material. The bucket elevators are used for elevating of material upto heights of 50 m and its capacity is upto 1000 tonnes/hr. In pivoted bucket elevator, the large buckets are pivoted to remain in horizontal position except at discharge point where they are completely overturned.

(c) Scraper or Flight conveyors : These conveyors use scraper plates or flights carried by one or two stands of chain to push the material along the troughs, which may be horizontal, inclined or combination of both. It is simplest and cheapest type of conveyor. It has low initial cost and can be used for steeper inclines. Its disadvantages include high power requirement and maintenance cost. It is not suitable for transport of heavy loads at long distance but suitable for light or intermediate load transport over a short distance.

15.3.4 Roller Conveyors :

It is the conveyor for packages and not for bulk solids. The unpowered roller conveyors, inclined or horizontal are referred to as 'gravity rollers'. It consists of steel or plastic rollers having diameters in the range of 1 inch to 3 inch and tube gauge depends on the carrying capacity. The pitch of the roller i.e. distance between the centres of two rollers is an important factor deciding the performance of the roller. If the pitch is too great the articles will bump or even dig-in. If the pitch is too small, the cost of the conveyor will be unnecessarily high. If the articles are irregular the roller pitch may have to be decreased. For wide articles a double row of rollers can be used. Horizontal conveyors require manual supervision and are commonly used for processes such as labelling, packing etc. where stopping and starting are frequent. Gravity rollers are one of the simplest conveying methods but they are not always easy to handle.

Powered rollers as used in rolling mills are also suitable for package handling where stopping and manipulation of articles is necessary without stopping the conveyor or where an economical way of moving heavy loads in limited space is required. The rollers may be belt driven or chain driven. A belt driven powered roller is a combination of a gravity roller track and a belt conveyor. The carrying rollers are present on the surface of pressure belt which is driven by pressure rollers. The width of the pressure belt is about 25% of the carrying rollers. The carrying roller pitch is decided in the same way as for gravity rollers. The rollers which are too large or too small are difficult to rotate. The large rollers are too heavy, whereas the smaller ones do not provide enough leverage. Generally, the roller diameter is around 38 mm to 64 mm.

Chain driven conveyors are suitable for heavy loads. The chain size depends on several factors such as roller pitch, revolutions per minute, number of rollers, length of conveyor etc. The efficiency of the conveyor drops markedly as the number of rollers or conveyor length increases.

15.3.5 Package Elevators :

Vertical package elevators are used for continuous movement of packages, up or down. Economically, elevators are more expensive to design, install and maintain than the inclined conveyor. But its main advantage over inclined conveyor is that they occupy little space.

Different types of package elevators include :

(i) arm or fork elevator,

(ii) twin-lift or tray elevator,

(iii) swing tray and stabilized tray elevator.

The fork elevator consists of two chain strands to which carriers are attached (Fig. 15.9). It is simple in principle, economic and has good capacity. It is not much wider than the articles to be handled. But feed and discharge can only be on one side. Intermittent motion is required for high capacity. It is difficult to carry heavy articles.

Fig. 15.9 : Arm of fork elevator

A twin lift elevator uses four strands of chain and in essence it is two 'fork elevators' moving synchronously. (Fig. 15.10). It is good for heavy loads, feed and discharge may be on same sides or opposite sides. But its width is considerable as compared to fork elevators.

Fig. 15.10 : Tray or twin-lift elevator

In swinging tray elevator (Fig. 15.11) the carriers are pivoted and hanging between two chain strands. The carriers are free to retain their horizontal attitude where the chain travels around the wheels. In contrast to fork and tray elevator, it is possible to use swing tray as a lowerator. But in this case, feed and discharge can only be on opposite sides. Though it is called as swing tray, the carriers are not free to swing.

Fig. 15.11 : Swing-tray elevator

In stabilized tray elevators (Fig. 15.12), the carriers are pivoted in the primary chain circuit but are prevented from rotating by cranked arms fastened to a secondary chain. This ensures that the carriers remain horizontal throughout their travel. But capacity of swing tray and stabilized tray is lower than the fork and twin lift elevators.

Fig. 15.12 : Stabilized-tray elevator

Lowerator : A simple form of lowerator which does not require any power, consists of a hollow post in which slides a counterbalance attached to a cable. The other end of the cable is passed over a pulley mounted at the top of the post, then fixed to a carriage. When an article is run on to the carriage, its weight overcomes that of the counterbalance and the carriage travels down and discharges itself at the bottom. When the weight of the article is removed, the counterbalance takes the carrier back to its original position. It can be loaded and discharged to side or front.

***

CHAPTER 16

CORROSION

16.1 INTRODUCTION

In nature metals are present in the form of their oxides, sulphides, hydroxides etc. By different processes, metals are extracted from the ores. Process of extraction increases energy of the metal. This high energy state has tendency to get transformed into a low energy form, such as oxides of the metals. This causes corrosion of the metal. Therefore, corrosion may be defined as *unintentional destruction in part or completely of a metal due to chemical or electrochemical reactions with the environment.*

Depending on the environment with which the metal reacts, the corrosion is termed as 'dry corrosion' and 'wet corrosion'.

16.2 DRY CORROSION

Dry corrosion occurs in the absence of aqueous medium. It occurs due to reactions with gases and vapours. Reaction between metal and gaseous state reactants leads to formation of an oxide film on the surface of the metal. The properties of this oxide film formed, play an important role in controlling further rate of corrosion. For example, if density of the film is low, the gases may easily pass through film and corrode the metal surface. Thus, higher is the density of film, lower is the rate of corrosion. If the film formed is highly reactive, rate corrosion will be high. The low reactivity film protect the metal hence termed as protective films. Adhesivity of film to the metal surface is also important. Dense and highly adhesive films can protect the metal better.

16.3 WET CORROSION

Wet corrosion is the corrosion due to purely electrochemical reaction, which occurs when the metal is exposed to an aqueous solution of acid or alkali. The electrochemical reaction transforms the metal into it's ionic state. For example, piece of zinc when comes in contact with dilute hydrochloric acid, the electrochemical reaction will be as follows :

$$Zn + 2\,HCl \rightarrow ZnCl_2 + H_2\uparrow$$

This reaction involves formation of zinc ions i.e. oxidation, which occurs at anode and liberation of hydrogen by accepting electrons at cathode. The Zn–HCl reaction can be analysed as follows :

At anode : $Zn \rightarrow Zn^{++} + 2e^{-}$

(315)

At cathode : $2H^+ + 2e^- \varnothing H_2$

Thus, for any metal such electrochemical reaction causes wet corrosion.

Different mechanisms have been proposed for wet corrosion explaining different cathodic reactions. These reactions at cathode include :

1. Hydrogen evolution.
2. Oxygen absorption.
3. Metal ion reduction.
4. Metal deposition.

16.3.1 Hydrogen evolution :

This reaction is displacement of hydrogen ions from the solution. Zn–HCl reaction discussed above, is of this category (Fig. 16.1)

Fig. 16.1 : Hydrogen evolution mechanism in corrosion

16.3.2 Oxygen absorption :

This reaction generally occurs when the electrolyte solution contains dissolved oxygen. The oxygen absorption reaction which occurs in neutral or alkaline medium are given below :

(a) In neutral medium : Iron in contact with water will show rusting due to oxygen absorption. An oxide film is formed on the surface of iron. If the cracked oxide film comes in contact with a drop of water, then water is neutral electrolyte, cracked film becomes anode and oxide covered is cathode (Fig. 16.2). The reaction takes place as follows :

At anode : $\quad Fe \rightarrow Fe^{++} + 2e^-$

At cathode : $2 H_2O + O_2 + 4e^- \rightarrow 4 OH^-$

$\qquad Fe^{++} + 2 OH^- \rightarrow Fe(OH)_2$

Fig. 16.2 : Oxygen absorption

(b) In basic medium : Consider that iron piece is exposed to sodium chloride solution. Then the cracked oxide film becomes anode, oxide film as cathode and solution of sodium chloride as an alkaline electrolyte. The reactions will be as below :

$$NaCl \rightarrow Na^+ + Cl^-$$

At anode : $\quad Fe \rightarrow Fe^{++} + 2e^-$

$\qquad Fe^{++} + 2 Cl^- \rightarrow FeCl_2$

At cathode : $4e^- + O_2 + 2 H_2O \rightarrow 4 OH^-$

$\qquad OH^- + Na^+ \rightarrow NaOH$

16.3.3 Metal Ion Reduction :

It is a step prior to metal deposition. It is a cathodic reaction, where trivalent metal ion gets reduced to divalent metal.

$$M^{+++} + e^- \rightarrow M^{++}$$

16.3.4 Metal Deposition :

Metal ions from the electrolyte get reduced and deposit on the cathode surface. The rate of cathodic deposition depends on rate of anodic dissolution.

16.4 TYPES OF CORROSION

Different types of corrosions are as follows :

1. Uniform corrosion

2. Galvanic corrosion
3. Crevice corrosion
4. Pitting corrosion
5. Intergranular corrosion
6. Selective corrosion
7. Erosion corrosion
8. Stress corrosion
9. Fretting corrosion
10. Corrosion fatigue
11. Caustic embrittlement
12. Cavitation corrosion.

Of these types ; crevice, pitting, intergranular and stress corrosion can cause process failure. Types of corrosion are explained below in brief :

16.4.1 Uniform corrosion :

It is also termed as general corrosion or chemical attack. It is a superficial, unlocalized attack on the entire exposed metal surface. This corrosion never causes unexpected or premature failure of the metal components. The rates of corrosion are high at higher temperatures.

Fig. 16.3 : Uniform Corrosion

16.4.2 Galvanic corrosion :

This type of corrosion occurs between two coupled dissimilar metals in the presence of an electrolyte. In such a couple, one of the metal acts as an anode; the other as a cathode. The tendencies of the metals to act as anode or cathode is derived from their relative positions in a galvanic series (Table 16.1). A potential difference exists between two metals depending on their distance in the electrochemical series. The less corrosion resistant metal becomes anodic and the more resistant metal cathodic. The intensity of corrosion depends on relative positions of the two metals in the series. The corrosion is accelerated if the anodic material exposes smaller surface area to the electrolyte than the cathodic material. The possibility of galvanic corrosion is less if the metal is coupled with its alloy, as the potential will be very low.

Table 16.1 : Standard electrode potential of metals (Electrochemical series) at 25 °C

Metal	Potential (Volts)	
Potassium	− 2.92	
Calcium	− 2.86	
Sodium	− 2.72	
Magnesium	− 2.35	
Aluminium	− 1.68	Active or
Manganese	− 1.01	Anodic end
Zinc	− 0.76	
Iron	− 0.45	
Cadmium	− 0.41	
Cobalt	− 0.26	
Nickel	− 0.26	
Tin	− 0.14	
Lead	− 0.12	
Hydrogen	0.00	
Copper (++)	+ 0.35	
Copper (+)	+ 0.55	Noble or
Silver	+ 0.81	cathodic
Mercury	+ 0.85	end
Platinum	+ 1.20	
Gold (+++)	+ 1.40	
Gold (+)	+ 1.70	

16.4.3 Crevice corrosion :

The crevices and other shielded areas of the material retain solutions and takes longer period to dry out. A galvanic couple can occur in such areas of the same metal at localized areas of widely divergent aeration or oxygen. The metal surface having more concentration of oxygen becomes cathode and the one with less oxygen becomes anode. It progresses at a very fast rate as compared to uniform corrosion. Crevice corrosion can also occur when a metal is in contact with different concentrations of the same environment.

Crevice corrosion is observed when the rivetted and bolted joints do not get exposed to atmosphere and the area with low oxygen becomes anode and gets corroded. Therefore gaskets are recommended. It can be observed at contact area of 316 stainless steel bubble caps with 316 stainless steel plates. In an agitated vessel, splashing of chemical occurs on inside of the vessel.

Some of the surface of the vessel gets covered with chemical while other is exposed to atmosphere. This condition creates difference in oxygen concentration.

16.4.4 Pitting corrosion :

It is a non-uniform corrosion resulting due to inhomogenities in the metal. It is a localized attack which results in holes or pits. It is generally caused by chloride or chlorine containing ions. In the pit the metal dissolves at an increasing rate and creates excessive positive charge that results in migration of chloride ions to maintain electro-neutrality. The chances of pitting are higher under stagnant conditions. Austenitic stainless steel T 316 and T 317 are resistant to pitting corrosion.

16.4.4 Intergranular corrosion :

During heat treatment or welding, some of the components get precipitated at the grain boundaries of the metal. Due to this precipitation, concentration of elements in the area near the grain boundaries decreases and grain boundary becomes anodic to the remaining area. For example, precipitation of chromium carbide at boundaries during heating of austenitic stainless steel between 800 to 1400 $^{\circ}$F causes depletion of chromium in the grains. This initiates intergranular corrosion, it is called as weld decay.

16.4.6 Selective corrosion :

It is a process where one element is selectively removed from the alloy by the corrosive environment. It is also called as selective leaching. For example, when brass comes in contact with sea water, or water containing high content of oxygen and carbon dioxide, zinc is selectively leached out from brass. This dezincification of brass occurring in the localized area leads to loss of strength of the alloy. Tin is added to brass to prevent this.

16.4.7 Erosion corrosion :

It is the increase in the corrosion rate due to relative movement between a corrosive fluid and metal. The material gets corroded in the direction of fluid flow, it is due to removal of metal ions due to abrasion action of the fluid. Higher is the turbulence, more are the chances of errosion corrosion.

16.4.8 Stress corrosion :

A certain area of metal may be subjected to thermal, mechanical or chemical stress. The areas which are stressed become sensitive to corrosive environment and act as anode. During stress corrosion, very fine cracks are observed in the initial stages. Hence, it is termed as stress corrosion cracking.

16.4.9 Fretting corrosion :

This type of corrosion occurs at contact areas between materials under load, subjected to vibrations. Pits form at the contact points, as a result of the continuous breakdown of the protective film. It is responsible for destruction of bearings. Therefore, equipments showing high vibrations such as sieve shaker, vibratory feeders are prone to such corrosion. Use of rubber gaskets and rigid foundation may aid in reducing fretting corrosion.

16.4.10 Corrosion fatigue :

This is a form of stress corrosion in which the stress is applied in a cyclic manner and is within the elastic range. The cyclic stress breaks the protective film which normally retards corrosion. Oxygen content, temperature, pH and solution composition affect corrosion fatigue.

Highly reactive gases such as hydrogen sulphide cause loss of resistance of metal to corrosion fatigue. Chromium steels have higher corrosion fatigue resistance than carbon steels.

16.4.11 Caustic embrittlement :

It is intergranular stress corrosion. It is observed in carbon steels when they are exposed to concentrated alkaline solutions at the temperature of 200 to 250 °C. It is also termed as caustic cracking. It can be reduced by reduction in stress, avoiding crevices and controlling stress conditions.

16.4.12 Cavitation corrosion :

Cavitation is a *process of formation and rapid collapse of air bubbles in the liquid, at the surface which is in contact with the metal.* The collapse of bubbles during cavitation produces high impact and removes the particles of metal surface forming deep pits or depressions.

This type of corrosion is common with high speed impellers, where cavitation occurs due to vaporization of liquid in the low pressure zone created in the viscinity of an impeller. Therefore, hydrodynamic pressure difference should be maintained low so as to minimize cavitation.

16.5 PREVENTION OF CORROSION

Following methods should be adopted for prevention or combating corrosion :

16.5.1 Material Selection :

Alongwith the working conditions and application, following points should be considered while selecting the material for equipment fabrication.

(a) Pure materials have less tendency towards pitting, but they are expensive and soft. Therefore, only metals like aluminium can be used in its pure form.

(b) Improved corrosion resistance can be obtained by addition of corrosion resistant element. For example, intergranular corrosion occurs in stainless steel. This tendency can be reduced by addition of small quantities of titanium, and tantalum. These elements preferentially combine with carbon and prevent chromium depletion responsible for intergranular corrosion.

(c) Use nickel, copper and their alloys for non-oxidizing environment, whereas chromium containing alloys for oxidizing environment.

(d) Materials which are close in electrochemical series should be used for fabrication.

(e) Particular material should be selected taking into consideration the corrosive environment as shown in Table 16.2.

Table 16.2

Corrosive Material	Suitable Material

Nitric acid	Stainless steel
Hydrofluoric acid	Monel
Distilled water	Tin
Dilute sulphuric acid	Lead
Caustic	Nickel

16.5.2 Proper Design and Fabrication of Component :

(a) To minimize galvanic corrosion, use rubber and plastic gaskets, insulate the materials, and keep the anodic area larger than the cathodic area.

(b) During fabrication avoid sharp corner, rivetted joints and minimize vibrations.

(c) Tanks and containers should be designed for easy draining and cleaning.

16.5.3 Alteration of Environment :

(a) Keep the moisture content and temperature of working low.

(b) Liquids should be deaerated.

(c) Alkali neutralizer should be used to reduce effect of acidic environment.

(d) Concentration of corrosive environment should be reduced.

For example, tap water contains high chloride ions concentrations which corrodes stainless steel.

16.5.4 Cathodic and Anodic Protection :

(a) Cathodic Protection : The metal which is to be protected is made cathode i.e. electrons are supplied to this metal. Addition of electrons to the metal suppresses its dissolution. Two methods used for cathodic protection are impressed current method and sacrificial anode method.

In impressed current method (Fig. 16.4), the negative terminal of power supply is connected to the material to be protected and positive to an inert anode e.g. graphite. Therefore, current passes to the metal to the protected and corrosion is suppressed.

Fig. 16.4 : Impressed current cathodic protection

In sacrificial anode method, the metal to be protected is coupled with a more anodic material. For example, magnesium is more anodic as compared to steel, and can be used as sacrificial anode for steel.

(b) Anodic Protection : In this method, the metal to the protected is made more anodic due to which it forms a passive film which decreases corrosion rate. But all metals can not form passive film. Anodic protection is carried out using a potentiostat, which maintains a metal at a constant potential with respect to reference electrode.

16.5.5 Use of Inhibitors :

Corrosion inhibitors are the chemical agents, which when added to the corrosive atmosphere (gas or liquid), causes decrease in corrosion rate. Inhibitors generally form a protective film. There are different types of inhibitors. Adsorption type inhibitors get adsorbed on the metal surface. Scavengers are used to remove corrosive agents from electrolytes e.g. sodium sulphate removes dissolved oxygen from electrolyte. Vapour phase inhibitors are agents with high vapour pressure and therefore sublime and condense on metal surface. These are useful for protection of metal surfaces in closed spaces.

16.5.6 Use of Surface coatings :

Metal surface is coated using corrosion resistant materials. Coating of metal using a corrosion resistant material improves corrosion resistance, at the same time it prevents direct contact between the metal and the corrosive environment.

Various methods used for coating include electroplating, cladding, vapour deposition, organic coating etc. In electroplating or electrodeposition, the metal to be protected is made cathode while the coating metal is made anode or its aqueous solution as electrolyte. Current density, time, temperature and concentration of electrolyte are the factors affecting electroplating.

Cladding involves mechanical bonding of a sheet of corrosion resistant material with the material to be protected ; e.g. nickel sheet is hot rolled with steel to impart corrosion resistance to steel. Vapour deposition is a process where the metal to be deposited is vaporized under high vacuum and deposited on the surface to be protected.

Organic coatings like paints, varnishes and lacquers are also commonly used. Coating with various polymers is also common.

***

FIRE HAZARDS

17.1 TYPES OF FIRES

Fires are divided into four categories on the basis of the nature of combustible material.

17.1.1 Class A Fires :

These are fires in ordinary combustible materials such as wood, cloth, paper etc. which produce glowing embers.

17.1.2 Class B Fires :

These are fires of flammable petroleum products or other flammable liquids, greases etc. Flammable gases are also practically categorised in class B only.

17.1.3 Class C Fires :

Class C fires are fires involving energized electrical equipment where the electrical non-conductivity of the extinguishing media is of importance.

17.1.4 Class D Fires :

These are fires in combustible metals.

17.2 FIRE EXTINGUISHERS

The fire extinguishing agents are classified as

(a) Water and water based agents.

(b) Dry chemicals.

(c) Carbon dioxide.

(d) Halon 1301

(e) Vaporizing liquids

(f) Dry powders for combustible metals

(g) Steam.

These extinguishing agents carry out extinguishment by

(i) removal of fuel e.g. blanketing with foam or interposing a layer of gas between the fuel and the flames, or

(ii) by removal of oxygen e.g. by dilution with inert gases or vapours, or

(iii) by removal of heat by cooling with water or other extinguishing agents.

17.2.1 Water and water based extinguishers :

(i) Portable Fire Extinguishers : Fire extinguishers containing water, calcium chloride or soda and acid solutions are effective on class A fires and fires in wood soaked with oil or greases.

In these extinguishers, water or water solutions are expelled from the extinguisher by a manually operated pump or by CO_2 generated from chemical reaction of sodium bicarbonate and sulphuric acid or by air stored under pressure in the same chamber.

(ii) Soda–Acid Extinguishers : These extinguishers contain acid and sodium bicarbonate solution; when inverted acid gets mixed with the sodium bicarbonate solution and forms CO_2. Because sodium bicarbonate in solution loses carbon dioxide as it slowly converts to sodium carbonate. These extinguishers should be recharged annually in order to insure that there will be a sufficient quantity of expellant gas produced when the solution is mixed with acid. Soda and acid extinguishers must be protected against freezing.

(iii) Antifreeze Extinguishers : Calcium chloride antifreeze solution cartridge operated extinguishers are pressurized by inverting and bumping on a firm surface in order to puncture the seal of the cartridge and release the pressurizing CO_2. As calcium chloride solution is corrosive, extinguisher should be constructed for corrosion-resistant materials. These extinguishers are suitable for use upto temperatures of $-40\,°F$.

(iv) Foam : There are two types of fire fighting foams, chemical foam in which the bubbles are filled with CO_2, and mechanical foam in which the bubbles are filled with air. Chemical foam is produced by chemical reaction which generates CO_2 bubbles in water solution containing a foaming ingredient. The reacting chemicals usually are sodium bicarbonate and aluminium sulphate. Chemical foam solutions should not be exposed to temperatures lower than $40\,°F$ and not higher than $120\,°F$. Foams form barrier and prevent contact of fuel vapours and air.

17.2.2 Dry chemicals :

The dry chemical extinguishing agents are finely divided powdered materials that has been treated to be water repellant and capable of being fluidized and free flowing so that it may be discharged through those lines or piping when under expellant gas pressure. These generally contain sodium bicarbonate, potassium bicarbonate and ammonium phosphate.

17.2.3 Carbon dioxide :

CO_2 is considered for all practical purposes to act as a diluent to both fuel vapours and oxygen. When sufficient CO_2 is introduced into the fire area, the reacting materials are diluted to the point where reaction cannot proceed with sufficient rapidity for the flames to exist.

17.2.4 Halon 1301 :

It is Bromotrifluoromethane, which is a liquefied compressed gas extinguishing agent. It acts due to its cooling action and dilution of fuel vapours and air.

The remaining classes are minor.

***

CHAPTER 18

POLLUTION FROM PHARMACEUTICAL INDUSTRY

18.1 INTRODUCTION

The pharmaceutical industry manufactures the products which belong to one of the categories such as medicinal chemicals and botanical products, pharmaceutical preparations (different dosage forms), in vitro and in vivo diagnostic agents and biological products (vaccines, sera etc.). Operations in these diverse areas gives rise to a wide variation in the wastes from pharmaceutical industry. There is little similarity between the effluents from different factories, and individual effluents show changes continuously as the process changes. This lack of homogeneity leads to difficulty in categorising, preventing and treatment method design for wastes from pharmaceutical industry. The characteristics of the waste from bulk drug manufacture and formulation manufacture are discussed below.

18.2 WASTE STREAM CHARACTERISTICS

18.2.1 Bulk Drug Manufacture :

The most common method in bulk drug manufacturing include chemical synthesis, natural product extraction and fermentation. The solvent wastes constitutes 75% of the waste loads from these operations.

18.2.1.1 Dirty Water :

One of the major waste in terms of volume is dirty water resulting from various sources that include boiler and cooling tower blowdowns. Usually, the volume of non-processed waste water in pharmaceutical manufacturing facility would be 5 to 10 times the volume of processed waste water. Due to batch operations, frequent equipment cleaning is necessary which contribute to a great extent to the waste water production.

18.2.1.2 Acids and Alkalies :

Certain waste streams give rise to effluents that may be highly acidic or alkaline. In many cases, these wastes contain little or no organic matter and pollutant load in terms of Biological Oxygen Demand (BOD) is negligible. The acids include mineral acids such as sulphuric and hydrochloric acids. Many times the amounts of these acids in effluents from drug manufacturing units may be as large as, 6500 kg/day of sulphuric acid and 3000 kg/day of hydrochloric acid. The organic acids in the effluents are acetic, formic and sulphanilic acids.

18.2.1.3 Dissolved salts :

The most predominant salts are sulphates and chlorides. Their concentrations may be upto 25000 – 30000 mg/lit. in the effluent flow. The maximum sulphate concentration should not be greater than 500 mg/lit. – 1000 mg/lit, above this concentration it may damage the sewer system. Chloride concentrations are not very critical.

18.2.1.4 General process liquors :

The effluent streams generate due to washings, accidental spillage and processing. All types of fine organic chemicals may be found in different wastes, in different concentrations. For example the effluent from a building having different production blocks for anit-TB drugs, antipyretics, sulpha drugs, vitamin B were found to contain 131 different chemicals. The effluent flow rate was 627 m^3/day. Many drugs and drug bases in these waste streams, may be toxic to bacteria. Dirty waste water may be considered under this heading also.

18.2.1.5 Strong process liquor :

These are concentrated process wastes from batch process. In synthetic process, it may be mother liquor which contains unreacted reactants, by-products and residual product in a solvent. In the fermentation operation, the aqueous wastes are produced from the spent fermentation broth, mainly comprising of unconsumed raw materials and cell debris. Natural product extraction generates the waste stream containing spent raw materials, organic waste rich in solvents, salts and natural products. These liquors can have BOD of 20,000 – 30,000 mg/lit. when it is biodegradable.

Emulsions may be present in the effluent, formed as a result of discharge of small quantities of oily effluents, or in some cases as a result of interaction of different components in wastes. The malting process produces discharges containing high carbohydrate concentrations.

18.3 FORMULATION MANUFACTURING

Characteristics of waste streams from different formulation manufacturing section are as follows :

18.3.1 Sterile Products :

The effluents contain mainly dextrose and salt solutions. They arise from washing out process equipment and breakages of vessels containing the actual preparation. Effluents also arise from bottle and container washing areas. These washing are dilute. The flow rates are generally 1 – 8 lit/hr with BOD of 12 – 85 mg/lit. The solids level is around 16 – 240 g/lit. and pH between 6.9 – 8.1.

18.3.2 Syrup Preparation :

The washing of equipments and vessels gives rise to an effluent stream with high pollution load. Effluent flows at the rate of 15 – 25 lit/hr. and has BOD values of 129 – 2280 mg/lit. The suspended solids level is around 70 – 260 mg/lit with pH range 6.4 – 8.4.

18.3.3 Pastilles :

The effluent contains sugar and starch. Though the washings are intermittent, BOD is about 2250 mg/lit with suspended solids level 150 mg /lit.

18.3.4 Tablet :

The rejected tablets are crushed and washed down the drain. There may be tablet rejects upto 50 kg at some occasions. Tablets may contain high carbohydrate percentage and can give rise to effluent with high BOD. The tablet - coating operation may be solvent intensive and could result in solvent waste and air emissions.

18.4 WASTE TREATMENT PROCESSES

18.4.1 Segregation and Balancing :

Segregation of waste streams is utilised as a saving cost. The basic principle is that, it is economical to treat small concentrated flow than a large dilute effluent stream, because it saves cost of pumping and settling tank capacities.

Balancing facilities are required as there is tendency for discontinuous effluent discharge. In the balancing tank, mixing facilities are provided to control sedimentation or a suitable method is provided for removal of sludge. The concentrated liquors are treated chemically to render them innocuous at this stage only.

18.4.2 Neutralization and Pretreatment :

Neutralization should be carried out wherever possible. If the effluent is acidic neutralization is carried out using sodium hydroxide or calcium carbonate. Sulphuric and hydrochloric acids are used for neutralization of alkali wastes. Neutralization is carried out in neutralization tank.

A separate reaction tank is designed for pretreatment of waste to remove emulsions, colloidal material etc. The coagulants such as ferric chloride, ferric sulphate and lime are used. If oil content of the waste is very high, then dissolved air floatation or electro-floatation technique is used. Special oil skimming devices are also available.

18.4.3 Dissolved salt removal :

Precipitation is generally adopted. Large quantities of sulphate are precipitated as calcium salt by lime addition. For removal of chloride and sulphate, ion-exchange technique can also be used. But if chloride and sulphate concentration is very high, which is not allowed in further biological treatment then dilution of waste is carried out.

18.4.4 Preaeration :

Volatile materials present in the effluent may be removed by stripping with aeration. This method is generally adopted for removal of volatile hydrocarbons.

18.4.5 Biological Treatment :

Biological treatment which involves degradation of organic chemicals using microbial organism is generally suitable for wastes from pharmaceutical and chemical industry. The majority of organic chemicals in the waste streams of these industries are biodegradable and allow growth of micro-organisms. In most cases, biological treatment is carried out using the activated sludge process. In this process, the pollutant is rapidly and completely mixed with the microbial population. Thus, rapid biodegradation of the chemicals occur. In the process the favourable physical and chemical environment is maintained for biological activity. pH, oxygen content are maintained in the limits. The nutrient balance is maintained by balance of BOD : nitrogen : phosphorus in the ratio of 100 : 5 : 1. Many effluents are deficient in nitrogen and these nutrients are added externally to the aeration tank.

Rate of biodegradation of effluents is also important, the effluents which is not readily biodegradable. The treatment rates are kept low. The loading of activated sludge is 0.18 kg/kg of effluent per day. Organic acids, their salts and esters readily undergo oxidation by micro-organism under aerobic conditions. Alcohols, aldehydes are easily degraded; whereas tertiary alcohols, ketones and ethers are resistant to microbial action. Cyanides and nitriles can be easily treated, whereas many amines are resistant.

***

CONVERSION TABLES

Where relevant in the following tables of conversion factors the SI unit or multiple there of can be used.

LENGTH

Millimetre mm	Centimetre cm	Metre m	Inch in	Foot ft	Yard yd
1	0.1	0.001	0.0394	0.0033	0.0011
10	1	0.01	0.3937	0.0328	0.0109
1000	100	1	39.3701	3.2808	1.0936
25.4	2.54	0.0254	1	0.0833	0.0278
304.8	30.48	0.3048	12	1	0.3333
914.4	91.44	0.9144	36	3	1

1 kilometre = 1000 metres = 0.62137 miles

1 mile = 1690.34 metres = 1.60934 kilometres

AREA

Square millimetre mm^2	Square centimetre cm^2	Square metre m^2	Square inch in^2	Square foot ft^2	Square yard yd^2
1	0.01	10^{-6}	$1.55 \infty 10^{-3}$	$1.076 \infty 10^{-6}$	$1.196 \infty 10^{-6}$
100	1	10^{-4}	0.155	$1.076 \infty 10^{-3}$	$1.196 \infty 10^{-4}$
10^6	10000	1	1550	10.764	1.196
645.16	6.4516	$6.452 \infty 10^{-4}$	1	$6.944 \infty 10^{-3}$	$7.716 \infty 10^{-4}$
92.903	929.03	0.093	144	1	0.111
836.127	8361.27	0.836	1296	9	1

VOLUME

Cubic millimetre mm^3	Cubic centimetre cm^3	Cubic metre m^3	Cubic inch in^3	Cubic foot ft^3	Cubic yard yd^3
1	0.001	10^{-9}	$6.1 \infty 10^{-5}$	$3.531 \infty 10^{-8}$	$1.308 \infty 10^{-9}$
1000	1	10^{-6}	0.061	$3.531 \infty 10^{-5}$	$1.308 \infty 10^{-6}$
10^9	10^6	1	61 024	35.31	1.308
16 387	16.39	$1\,639 \infty 10^{-5}$	1	$5.787 \infty 10^{-4}$	$2.143 \infty 10^{-5}$
$2.832 \infty 10^7$	$2.832 \infty 10^4$	0.0283	1728	1	0.0370
$7.646 \infty 10^8$	$7.646 \infty 10^5$	0.7646	46 656	27	1

VOLUME (CAPACITY)

Litre l	Cubic metre m^3	Millilitre ml	UK gallon UK gal	US gallon US gal	Cubic foot ft^3
1	0.001	1000	0.22	0.2642	0.0353
1000	1	10^6	220	264.2	35.3147
0.001	10^{-6}	1	2.2×10^{-4}	2.642×10^{-4}	3.53×10^{-5}
4.546	0.004 55	4546	1	1.201	0.1605
3.785	0.00378	3785	0.8327	1	0.1337
28.317	0.0283	28 317	6.2288	7.4805	1

1 US barrel = 42 US gallons (petroleum measure)
1 litre = 10^6 mm^3 = 10^3 cm^3 or 1 cubic decimetre (1 dm^3)
1 litre = 1.76 UK pints

VELOCITY

Metre per second m/s	Foot per second ft/s	Metre per minute m/min	Foot per minute ft/min	Kilometre per hour km/h	Mile per hour mile/h
1	3.281	60	196.85	3.6	2.2369
0.305	1	18.288	60	1.0973	0.6818
0.017	0.055	1	3.281	0.06	0.0373
0.005	0.017	0.305	1	0.0183	0.0114
0.278	0.911	16.667	54.68	1	0.6214
0.447	1.467	26.822	88	1.6093	1

MASS

Kilogram kg	Pound lb	hundred weight cwt	Tonne t	UK ton ton	US ton sh tn
1	2.205	0.0197	0.001	9.84×10^{-4}	0.0011
0.454	1	0.0089	4.54×10^{-4}	4.46×10^{-4}	5.0×10^{-4}
50.802	112	1	0.0508	0.05	0.056
1000	2204.6	19.684	1	0.9842	1.1023
1016	2240	20	1.0161	1	1.12
907.2	2000	17.857	0.9072	0.8929	1

MASS FLOW RATE

Kilogram per second kg/s	Pound per second lb/s	Kilogram per hour kg/h	Pound per hour lb/h	UK ton/hour ton/h	tonne/hour t/h
1	2.205	3600	7936.64	3.5431	3.6
0.454	1	1633	3600	1.607	1.633
2.78×10^{-4}	6.12×10^{-4}	1	2.205	9.84×10^{-4}	0.001
1.26×10^{-4}	2.78×10^{-4}	0.454	1	4.46×10^{-4}	4.54×10^{-4}
0.282	0.622	1016	2240	1	1.016
0.278	0.612	1000	2204.6	0.9842	1

VOLUMETRIC RATE OF FLOW

Litre per second l/s	Litre per minute l/min	Cubic metre per hour m^3/h	Cubic foot per hour ft^3/h	Cubic foot per minute ft^3/min	UK gallon per minute UK gal/min	US gallon per minute US gal/min	US barrel per day US barrel/d
1	60	3.6	127.133	2.1189	13.2	15.85	543.439
0.017	1	0.06	2.1189	0.0353	0.22	0.264	9.057
0.278	16.667	1	35.3147	0.5886	3.666	4.403	150.955
0.008	0.472	0.0283	1	0.0167	0.104	0.125	4.275
0.472	28.317	1.6990	60	1	6.229	7.480	256.475
0.076	4.546	0.2728	9.6326	0.1605	1	1.201	41.175
0.063	3.785	0.2271	8.0209	0.1337	0.833	1	34.286
0.002	0.110	0.0066	0.2339	0.0039	0.024	0.029	1

FORCE

Newton N	Kilonewton kN	Kilogram-force* kgf	Pound-force lbf
1	0.001	0.102	0.225
1000	1	101.97	224.81
9.807	0.0098	1	2.205
4.448	0.0044	0.454	1

* The kilogram-force is sometimes called the kilopound (kp)

MOMENT OF FORCE

Newton metre N m	Kilonewton metre kN m	Kilogram-force metre kgf m	Pound-force inch lbf in	Pound-force foot lbf ft
1	0.001	0.102	8.85	0.738
1000	1	101.972	8851	737.6
9.807	0.0098	1	86.8	7.233
0.113	1.13×10^{-4}	0.0115	1	0.083
1.356	0.0014	0.138	12	1

ENERGY, WORK, HEAT

Joule J	Kilojoule kJ	Megajoule MJ	Foot pound-force ft lbf	British thermal unit Btu	Therm	Kilowatt hour kWh
1	0.001	10^{-6}	0.738	9.48×10^{-4}	9.48×10^{-9}	2.478×10^{-7}
1000	1	0.001	737.56	0.9478	9.48×10^{-6}	2.478×10^{-4}
10^6	1000	1	737.562	947.82	9.48×10^{-3}	0.2778
1.356	0.0014	1.36×10^{-6}	1	0.0013	1.28×10^{-8}	3.77×10^{-7}
1055.1	1.0551	0.0010	778.17	1	10^{-5}	2.931×10^{-4}
1.0551×10^8	105 510	105.51	7.78×10^7	100.000	1	29.307
3.6×10^6	3600	3.6	2.65×10^6	3412.1	0.03412	1

1 joule = 1 newton metre

POWER

Watt W	Kilogram-force metre per second kgf m/s	Metric horsepower	Foot pound-force per second ft lbf/s	Horsepower hp
1	0.102	0.00136	0.738	0.00134
9.806	1	0.0133	7.233	0.0131
735.5	75	1	542.476	0.9863
1.356	0.138	0.00184	1	0.00182
745.70	76.04	1.0139	550.0	1

1 watt = 1 joule per sec = 1 newton metre per second

HEAT FLOW RATE

Watt W	Calorie per second cal/s	Kilocalorie per hour kcal/hr.	British thermal unit per hour Btu/h
1	0.239	0.86	3.412
4.187	1	3.6	14.286
1.163	0.278	1	3.968
0.293	0.07	0.252	1

1 watt = 1 joule per sec = 1 newton metre per second

PRESSURE AND LIQUID HEAD

Bar (10^5 N/m²) bar	Millibar (10^2/Nm²) m bar	Pascal (1 N/m²) Pa	Kilogram-force per square centimetre kgf/cm²	Pound-force per square inch lbf/in²	Foot of water ft H₂O	Metre of water m H₂O	Milli-metre of mercury mm Hg	Inch of mercury in Hg
1	1000	10^5	1.02	14.5	33.455	10.2	750.1	29.53
0.001	1	100	1.02×10^{-3}	0.0145	0.033	0.0102	0.75	0.029
10^{-5}	0.01	1	1.02×10^{-5}	1.45×10^{-4}	3.3×10^{-4}	1.02×10^{-4}	0.0075	2.95×10^{-4}
0.981	980.7	98067	1	14.22	32.808	10.0	735.6	28.96
0.069	68.95	6895	0.0703	1	2.307	0.703	51.71	2.036
0.03	29.89	2989	0.0305	0.433	1	0.305	22.42	0.883
0.098	98.07	9807	0.1	1.42	3.28	1	73.55	2.896
0.0013	1.333	133.3	0.0014	0.019	0.045	0.014	1	0.039
0.0339	33.86	3386	0.0345	0.491	1.333	0.345	25.4	1

One millimetre head of mercury (1 mm Hg) is also known by the name 'torr'.

The international standard atmosphere (1 atm.) = 1.01325 bar = 14.6959 lbf/in².

The technical (metric) atmosphere (1 atm.) = 0.980 66 bar = 14.2233 lbf/in².

The conventional reference conditions known as 'standard temperature and pressure'(s.t.p.) are : 1.01325 bar (14.6959 lbf/in^2) at 0°C.

The standard reference conditions (s.t.) for gas, as defined by the International Gas Union, are : 1.01325 bar at 15 °C and dry. These conditions may also be referred to as 'Metric Standard Conditions' (MSC).

STRESS

Megapascal (10^6 N/m^2)	Pound-force per square inch lbf/in^2	UK tonne-force per square inch UK tonf/in^2	Kilogram-force per square centimetre kgf/cm^2	Kilogram-force per square millimetre kgf/mm^2
1	145	0.0647	10.197	0.102
0.0069	1	4.464 × 10^{-4}	0.0703	7.031 × 10^{-4}
15.44	2240	1	157.5	1.575
0.0981	14.22	0.0063	1	0.01
9.807	1422	0.6350	100	1

A 'Pascal' is the special name for one newton per square metre (1 Pa = 1 N/m^2)

One megapascal is equal to one newton per square millimetre (1 MPa = 1 N/mm^2)

SPECIFIC ENTHALPY (AND SPECIFIC ENERGY)

Kilojoule per kilogram kJ/kg	Kilocalorie per kilogram kcal/kg	British thermal unit per pound Btu/lb	Kilogram-force metre per kilogram kgf m/kg	Foot pound-force per pound ft lbf/lb	Kilowatt hour per kilogram kWh/kg
1	0.239	0.4299	101.97	334.55	2.78 × 10^{-4}
4.187	1	1.8	426.93	1400.7	11.63 × 10^{-4}
2.326	0.555	1	237.19	778.17	6.46 × 10^{-4}
0.009 81	0.002 34	0.004 22	1	3.28	2.72 × 10^{-6}
0.002 99	7.139 × 10^{-4}	0.001 28	0.305	1	8.30 × 10^{-7}
3600	859.845	1547.72	3.671 × 10^5	1.204 × 10^6	1

SPECIFIC VOLUME

Cubic centimetre per gram cm³/g	Cubic centre per kilogram m³/kg	Cubic inch per pound in³/lb	Cubic foot per pound ft³/lb	Cubic foot per UK ton ft³/ton	UK gallon per pound U K gal/lb	US gallon per pound USgal/lb

1	0.001	27.68	0.016	35.88	0.0998	0.1198
1000	1	27 680	16.018	35 881	99.776	119.83
0.036	3.613×10^{-5}	1	5.787×10^{-4}	1.296	0.0036	0.0043
62.428	0.062	1728	1	2240	6.229	7.481
0.028	2.787×10^{-5}	0.771	4.464×10^{-4}	1	0.0028	0.0033
10.022	0.010	277.4	0.160	359.6	1	1.201
8.345	0.0083	231.0	0.134	299.4	0.833	1

1 cm^3/g = 1 ml/g = 1 dm^3/kg = 1 litre/kg = 1 m^3/tonne

1 m^3/kg = 1 dm^3/g

DENSITY

Gram per cubic centimetre g/cm^3	Kilogram per cubic metre kg/m^3	Pound per cubic inch lb/in^3	Pound per cubic foot lb/ft^3	UK ton per cubic yard ton/yd^3	Pound per UK gallon $lb/UKgal$	Pound per US gallon $lb/USgal$
1	1000	0.036	62.428	0.752	10.022	8.345
0.001	1	3.613×10^{-5}	0.062	7.525×10^{-4}	0.010	0.0083
27.68	27 680	1	1728	20.829	277.42	231
0.016	16.018	5.787×10^{-4}	1	0.012	0.160	0.134
1.329	1328.9	0.048	82.963	1	13.319	11.090
0.0998	99.78	3.605×10^{-3}	6.229	0.075	1	0.833
0.1198	119.83	4.329×10^{-3}	7.480	0.090	1.201	1

1 g/cm^3 = 1 g/ml = 1 kg/dm^3 = 1 kg/litre = 1 tonne/m^3

1 kg/m^3 = 1 g/dm^3

MASS PER UNIT LENGTH

1 kg/m = 0.6720 lb/ft

1 lb/ft = 1.488 kg/m

CALORIFIC VALUE (VOLUME BASIS)

1 MJ/m^3 = 26.84 Btu/ft^3

1 Btu/ft^3 = 0.037 26 MJ/m^3 or 37.26 kJ/m^3

MASS PER UNIT AREA

1 kg/m^2 = 0.2048 lb/ft^2

1 lb/ft^2 = 4.882 kg/m^2

THERMAL CONDUCTIVITY

1 $W/(m\ ^\circ C)$ = 6.934 Btu in / (ft^2 h $^\circ F$)

1 Btu in/ft^2 h $^\circ F$ = 0.1442 W / (m $^\circ C$)

[i.e., 0.1442 W m / (m^2 $^\circ C$)]

***

INDEX

Agitated tank crystallizer	212
Angle of nip	87
Apron conveyor	308
Azeotrope	272
Azeotropic distillation	294
Baffles	151
Bag filters	139
Balanced pressure trap	63
Ball mill	82
Basket centrifuge	112
Belt conveyor	306
Bernoulli's equation	16
applications	17
Bimetallic trap	63
Black body	45
Boiling point diagram	266
Bond's law	78
Boundary layer	51
Bourdon gauge	12
Bubble cap plate	279
Bubble point test	135
Bucket conveyor	309
Burnout point	53
Centrifugal pumps	298, 301
Centrifugal rotory evaporator	239
Centrifugation	
theory	109
pressure differential	111
equipments	112
Chain conveyor	308
Circulating magma crystallizer	216
Climbing film evaporator	234
Closed circuit milling	91
Coefficient of contraction	20
Collision breeding	207
Colloid mill	155
Conduction	38
steady state	40
unsteady state	44
pipes and tubes	42
Continuity equation	15
Convection	47
natural	47
forced	47
dimensional analysis in	48
Conveyors	304
pneumatic	304
mechanical	306
chain	308
Corrosion	
definition	315
dry	315
wet	315
types	317
prevention	321
Critical temperature drop	53
Crystal	199
forms	200
habit	201
growth	208
caking	222
Crystal growth theories	208
Crystal lattice	199
Crystallization	199
equipments	210
by cooling	211
by evaporation	215
by adiabetic evaporation	215
Cutter mill	89
Cyclone separator	107
Deaeration	171
Defoaming	171
Degree of mixing	166
Diaphragm pump	299
Diasona mixer	163
Diffuser pump	301
Dimensional analysis	5, 48, 70
Dimensional correlation	49
Dimensions	4
Discharge coefficient	20
Dislocation theory	209
Distillation	
immiscible systems	296
definition	264
simple	272
flash	272
fractional	277
vacuum	292
molecular	292
non-ideal system	294
DOP test	143
Drop-wise condensation	55
Drum dryer	262
Dry grinding	90

Drying		Extractive distillation	295
definition	242	Extractors	
significance	242	Solid-Liquid	
mechanism	242	Mixers	178
theory	244	Vortical	178
curves	244	Ultrasound	178
equipments	246	Electrical Discharge	179
DTB - crystallizer	219	Percolation Battery	179
Duhring rule	225	Rotocel Extractor	180
Edge filter	129	Robbert diffusion battery	180
Edge runner mill	88	Carousel extractor	180
Electromagnetic flow meter	26	Basket extractor	182
Electrostatic precipitators	140	Screw extractor	183
Elutriation	104	Silver continuous battery	183
End runner mill	89	Hilderbrandt extractor	184
Energy balance	2, 15	Pulsation column extractor	184
Energy losses		Centrifuge	185
frictional	32	Liquid-Liquid	
pipe fittings	33	Mixer-settler	188
enlargement	33	Spray columns	189
contraction	33	Packed column	189
Enfleurage	198	Tray column	189
Entrainment	279	Reciprocating plate column	190
Equilibrium curve	266	Schiebel column	191
Equilibrium distillation	272	Mixco extractor	191
Evaporation		Rotating disc contactor	191
definition	224	Pulsed packed column	192
theory	224	Podbielniak	192
factors affecting	224	Falling film evaporator	235
Evaporators	226	Fanning equation	31
pan	226	Fick's law	67, 69, 146
tubular	227	Film-wise condensation	54
horizontal tube	227	Filter aids	123
vertical tube	227	Filter medium	119
short tube	227	surface type	120
long tube	233	depth type	121
multiple effect	229	cake type	122
economy	225	Filter press	125
capacity	225	plate and frame	125
forced circulation	236	chamber	127
wiped film	237	Filtration	
centrifugal rotory	239	definition	118
Extraction	172	mechanisms	119
Solid-liquid	172	types	119
Liquid-liquid	172	theory	122
Continuous counter current	173, 176	equipments	125
Calculations	173	Fire extinguishers	324
Super fluid gases	194	Fire hazards	324

Fire types	324
Flight conveyor	309
Float and thermostatic trap	62
Flow patterns	147
Flowmeters	19
classification	19
pressure differential	19
variable area	24
quantity	26
nuclear technique	28
Fluid dynamics	7
Fluid energy mill	85
Fluid flow	
through pipe	28
laminar	14, 28
turbulent	14, 30
energy losses	30
Fluid statics	7
Fluidized bed dryer	248
Forced circulation evaporator	209
Form friction	30, 34
Fourier's law	39
Fractional distillation	277
Fractionating columns	278
Freeze dryer	256
Freeze grinding	90
Friction factor	31, 32
Frictional energy loss	32
Froude number	158
Gate meter	25
Gear pump	300
Gilliland correlation	284
Gral mixer	165
Grashof number	48
Griffith's theory	75
Growth type crystallizer	220
H.E.T.P.	290
H.T.U.	290
Hammer mill	80
Harris law	79
Heat exchangers	
classification	55, 57
heat transfer in	56
Heat transfer	38
equipments	55
mechanisms	38
radiation	45
conduction	38
convection	47
coefficient	50
to boiling liquids	52
from condensing vapours	54
HEPA filter	142
Heterogenous nucleation	207
High speed mixer	163
Holmes law	79
Homogenizer	153
Homogenous nucleation	206
Hydraulic separator	104
Ideal binary system	265
Impellers	147
Initial breeding	207
Integrity tests	135
Intensifier	163
Intensity of segregation	167
Inverted bucket trap	62
Jet mixer	152
Kick's law	77
Kirchoff's law	45
Kozeny's equation	36
Krystal crystallizer	221
Leaching	172
Leaf filter	130
Liquid mixing	
mechanisms	144
equipments	146
power requirement	158
Lobe pump	300
Lodige mixer	164
Louvers	141
Manometer	9
simple	10
differential	10, 12
inclined	11
U-tube	11
Mass transfer	66
Material balance	2, 15, 98, 282, 291
Mc-Cabe Thiele method	282
Mechanical classifiers	105
Membrane filter	134
Metafilter	129
Microfiltration	139
Mier's theory	213
limitations	215
Mirer's theory	213
methods	220

Mixing		Poiseulli's equation	30, 35
definition	144	Pollution	326
liquid	144	Ponchon-Savarit method	384
solid-liquid	160	Pool boiling	52
solids	165	Positive displacement pump	298
Mixing index	168	Power curve	159
Mixing rate	169	Power number	158
Mogensen sizer	100	Prandtl number	48
Molecular diffusion	66	Pressure	7
in gases	66	absolute	8
in liquids	68	gauge	8, 9
in laminar and turbulent flow	68	Pressure energy	3, 16
interfacial	70	Pressure homogenizer	154
Molecular distillation	292	Propellers	148
Multiple effect evaporator	229	Pseudo-equilibrium curve	287
economy	229	Pumps	298
working	230	types	298
capacity	230	comparison	302
feeding methods	231	Rake classifier	106
Nauta mixer	162	Random packing	288
Needle breeding	180	Raoult's law	265
Non–ideal systems	268	Rayleigh's equation	274
Nucleation		Reciprocating pump	298
primary	206	Rectification	277
secondary	207	Relative volatility	264
Nusselt number	48	Reverse osmosis	137
Nutsch filter	128	Reynolds experiment	14
Open circuit milling	91	Reynolds number	14, 48, 70
Orifice and plug meter	25	significance	15
Orifice meter	21	Ribbon blender	170
Package elevators	310	Rittinger's law	77
Packed column	288	Roller conveyor	310
Paddles	150	Roller dryer	262
Penetration theory	72	Roller mill	86
Pipe mixer	156	Rotameter	24
Piston pump	298	Rotory drum filter	131
Pitot tube	23	Rotory pump	298
Planetary mixer	161	Sambay evaporator	238
Plate and disc centrifuge	115	Scale formation	240
Plate columns	278	Scale of scrutiny	167
Plate efficiency	286	Scale of segregation	167
Plate heat exchangers	59	Schmidt number	70
flat plate	59	Screw conveyor	307
spiral plate	60	Screw dislocation	210
applications	61	Screw mixer	161
Plate separator	116	Sedimentation	101
Plunger pump	299	theory	101
Pneumatic dryer	250	equipments	103

Sedimentation tank	103	Tray dryer	246
Segregation	165	Triangular diagrams	174, 187
Sieve bend	95	Triple roller mill	87
Sieve plate	280	Tube centrifuge	117
Sieve shaker	96	Tubular heat exchangers	58
vibratory	96	concentric tube	58
gyratory	97	shell and tube	58
alpine jet	98	Tumbler mixers	169
Sieves	92	Tumbling mills	82
effectiveness	98	Tunnel tray dryer	247
factors affecting	100	Turbines	148
Sieving	92	Turbo tray dryer	248
Sigma mixer	160	Two-film theory	70
Simple distillation	272	Ultrafiltration	136
Size reduction		Ultrasonic flowmeter	27
definition	73	Ultrasonic homogenizer	155
significance	73	Unit cell	199
theory	73	Unit operations	1
energy requirement	76	Units	4
equipments	79	Vacuum crystallizer	215
mechanisms	79	Valve plate	281
control	91	Vane pump	300
Size separation	92	Vapour - liquid equilibrium	
Skin friction	30, 34	miscible system	265
Smoker's method	284	partially miscible system	272
Solid mixing	165	immiscible system	271
mechanisms	165	non-ideal system	268
equipments	169	Vapour recompression	240
Solubility	202	Velocity distribution in pipe	29
Spray dryer	252	Venturi meter	22
Static mixer	156	Versator	171
Steam distillation	297	View factor	47
Steam traps	61	Viscous drag	30, 34
mechanical	61	Volumetric meters	26
thermostatic	63	Volute pump	300
thermodynamic	64	Waste treatment processes	328
Stefan - Boltzman law	46	Weighing meters	26
Stoichiometry	1	Wet grinding	90
Stokes law	35	Wet scrubber	141
Streamline filter	130	Wiped film evaporator	237
Structured packing	288	Wurster technique	250
Supersaturation	202	Z - blade mixer	160
Surface renewal theory	72	Zig-zag sifter	105
Swenson Walker crystallizer	213		
Tank crystallizer	212		
Thermal conductivity	40		
Thermodynamic trap	65		
Transducers	12		

***

www.ingramcontent.com/pod-product-compliance
Lightning Source LLC
Chambersburg PA
CBHW081345230426
43667CB00017B/2728